MW00780242

"Thomas Gaulke has crafted a s
a theologian and a creative arti
unbelief that Christian believer
with myriad ways of understanding the big questions of life. His insight
leads the reader to consider the ways that all lives are part of an ecosystem
that is beyond the boundaries of the beingness of humans and other living
things. Provocative. Essential reading for these times of un-hope and hope."

—**Linda E. Thomas**, Professor of Theology and Anthropology, Lutheran School of
Theology at Chicago

"Thomas Gaulke's exploration of hope is exactly what is needed in the
church today. He weaves together a variety of frameworks for finding and
defining hope with brilliant insights and a pastoral heart. As a person of
faith who sometimes finds herself despairing, this book is balm for my soul.
I can't wait to share Gaulke's work with the people I serve."

—**Laila Barr**, Pastor of Lifelong Learning, Shepherd of the Lake Lutheran Church,
Prior Lake, Minnesota

"*An Unpromising Hope* stands squarely at the intersection of rich scholarship and deep pastoral insight. Gaulke enters into a global conversation
of theologians and philosophers to explore the questions of hope and
hopelessness that are felt so powerfully in contemporary churches and,
crucially, at their margins."

—**Marvin E. Wickware Jr.**, Assistant Professor of Church and Society and Ethics,
Lutheran School of Theology at Chicago

"Two questions guide Thomas Gaulke's book: Where might we look for hope outside of promise? Where might we find hope for an agnostic church and for those of us who find it hard to believe? In different ways, Gaulke shows us how hope is possible in a space that is, perhaps, closer to the gospel—that is closer to Jesus—than the frail forms of hope we hear everywhere. Against a Christian tradition that seals the promise to a few and circumscribes hope to a proper belief, Gaulke shows us that hope is only possible where hope is not given. The Thomas of this book shadows the Thomas of the Gospel, and the results are strikingly close. Both of them have had a hard time believing, but both have also touched Jesus. Don't be mistaken: this is a mighty book!"

—**Cláudio Carvalhaes**, Associate Professor of Worship, Union Theological Seminary, New York City

"Theologies of 'hope' have served to frame strong ethical imperatives toward activism for many decades now; however, in an increasingly broken world, we have long needed a more grittily realistic appraisal of how faith can coexist alongside work for justice. Not only does Thomas Gaulke's book provide such an intensely searching and fearless appraisal of our prospects, but his unflinching realism exists—exuberantly—alongside a virtuoso demonstration of theological creativity and synthesis drawing on spatialized eschatologies, womanist ethics, and liberation narratives enshrined in both theology and popular culture. His book will be especially helpful for activists who are in need both of theological inspiration and of resilience in the absence of guarantees, and should marvelously disrupt theological conversations about hope, its limits, and its horizons in the years to come."

—**Robert Saler**, Research Professor of Religion and Culture, Christian Theological Seminary, Indianapolis

An Unpromising Hope

An Unpromising Hope

Finding Hope outside of Promise for an Agnostic Church
and for Those of Us Who Find It Hard to Believe

Thomas R. Gaulke

PICKWICK *Publications* · Eugene, Oregon

AN UNPROMISING HOPE
Finding Hope outside of Promise for an Agnostic Church
and for Those of Us who Find it Hard to Believe

Pickwick Publications
An Imprint of Wipf and Stock Publishers
199 W. 8th Ave., Suite 3
Eugene, OR 97401

www.wipfandstock.com

PAPERBACK ISBN: 978-1-7252-9693-0
HARDCOVER ISBN: 978-1-7252-9692-3
EBOOK ISBN: 978-1-7252-9694-7

Cataloguing-in-Publication data:

Names: Gaulke, Thomas R., author.

Title: An unpromising hope : finding hope outside of promise for an agnostic church and for those of us who find it hard to believe / by Thomas R. Gaulke.

Description: Eugene, OR : Pickwick Publications, 2021 | Includes bibliographical references.

Identifiers: ISBN 978-1-7252-9693-0 (paperback) | ISBN 978-1-7252-9692-3 (hardcover) | ISBN 978-1-7252-9694-7 (ebook)

Subjects: LCSH: Hope—Religious aspects—Christianity. | Christianity and atheism.

Classification: BV4638 .G38 2021 (print) | BV4638 .G38 (ebook)

09/17/21

To Daisy and Hannah, and to the communities who are First Trinity, Bethlehem, Gethsemane, and South Loop Campus Ministry.

Contents

Acknowledgments

I OWE ENDLESS THANKS to the many people who have been my support, my encouragement, and my lifeboat on the journey to completing this book.

Dr. Vítor Westhelle and Dr. Kadi Billman first pushed me toward the question of hope in 2006. When I returned to the Lutheran School of Theology at Chicago from my vicarage in Nebraska, it was in their classroom, organized around the topic *Fostering Narratives of Hope*, that I read Rubem Alves for the first time. It was there, also, that we read other poets, Neruda, and Bloch, and listened for the whispers of the divine beneath their words. I put these authors away for years, but the memories followed me into ministry and informed my practice in the parish.

After years immersed in congregational life and in organizing communities, I nervously started to wonder about working on a PhD. I returned to LSTC, meeting with as many professors as I could, hoping and fearing that they, too, might think that this was a good idea. Among those I had conversations with were Dr. Westhelle and Dr. Billman, as well as Dr. Linda Thomas, Dr. Ray Pickett, and Dr. Robert Saler. Each, in their way, affirmed this new vocational direction.

When I announced that I was going back to school, I also announced that I would be leaving South Loop Campus Ministry, one of the ministries to which I had been called. I owe endless gratitude to the board of SLCM who gave thanks for my time and graciously sent me on my way. I am humbled by the work of Pastor Ben Adams, who came after, and has wonderfully built up that ministry in the South Loop of Chicago.

The people of First Lutheran Church of the Trinity (my first call and a community that I will always hold near and dear), responded to the news of my return to school only with excitement and joy, often jesting about how

Pastor Tom will one day be "the Reverend Doctor." They were more than generous in allowing me time away to prepare for exams and assignments. Indeed, they are the image of a community of hope, for me. I cannot write about hope and church without seeing the people of First Trinity. Though throughout my program I discerned that I was being called away from the ministry there, the spirit of the place still permeates my every day.

School is not free. When I first began, I created a Go Fund Me called "Ph.D. Me A.S.A.P." Friends and family flooded the page with support. I will not list every contributor here, but needless to say, without their support, and the support of my parents, Tom and Cristine Gaulke, this process would have been much more difficult, and perhaps impossible. Special thanks are due to Jim Peters who, in addition to helping with costs, also bought me a laptop that worked. I am writing on it now. Without the proper tools, it is difficult to do a good job, and I am grateful for this lasting tool and the creative possibilities it has allowed. Thanks are due also to the Lutheran School of Theology at Chicago, who granted me a scholarship after the completion of my ThM, and the Evangelical Lutheran Church in America, who also offered grants along the way.

My readers and mentors in this process have been many, especially as health has waxed and waned in our academic community. In addition to Dr. Westhelle, Dr. Billman, Dr. Saler, and Dr. Thomas (listed above) thanks are due to Dr. José David Rodriguez, Dr. Marvin Wickware, Dr. Ben Stewart, Dr. Mark Swanson, and Dr. Cláudio Carvalhaes. Each of these has had a hand in this process and offered encouragement and kindness along the way. Dr. Kim Wagner was a good neighbor, who also taught me about footnoting software. This was a lasting gift.

Dr. Thomas allowed me to teach with her while I was writing. This gesture of confidence and kindness was incredible. The experience in the classroom, while still completing the process, helped to affirm that the process, indeed, might be worthwhile. I am ever grateful.

I could not have written any of this without the GSA "study party" people here at the seminary. Adam Braun, Mayuko Yasuda, Eddie A. Rosa Fuentes, Denise Rector, and S. Hellen Chukka have been a gift in my life and have added joy and laughter to this often isolating and lonely process. Their constant critiques of my ideas have no doubt shaped them into their present form. Though they may not find their way into the footnotes, many pages were written after study breaks in which we engaged these ideas, and many of my sources were suggested by them. Likewise, I have had countless conversations with Benjamin Taylor. We spoke nearly every time I went to the JKM library to write. He also listened to me worry often about the project, more than one might expect from any friend. When we lost Dr. Westhelle to cancer, it was good to have a friend who also missed him dearly and shared an ongoing love for Westhelle's work.

Gloria Vicente in the Advanced Studies Office at LSTC has been a great source of help and encouragement. I am ever grateful for her reminders, follow-through, and kindness. Her pastoral ability has made the sharp edges of academia much more tolerable.

Lastly, I must thank the love of my life, Dr. Daisy Varughese. We started dating, got engaged, and experienced the birth of our beautiful baby, Hannah Sofia, while I was working toward this project. Daisy supported me when I left my call at First Trinity to prepare for field examinations and finish this book. She has constantly been a loving partner and support. I can't imagine life being as good, or this book getting done, without her love in word and deed.

Certainly, there are those I have not listed. Nonetheless, each act of support and act of generosity is embedded in my heart, and I am grateful for the love of each friend and colleague who has helped me through.

Introduction

I COUNT MYSELF AMONG the many in my generation of Lutherans, raised in the US, who may be seen as the inheritors of the Moltmannian promise of the reign of God, and of the varied expressions of this promise which from it flowed. Insofar as we have had this promise written upon our hearts, many of us have also faced our own *delayed parousia* as a result. Utopia has not been realized. Justice is not established in all the earth. Many of us feel as if we live in the shadow of the frustrated hopes and aspirations of those who came before us.

Some of our congregants are turning to (or back to) white nationalism and other racist ideologies for answers to, and explanations of, their pain, allowing neofascist movements to be the authors and authorities of their hope. These forces are casting for them new visions and dreams of a "greatness" that is to be yet "again." These hopes require strong beliefs in quite dangerous ideological frames. They are leading Christian people to create concentration camps for refugees and to open fire in Black churches, in synagogues and in grocery stores.[1]

Some among us have turned from the world all together, insulating ourselves from the fear, the pain, the violence, and the rhetoric that continues to flare up all around us. It is easier to lose ourselves in TV or movies, entertainment or work. Perhaps we lose ourselves in drugs. It is easier to turn off and tune out, so we do not have to feel the call to responsibility or enter into the anxiety and the pain that compassion so often demands. We reject faith, hope, and love, in exchange for a new opiate: escape into self-isolation. We arrive at a time not unlike Bloch's Germany: How do we hope? How do we hope so that all might live?

1. White, "When I Found Out."

This book intends to be a small contribution to a larger conversation about hope. It also intends to be useful for pastors and church-builders as well as those who work in community organizing and movement building. Such work depends upon hope and spiritual strength, whatever dogma one does or does not believe. My desire is that this book might be a source of hope, hunger, and desire for a better life, especially for those who skew agnostic or atheist, for those who are belief-fluid, and for those (like me) who find it hard to believe.

After Moltmann

When Jurgen Moltmann set out to write *A Theology of Hope* (published in 1964), he explicitly did so under the philosophical influence of both Ernst Bloch's philosophy of hope *and* the praxis and ideologies of the student movements of his day.[2] Bloch's ability to bridge personal spirituality with collectively utopian dreams left a new opening for people of faith to enter a conversation about changing the world. For Bloch, the mystical life was not only for those who would wait for the by-and-by. It also contained a spirit that could stir a body of people, filling them with longing for a better society and solidaritous dreams of a better life.[3] Moltmann perceived this opening in Bloch. Entering, he began to build a theology that would be explicitly Christian and explicitly hopeful in a this-worldly sense.

Moltmann came to the conversation with special concern for two practical questions, "Why don't protesting students pray?" he wondered, and "Why don't praying students protest?"[4] Implicit in these questions is Moltmann's conviction that both prayer and protest are outward as well as potentially communal expressions of an inward hope. Moltmann's task, flowing from these questions, was then to write theologically in a manner that would feed and nourish Christian hopefulness, leading praying Christians to protest for change, while naming the sacred in the work of the already politically active.

Attempting to lay a foundation, Moltmann posited that any Christian theology of hope, including his own, should contain and engage at least three essential concepts: "a), the concept of the divine promise in the Old

2. Moltmann, *A Broad* Place, 97–130.

3. *Dreams of a Better Life* was Bloch's intended title for his work published as *The Principle of Hope*.

4. Moltmann, *A Theology of Hope (Love)*, 8:19.

Testament; b) the concept of the raising of the crucified Christ as God's future for the world, in the New Testament; and c) an understanding of human history as the mission of the Kingdom of God today."[5] In Moltmann, the promise of God instills and verifies a Christian hope which leads the faithful into participation in God's missiological activity in the world.

This promissory-missiological motif, with its movement from divine promise to human participation in and agitation toward the promise (from praying to protesting), from 1964 onward, was quickly picked up from Moltmann's work and spread to various corners of Christendom. Here it took on a life of its own in the global south as it was incorporated into various liberation theologies and faith-led social and political movements. Subsequently, it found linguistic expression in the congregational and denominational mission statement projects of the ecumenical West. Missiological paradigms shifted among denominations of the mainline churches. From "going to all nations baptizing," many now began to emphasize "participation in God's kingdom work"—relocating emphases from the "going out" of *The Great Commission* to some combination of the love presented by Jesus in *The Greatest Commandment* and participation in the "kingdom work" of the *Missio Dei*, often as expressed in Jesus' "mission statement," adapted from Isaiah in Luke 4:18–19, with a special emphasis on bringing good news to the poor.[6]

In this frame, the mission is God's. The prayer for God's reign to come is about hope for the here and now, even as God's people participate in the promise of the reign's in-breaking fruition. In other words, piety and praxis become inseparable. "Christianity [becomes] the community of those who on the ground of the resurrection of Christ wait for the kingdom of God *and* [so it follows] whose life is determined [directed, shaped, moved] by this expectation."[7] God's promise gives the life and the activity of the believer meaning and shape.

There is no doubt that Moltmann gave shape to an important Christian theology. Grounded in promise, in Christ, and in resurrection hope, this theology helps the praying Christians of the world to be moved into faithful protest and action. No doubt this theology has inspired believers

---

5. Moltmann, *A Broad Place*, x.

6. Bosch, *Transforming* Mission, 442–57; Bevans and Schroeder, *Constants in Context*, 313–14, 387.

7. Moltmann, *Theology of Hope*, 288.

to live into the promise of God as received by faith, and to participate in world-changing work.

Yet Moltmann retains something of an air of Christian supremacy. Early in his work, he claims that "Christian hope alone is realistic."[8] There he also speaks of the "sin of despair."[9] For all of the hope that Moltmann offers, it is still, in the end, hope meant for a church full of believers, and hope that is to be dispensed, stewarded, and enacted by the church community, a community that counts despair as an alienation from or an offense toward God. This is curious for a man who relied so heavily on Bloch, a Jewish atheist, as he penned his own theology.

Beyond Moltmann's Promise

The questions I will raise in the following chapters are distinct from those Moltmann asked so many decades ago. This is because my task is different. I want to speak of a hope that is not so much for the already-believers (or aspiring believers), as it is for those who don't, who can't, or who won't believe. That is, here I am less worried about the ones who pray being moved to protest, than I am about agnostics, atheists, and belief-fluid folks finding and fueling a hope of their own—a hope that does not require belief in the coming fruition of a promise, or in an understanding of a god, a hope that does not cast shame or judgement on those of us who experience despair, and that does not mark the hopeless as the ones who are lost to sin. As a pastor, it is clear to me that despair is no sin against God or against hope. Indeed, the experience of despair is one of the primary reasons we summon hope and gods in the first place.

I am concerned also with those in faith communities who are fed by faith communities, and yet remain uncertain about God and uncommitted to dogma. In my own experiences in Lutheran churches in Nebraska, Wisconsin, and Chicago, there are often more community members who fit this agnostic description than those who do not. As a pastor and as a person, I usually fit this description myself. Yet, like these community members, I am committed to building a spiritual community that is grounded in love, a church community that feeds people now (literally) and works for a world where none will go hungry. Where our beliefs remain uncertain, we

8. Moltmann, *Theology of Hope*, 14.

9. Moltmann, *Theology of Hope*, 7–10.

nevertheless share a hope without belief. Our shared hope shapes our shared community and our shared mission, simultaneously.

From my concerns for agnostic hopers, for those who cannot cling to a promise tightly, and for uncertain faith communities, arise two guiding questions. These will shape my inquiry throughout. *Where might we look for hope outside of promise? Where might we find hope for an agnostic church and for those of us who find it hard to believe?* The unpacking of these questions, I call the pursuit of an *unpromising hope*. An unpromising hope does not need a promise in order to hope, though the hope itself might still "hold promise" in the sense that, in due season, it may bear fruit.

My aim is to find a few answers to these questions, and to do so by mining the works of thinkers and theologians who were each a part of spiritual communities (loosely defined), and yet sought after and spoke about *hope* in a way that was set apart from belief in promises or a belief in a well-defined god. I will find along the way that hope has more to do with homesickness, hunger, holler, pain, and even trepidation, than it has to do with belief or certainty—at least among my chosen interlocutors—as do the communities we call church.

Approaching Hope

There is a German appellation given to those whose vocation it is to become pastors. *Seelsorger* translates as *soul-carer*, one who cares for souls. In this sense, my approach as I write about hope is primarily pastoral. It is concerned with the spirit of our people and our church communities. It is concerned with feeding the spirit that fuels communal works of love and liberative justice. This concern is shared with my primary interlocutors as each one thinks theoretically and/or theologically about hope as hope takes place in and through the individual, the individual's community, and the wider world.

As stated above, this work is pastorally concerned especially for those who cannot or will not believe in a promise or in a god-of-promises. I am happy for the hope of believers, yet I am searching for a hope that will belong to a more deeply agnostic church, and for those, like me, who find it difficult to believe.

On this journey, I engage philosophers, queer theorists, activists, and those who reject the theological, as well as a number of Christian-identifying theologians. Though I come to this work as a pastor and theologian, my focus is upon finding unpromising hope, wherever if might be found. It is important for me to engage those outside strictly theological realms both because the question of hope is a question that transcends theological discourse (it is a human question), and because theological discourse has often listened quite poorly, ignoring the voices of those outside of theological circles, or distorting them quite badly (as I believe Moltmann did to Bloch). My intent is not to build a theology from atheists' ideas, but rather to engage in these ideas as an uncertain and agnostic theologian and pastor. My intent is that this study will be useful to theists, atheists, and agnostics alike.

Structure

Where might we look for hope outside of promise? Where might we find hope for an agnostic church and for those of us who find it hard to believe? In each chapter ahead, we will highlight a primary author or group of authors who have in some way addressed these questions in their own contexts. Each chapter will lift up an approach or approaches to hope that do not require belief in a promise, and sometimes do not require belief in a god (or in a god that is well-defined). Each remains committed to community.

Additionally, each chapter will be set in a "key." This is a practice I have adopted from Vítor Westhelle. Naming a *key* does at least two things. First, as a musical key, it names an emotional context and mood. A key expresses the emotional matrices from and in which a theology is formed. Musical, it names that more is communicated on the page than the words alone. Second, as a key to understanding, naming the key, placing it in our hands, helps us to unlock our minds in order that we might receive information that we might usually shut out.

In the first chapter, "Hope in the Key of *Heimweh*: Utopian Surplus," my primary source is Ernst Bloch. To dig beyond the promise in Moltmann, it became important for me to go back to this important source and to see what may have been missed by Moltmann or overshadowed by his promise motif. Adding to Bloch, I also look at José Esteban Muñoz and M. Shawn Copeland, especially as they interact with Bloch's concept of *utopian surplus*. These each name spaces and moments of becoming in which one might come to hope the revolutionary hopes left to humanity by humanity's aspirational ancestors.

In the second chapter, "Hope in the Key of *Saudade*: Dreaming the Messiah's Dreams," my primary source is Rubem Alves. I will explore a number of Alves' approaches to hope, concluding that his call that we might dream the messiah's dreams is most helpful in the pursuit of an unpromising hope. Sacramentally, when one takes in the messiah's dreams, these dreams might become infused with those of the dreamer. When this takes place, our dreams and the messiah's *become* together. For Alves, hope is fed in *aperitif* or sacramental communities, communities that bring us pleasure, while making us hungry for a better world, a world often envisioned as a banquet or a garden where children can freely play.

In the third chapter, "Hope in the Key of *the Holler*: A Countercultural Passion for the Possible," I will primarily dig into the work of Delores Williams, Emilie Townes, and A. Elaine Brown Crawford, returning as well to M. Shawn Copeland. I'll briefly look at both James Cone and Franz Fanon in order to clearly name the Manichean framework from which womanist theologies departed, forming a distinct framework and logic for ethical and theological reflection. The chapter's title is a nod to Crawford's work, *Hope in the Holler*. These authors will offer to the search for an unpromising hope their own *hope in the holler* for survival and quality of life and a passion for the possible right now, grounded in counter-hegemonic spaces and a counter-cultural, slavery-denouncing faith received from their Black Christian forebears.

The fourth chapter, "Hope in the Key of *Chōra*: So Close You Can Touch It," will turn the questions of an unpromising hope toward Vítor Westhelle's eschatological work. Unpacking some of his key concepts, I will find a hope that, unlike Bloch's revolutionary dreams, Alves' messianic dreams, or Williams' and Crawford's desires for survival and quality of life, is a hope that is thoroughly spatialized, and so hopes expectantly but without any image of certainty. It is a hope that fills the body with as much fear as anticipated joy. It is a hope that risks and "hopes against hope," in choratic spaces, in the crossing, even though hope's end may be death or increased despair.

In the form of a conclusion, I will reiterate the unpromising hope found in the works of these interlocutors, drawing implications for speaking of hope pastorally and building communities of hope today. Where might we look for hope outside of promise? Where might we find hope for an agnostic church and for those of us who find it hard to believe? Perhaps something of an answer will be received in the turning of these pages and in the pages of those who have struggled with faith, injustice, and hoping agnostically before us.

CHAPTER ONE

Hope in the Key of *Heimweh*

Utopian Surplus

HEIMWEH: THIS IS THE emotion that runs through Ernst Bloch's philosophical, mystical, and poetic work.[1] Translated to English, *heimweh* is "homesickness." It is a longing for a place of belonging, of safety, of joy. *Heimweh* is born from something lacking, from alienation, from a space of physical or spiritual homelessness.[2]

Bloch's own biography is full of existential and geographical displacement and alienation. Whether speaking of estrangement from the work of one's hands via the appropriation of labor and labor's fruits by industry, or his own expulsion from his physical homeland by fascist rule, homesickness, *heimweh*, for Bloch, is never simply theoretical.[3]

Without *heimweh*, Bloch's poetry, Bloch's spirituality, and Bloch's philosophy will seem out of tune and perhaps even weird. It will not make sense or resonate for anyone who feels perpetually rooted or fully at home. Perhaps most importantly, without a sense of *heimweh* there is no understanding Bloch's hope, for hope and *heimweh*, for Bloch, are inseparably intertwined. *Heimweh* is the emotional space where we meet, longing, to aspire.

Yet, for Bloch, *heimweh* is no longing backward toward a lost sense of belonging or being at home. There is no Eden, no Paradise lost. If Eden holds any meaning it may be only this: that estrangement and alienation mark our very beginnings. Estrangement is the world as it is. With no

1. Bloch, *The Spirit of Utopia*, 157, 192.
2. Bloch, *The Principle of Hope*, 1:76.
3. Bloch, *The Heritage of Our Times*, 1–15; Bloch, *The Spirit of Utopia*, 9, 239.

backward glances, *heimweh* longs forward for Bloch, desiring a Not Yet home, a home we have never known.[4]

"Next year in Jerusalem!" This phrase is said in exile, year after year at Seder tables around the globe. His chair is there. Elijah is gone. Nonetheless, the presence of his absence speaks loudly to our forward-reaching desire: "The world at hand cannot overpower the potential light [which shines into history] from the end of the Bible: with *l'ordre du coeur* [the order of the heart and with a hunger for] the New Jerusalem instead of the old Rome."[5] *Heimweh* longs for the new, the novum, for a society where humans feel at home, a city which is not yet. Longing, therefore, it negates what is and becomes the source of radical and revolutionary dreams.

Utopian Surplus: An Unpromising Hope Repository

Where might we look for hope outside of promise? Where might we find hope for an agnostic church and for those of us who find it hard to believe? These are the questions we will address in the coming chapters. Ernst Bloch has been often cited as a muse for theologians of promise, most notably for Jürgen Moltmann. Perhaps despite this fact, or perhaps because of it, he is a helpful thinker for us to begin with. Though Bloch has been picked up by Christian promisers, he himself identified as an atheist, and his hope was not tied to a promising God.

From a space of estrangement, displaced by a world marked by rising fascism, Bloch conceptualizes Utopian Surplus. He speaks of its efficacy in contributing to the growth and augmentation of daydreams and hope. As this was crucial for Bloch, it is crucial for us, as, indeed, it was his path toward feeding hope in a time of hopelessness.

This chapter, then, pays particular attention to Utopian Surplus. Overlooked by Moltmann and the theologians of promise, Utopian Surplus will engage us in our quest for responses to our questions.

To help us along the way, we will briefly touch upon Bloch's own biography, Bloch's understanding of human drives, and Bloch's understanding of the relationship between Utopian Surplus, music, performance, innovation, and art. We will also investigate some of the ways Bloch

4. My use of capitalization is here in accord with Bloch's own. Bloch, *The Spirit of Utopia*, 168.

5. Bloch, *The Spirit of Utopia*, 172.

struggles against fascist hopes which ran rampant in his day, as they do in our own.[6] As we near the chapter's end, we will put Bloch in conversation posthumously with some recent interlocutors, engaging Utopian Surplus for new contexts. We will conclude with an affirmation that Utopian Surplus is an important concept for us to utilize as we seek to speak of an unpromising hope today.

I. Bloch's Hope

Ernst Bloch

Ernst Bloch began his work on hope in the context of rising fascist ideologies in Germany—and therefore in the context of fascist *hoping*.[7] Fascist hopes were hybrid in nature. They were born of an idealized and glamorized German past, a past understood by fascist dreamers as having been both "pure" and "true." Looking backward, toward a fantasy projected upon history, they simultaneously longed forward toward a future realization of the fantastic images that the glamorization of an idealized past evoked. That is, their desire was directed toward the fulfillment and/or completion of that which the image of the past simultaneously presented and promised.[8]

The sciences of the day helped to ensure that these hopes were well founded in scientific facts. At the time, scientists had constructed and produced a number of racial distinctions and hierarchies, taxonomies that proved to be useful to the fascist cause, confirming at once fascist values and fascist aspirations toward their realization.[9] These so-called truths and

---

6. What Bloch means by fascist hope will be unpacked later in the chapter.

7. It will become important to our conversation later that these propagated hopes, dreamt by the Nazi party, where they resonated with many, were not born from within the hoper, but rather were received from an outside authority. This authority named both the pains and the responses to pain for the hoper, thereby robbing the hoper from genuine personal dreaming. In other words, hope was imposed, received, and not born from within.

8. Bloch, *The Principle of Hope*, 1:235–36.

9. For "scientific racism," in Nazi Germany, see especially Günther's notorious work on the "ethnology of the German people." Günther was praised by Hitler, having been used largely as a basis for the Reich's eugenics policies. Ludwig Ferdinand Clauss was also a leading contributor to this conversation, claiming distinctions between Germans, Nordics, Arians and so-called inferior groups. Günther, *Rassenkunde des deutschen Volkes*; Clauss, *Race and Soul*.

facts of Arian supremacy were further augmented by the newly accepted and quite in-vogue theory of Social Darwinism.[10]

In the service of fascism, science and religion were not necessarily conflicted. Fascist ideologies and hopes were enabled and even propagated by churches who held to the ancient understanding that "all authority is given by God," and so taught that the Christian is to faithfully obey Hitler, to pray always for him without ceasing, never resisting the SS, and so on.[11] In addition, propagandizing preyed upon the already dominant conviction among many in the church, that the Christian is the superior and true believer, and indeed the bearer of salvation. Today this attitude and belief is called "Christian supremacy."[12]

Here was a vision of an Arian nation: The Third Reich, the final kingdom.[13] It was to be for these believers something of heaven on earth meant for the chosen, the few, the pure. "The eternal God created for our nation a law that is peculiar to its own kind," claimed church leaders in a public fashion, "It took shape in the Leader Adolf Hitler, and in the National Socialist state created by him. This law speaks to us from the history of our people . . . One Nation! One God! One Reich! One Church!"[14] The Third Reich for these Christians was the fulfillment of the promise, spoken from history, the fruition of fascist, supremacist hopes and dreams.

Of course, such hope was not exclusively for the Christian. Resourceful as they were, fascist hopes played similarly on the messianic impulses within communist dreams and socialistic anticipations: desire for power to the people, to the workers, the proletariat, the farmers, those born of sweat and blood and soil.[15]

10. For Bloch addressing this directly as "the europic principle," see Bloch, *The Principle of Hope*, 1:98–102.

11. As mentioned, although Protestantism remained diverse, there were concentrated attempts to erase the Hebrew Bible and the Hebrew origins of Christianity by the state and by self-proclaimed German Christian movements. The Confessing Church formed in distinction to the German Christians (the Deutsche Evangelische Kirche) and, later, the Reich Church, who colluded more directly with the Nazis. Beyond collusion by organizational structures, church members and party members overlapped. Bergen, *Twisted Cross*.

12. Fletcher, *The Sin of White Supremacy*; Heschel, "Nazifying Christian Theology."

13. Bloch, *The Principle of Hope*, 2:509, 3:856.

14. Remak, *Nazi Years*, 95–96.

15. Of course, this movement was as much a heresy to Marxists as it was to the Confessing Christians—both schools claiming, at their best, fidelity to the crucified and the poor, to those the regime wished to exterminate.

Hearing any claims to be of the people, we must always ask, with history, "Which people?" Fascist hopes simultaneously dehumanized and were willing to sacrifice, to kill, to incarcerate, to displace those deemed non-people or lesser people, according to their own scientific or theological classifications.[16] Such as these were not heirs to fascist hopes, they claimed. They were merely sacrifices toward hope's fulfillment, here and now, on earth, as it is in the imagined fascist heaven. In Germany these became the Jews, the Roma, those who were gay, and so on. These were rounded up, detained, tortured, and killed in the name of the kingdom, the Reich, the imagined paradise conceived by idealistic minds. To these hopes, Bloch, a Jew and a refugee who was forced into flight, sought to write alternatives.

The Subject of Hope: Hunger, Self-Preservation, Filled and Expectant Emotions

Seeking an alternative hope, Bloch did not begin with dream-images or pictures of a divergent promise or of a nearby promised land. He also did not begin contrasting God's reign to the reign of state terror that was arising all around him, although certainly he was aware of the distinctions. His initial question was not, "For what shall we hope instead of the Reich?" This is because Bloch's initial question was not about the *object* of hope at all.

Bloch begins by examining what it is inside the individual, inside the *subject* of hope, the one who gives birth to daydreams and anticipations in the first place. How might we understand more deeply the human impulse toward better possibilities? Where is it, in or among us, that the seeds of hope germinate? Are they planted? Do we carry them from birth? To engage such questions, Bloch turns his attention toward human drives and emotions.

Freud would become an obvious springboard for this project. Yet, Bloch took issue with Freud. Freud, felt Bloch, was far too obsessed with the libido (a not uncommon critique at the time).[17] Contrary to Freud, Bloch

---

16. Clauss, *Race and Soul*; Günther, *Rassenkunde des deutschen Volkes*.

17. Although he does not make explicit his move away from Freud's nearly platonic or Manichaean concept of the libido, Bloch does explicitly reject what he deems as Freud's "backward glances," including his reportedly shallow conviction that hope is grounded primarily in repressions. It is clear in Bloch's philosophy and in his mystical approach that the mind is never separate from the body. The mind is of the flesh. It is the body. At the same time, for Bloch, the body is not primarily dominated by the libido, as we will discuss below. Interestingly, as much as Bloch would come to speak of hunger, he,

argues that the two most basic drives in humans are (a) hunger and (b) self-preservation.[18] Anyone who has spent significant time with an infant will likely not be prone to disagree. These are basic to nearly every human experience, Bloch believes. Further, hunger is the one emotion that seems also to foster empathy between humans: one feels compassion for a hungry person in a way one does not feel for someone who is heartbroken.[19] Certainly it would have been easy for Freud to overlook hunger, Bloch emphasized, as Freud lived and moved only among the rich and culinarily satisfied.[20] Bloch was determined not to make this mistake.

Moving from these two basic drives (hunger and self-preservation), Bloch then divides human emotions into two basic categories. The first he calls "filled emotions." These are jealousy, anger, and the like. The second he calls "expectant emotions," those that anticipate. They include hope and fear (which correspond to one another), as well as belief/confidence and despair (which correspond to one another).[21]

The basic drives, hunger and self-preservation, Bloch says, feed the expectant emotions (hope, fear, belief, and despair). These emotions, in turn, engage the imagination. The imagination, by way of these emotions, then produces wishful and unwishful images. We come to envision, to picture, or to flesh out that which we first felt in our first anticipatory, presentimental, state. These images, produced by the imag-ination, might then morph into ideas. These wishful images and these ideas, if they do not flutter off too quickly, perhaps distracted by the goings on of the day, an interruption or an obligation, or a rough and endless day at the factory, may then become what for Bloch is one of the most beautiful things: daydreams.[22] It is with the emergence and arrival of daydreams that Bloch,

---

unlike Freud, commonly avoided using the term *desire* in a similar manner. For Bloch there remained a certain distinction. I find it helpful to know that one of Bloch's intellectual enemies also struggled with this tendency in Freud. Jung himself understood Freud's obsession with the libido to be his fall into dogmatism, which was undesirable for Jung. Bloch, likewise, could never stand the dogmatic. Any system "closed" and clear of inquiry and growth was a system that would eventually choke out hope, and even life itself. For a fascinating account of this, see Jung, *Memories, Dreams, Reflections*, 150–53.

18. Bloch, *The Principle of Hope*, 1:67.

19. Trading one set of universals for another may not have been Bloch's best choice, but it is the one that he made.

20. Bloch, *The Principle of Hope*, 1:65.

21. Bloch, *The Principle of Hope*, 1:74–75, 111–13.

22. Bloch, *The Principle of Hope*, 1:4, 21–44, 50.

the atheist mystic, can without irony proclaim with the messiah that the reign of God is near, that it is within and among those who are hungry now and those who hunger now for justice.[23]

Hungry, self-preserving, and anticipatory by nature, daydreams are always born of something lacking, from a pain (or absence), as mentioned above. Daydreams are aware, emotionally and intellectually, of a barrier to (or void of) joy, and therefore dream through the barrier, beyond the absence, *ex nihilo*, toward the presence or recreation of something new. They are dreams of a better life. Daydreams are the presence of the possible in human imagination and emotion.[24]

Distinct from night dreams which are dreamt with a compromised ego, says Bloch, constantly standing in need of a Freud or another accredited professional to interpret and analyze them, daydreams are dreamt while awake. Ego intact, they are dreams we dream while we are playing our roles in the waking world.[25] We don't forget them. We decide what they mean. They belong to us, and we need no higher authority to find in them inspiration and instigation.

Heimweh and the Not Yet Conscious, A Hunger for an At-Home Future:
From Self-Preservation to Self-Extension

Sometimes daydreams die. They are abandoned or forgotten. Yet if daydreams are "watered by a light-dark mood,"[26] says Bloch, they may emerge (the admixture of emotions + images + ideas + dreams) as what Bloch refers to as the Not Yet Conscious.[27] The Not Yet Conscious possesses the body and mind as a ghost—the Spirit—from which Bloch's early work, *The Spirit*

---

23. This hunger and pain that gives birth to a dream for a better life is for Bloch the messianic impulse—the impulse within humans that holds the potential of igniting a collective uprising, the collective resurrection of the body of the oppressed. At least some credit for Bloch's understanding of this impulse must be attributed to Tolstoy's interpretation of Jesus' proclamation that, "the kingdom of God is among you," meaning both that it is "within you" (singular) and "among you all" (plural). The aim of this use is poetry more than precision. Tolstoy, *Walk in the Light*, 11–12; Tolstoy, *The Gospel in Brief*, 29–34; Tolstoy, *The Kingdom of God*, 234–325.

24. Bloch, *The Principle of Hope*, 1:76.

25. Bloch, "Man as Possibility," 50–51.

26. Bloch, *The Principle of Hope*, 1:107.

27. Bloch, *The Principle of Hope*, 1:64, 117, 145.

of Utopia, derives its name. The Spirit is music, "melodies of the future."[28] The Spirit moves and enlivens. It animates the body. The Spirit is homesickness (*heimweh*), presentiment for a home not yet here. It is an anticipatory feeling of belonging and being where one belongs, of placed-ness, of feeling (momentarily) no longer a stranger on the earth. This Spirit possesses the would-be utopian before she conjures an image of just how home might look or appear. The utopian dream precedes concrete blueprints.[29] Indeed, the blueprints proceed from the dream. Possessed by these dreams, by this homesickness, this *heimweh*, this spirit of utopia, the body might finally be instigated toward motion. It might come to imagine what could and perhaps even what should become in the world.

Once the image is cast, the body, the individual, may fall in love with this vision.[30] Falling in love, it might be moved—to live, to fight, even to die for the vision.[31] When this happens, hunger for the possible has overcome the self-preservation drive. The Not Yet Conscious and daydreams of a better life, make possible the critical utopian move "from self-preservation to self-extension."[32] The adventurer is born! Here is the one who is able to "venture beyond," even beyond her own self-preservation, for the sake of a Not Yet home.[33]

Hunger and the Question of Hope

Said differently, what begins inside the body now extends beyond it. "Glossolalia becomes prophecy. . . . Each is born of the same Spirit."[34] The body,

---

28. This phrase—regarding the musicality of forward-summoning hope, will become important for Rubem Alves, the focus of our second chapter. Bloch, *The Principle of Hope*, 1:117; Alves, *Tomorrow's Child*, 195.

29. Bloch, *The Spirit of Utopia*, 157, 191, 206.

30. Such longing hope stands in contrast for Bloch, to the backward longings of fascism and glorification of a German "Vaterland." It is not the "Fatherland" Bloch desires but a new and "virgin" one. Alves, *Tomorrow's Child*, 115; Bloch, *The Principle of Hope*, 1:236.

31. For critiques of a world "to die for" and an ethics of giving one's life for a cause (in contrast to *living for* a cause), see Beale, "Double Jeopardy," 90–100; Douglas, *The Black Christ*, 21–22; Baker-Fletcher, *Dancing With God*, 146–52; Grant, "Black Women and the Church"; Williams, *Sisters in the Wilderness*, 161–66.

32. Bloch, *The Principle of Hope*, 1:75–76.

33. Bloch, *The Principle of Hope*, 1:77.

34. Bloch, *The Principle of Hope*, 1:187, 237.

the person, moving outward from turned-inwardness dreams to create a world that is a homeland, where skeletons dance; a world, for Bloch, where all things are common: *omnia sunt communia*;[35] a world transformed from Hegel's Thing in Itself into Engels' Thing For Us.[36]

Such messianic hope, born of the Utopian Spirit, has no desire simply to see the world as it *is* and describe it, but as it should be—and change it.[37] Said differently, hope is no food critic, but a chef. It is hungry. It is *presentiment*,[38] forehunger. It can taste the future it desires. So it sets the table. It salivates. The stomach growls. The feast, hope says, is at hand.

The question of fostering hope, it follows, becomes a question about instigating hunger: hunger for the absent, imagined, anticipated ought; hunger that dreams through walls and pain and chains. The hungry are filled and the tyrants are torn from their thrones.[39] Yum! Delicious! This is the feast we desire. More than hunger for bread, however, in the vision of the banquet itself there is sustenance. Such hunger is a body, as a plant, stretching toward the sun.[40] The body is enlivened, fed by the sun, though the object of hope remains distant and yet un-obtained.

This is the question of fostering hope: How is one to feed, to instigate such hunger? For Bloch the answer is not with promise. Rather, it is with Utopian Surplus. Utopian Surplus, for Bloch, is found in many wells, many suns, and many repositories. And among the most important, for Bloch, is music.

II. Utopian Surplus

Music carries in itself Utopian Surplus, the concept in Bloch that will become something of an answer for us as we ask, *Where might we look for hope outside of promise? Where might we find hope for an agnostic church and for those of us who find it hard to believe?* In brief, Bloch uses this

---

35. Meaning, "All Things in Common," a slogan to which Bloch clings, popularized by Münzer at the time of the Peasants' Revolt, and found in Acts 2 and 4. Bloch, *The Principle of Hope*, 3:582; Bloch, *Thomas Münzer*.

36. Bloch, *The Principle of Hope*, 1:7, 336.

37. Bloch recalls Marx's Thesis 11 on Feuerbach: "The point is to change it." Marx, "Contribution to the Critique," 145.

38. Bloch, *The Spirit of Utopia*, 156–58.

39. Luke 1:52–53; Bloch, *The Principle of Hope*, 2:490.

40. Bloch, *The Principle of Hope*, 1:132.

concept to convey his conviction that in every piece of art, in every created object, in any creation dreamt by the heart and created from the hunger formed in the presence of its absence (be it a painting or a piece of music or a sermon or a political speech), that there exists something of a surplus. There remains there, even after the artist or creator is long gone, a residue, left-overs, traces of the hopes and dreams of the one who created it. That is, the artists' utopian daydreams become infused into the artists' art. For Bloch, then, if we can find a way to access that surplus, to approach and enter the piece from just the right angle and so to tap into it, we might be able, then, to imbibe it. We can eat and drink those residual hopes and dreams. Taking them in, those hopes and dreams might then both shape and feed our own hopes and dreams. Hope inspires hope. Hope feeds hope. Dreams of a better world exponentially give birth to deeper and wider messianic, utopian, and revolutionary dreams.

In brief, hopes and dreams lay hidden all around us in works of love from artists and ages gone by. We may access and ingest the surplus left in these objects. In turn, the hopes, the utopian dreams found in them, feed our own. This is Utopian Surplus.

More than any other created thing, for Bloch, music is the primary source and well of human hope. It's cup runneth over. It awakens in the subject the Not Yet Conscious as perhaps nothing else in the entire world can do.

A Musical Shape for Written Words

Music is of such importance, that even Bloch's works, written words though they remain, are themselves shaped as a symphony. His words and pages take on musical form and notes, some reading lyrically, some rhythmically, some as poetry. One commentator speculates that the shape of Bloch's works is based on Goethe's Faust. "Reprises, refrains, codas, the musical gestures are unmistakable."[41] "Hope is to hear the melody of the future,"[42] claims Bloch, and the songs we sing now, the orchestras that swell, can help us to perceive it. Bloch hopes that his writing, not fully a symphony, will still summon at least something of the melodic.[43]

41. Plaice et al., "Translators' Preface," xxxi-xxxii.

42. Bloch, *The Principle of Hope*, 1:142.

43. Both Rubem Alves and Vítor Westhelle (subjects of following chapters) would model their larger works on Bloch's format. Similarly an homage is their refusal of neat

Clairaudience: Mystical Melodies and Scientific Sight

In Bloch, then, music and melody do not serve simply as similes or symbols, signifying that the imagined object of hope summons an expectant "presentiment," and, subsequently a will to dance or move into the Not Yet. This is the case. However, it is so because sound itself is also a way for Bloch to combat what Westhelle will later call, the obstruction of "scientific sight." We will return to this concept below.[44]

Poetically, Bloch laments that there is no clairvoyance in his time. Humans have lost abilities for foresight and forward-reaching visions. There are no more oracles. Yet there is a possibility of an inkling. There is a sense of an open future, a future that remains faintly, yet really, accessible.[45] This sense exists not as clairvoyance, Bloch says, but as a clairaudience.[46] Small and faint, humanity may yet listen for that which can break through our inabilities to visualize, to fully imagine the *new*.[47] So there is a chance that we might yet perceive—albeit differently. "Music is the only subjective theurgy."[48] Hunger for the banquet breaks in through the ears.

Yet, for Bloch, why is there no clairvoyance? Why can we no longer catch a glimpse of what is to come? A piece of our seeing as in a mirror dimly, is the frames we have inherited. Indeed, our lenses help us to perceive, but only by way of their distorting function. And we have mistaken our method of observing-distorting as truth itself, or as true perception. Westhelle calls this way of perceiving scientific sight.[49]

---

conclusions which are instead often exchanged for "the offing" or an Adieu. These follow suit with Bloch—to conclude a work, to close a system is the devil. The messiah is only to be found in an open system, an open future, in becoming. A hoped for and unseen Not Yet. The stylistic introductions that are more poetic than anything, and which express Bloch's *heimweh* or Alves' *saudade*, become the norm for these authors. Injected into even the driest of works is at least a poetic introduction, an instigation of longing, of presentiment, of song. This is the point of each: the medium is not only the message, but also a tool for the fulfillment of the mission: to make a group of playing children from the valley of scattered bones (Alves), to begin a venturing beyond lured by the melodies of the Not Yet (Bloch). Alves, *The Poet, The Warrior, The Prophet*; Westhelle, *The Scandalous God*; Westhelle, *Eschatology and Space*.

44. Westhelle, "Scientific Sight," 341–61.

45. Bloch, *The Spirit of Utopia*, 190.

46. Bloch, *The Spirit of Utopia*, 163.

47. Bloch, *The Spirit of Utopia*, 238.

48. Bloch, *The Spirit of Utopia*, 163.

49. It is good for us to create some distance here both from Westhelle's and Bloch's insistence on sensory metaphors. While there is no doubt, especially in Bloch, that sound

Scientific sight, he explains, first emerged at the wedding of colonization and scientific exploration. Going into a new habitat, scientists would observe species.[50] They would then categorize these species, simultaneously encapsulating them into two-dimensional sketches or diagrams.

A sketch itself (the representation of the observed object, of the *spectacle*), would be copied and recopied, then, by way of the printing press. This representation of the observed object (the spectacle), produced by the observer (and not the one spectated), would then become universally available for the consumption of other eyes in nearly all corners of the colonized world. This practice happened more frequently as technology advanced.

The representation, reproduction, and universal distribution of a spectated object became something of a Platonic ideal form of the object. To scientific sight, this *other* on the page was held as truer than the other's account of herself. This becomes evidently dangerous when the colonizer/scientist begins to define indigenous people in the Americas, in Africa, and so on. There, as elsewhere, scientific sight silences and distorts those it wishes to represent.[51]

Scientific sight in the colonizing world becomes the truth. Scientific representations become so well trusted that if an objectified person wished to deviate from her own idealized scientific sketch (her confining caricature—often as one who is meant to be detained/enslaved) she would become something of a transgression—or she would be caught in transgression—and one that requires a hefty penalty. To de-conform is to be abnormal. To become abnormal is to transgress. To transgress is to be criminal, to be labeled as illegal. To be criminal is to be potentially crucifiable.

Drawn, defined, described, and contained, the other to empire is taxonomically put in its place.[52] In its place, judgements are made about

---

is indispensable to Bloch's hope, his insistence on hearing most certainly would have changed had he become unable to hear. Each of these authors is in search of a less-limited knowledge and desire that breaks free from conventional frames and constraints, and for each this begins with tapping into the body and its sensory knowledges. The use of bodily senses transgresses conventional limits/rationalities for these two, even as it creates its own limitations.

50. Species, from *specere*, meaning "to look" refers here to the things the scientist-explorers would "spectate" or "look at," making the object of their scientific inquiry the *species* or the *spectacle*—that which was observed and that which was clearly object. Agamben, *Profanations*, 57–58.

51. Westhelle, "Scientific Sight," 346–61.

52. This is not dissimilar to how fascist hope looks to a glamorized image of a historic "Vaterland," and wants it in the future, fulfilled and "great again," as discussed above.

inferiority and superiority. Policy and legislation reflect these judgements. Such science aids fascist ideologies (such as Hitler's eugenics) and, as mentioned, worldwide colonization.[53] Such science aids fascist ideologies today.[54] Certainly Bloch and his family were targeted by such science. He, defined as a Jew, by rising fascist power, was subject to the fascist definition of what *Jew* or *Semite* meant and to the appropriate punishment for existing as a transgression.

In addition to its fascist proclivities, scientific sight, for Bloch, presents another problem. The delineation produced by scientific sight and description is for Bloch something of a still life. It is static, a snapshot. So, for Bloch, it is also untrue to actual human existence. Existence is no still life. Life and history are fluid, in flux, perpetually and forever only existing in a state of becoming.[55] Definition as delineation inhibits becoming insofar as it demands conformity, as it puts one literally and figuratively in a box. Not only does scientific sight prevent a genuine and holy encounter with the o/Other,[56] it also makes we who see in this way unable to perceive reality. We see only static beings in a world that is, in reality, dynamic becomings.

Scientific sight mistakes representation for life itself.[57] Students of hope must perceive differently. We must free ourselves and others from its chains. We are not to dissect and draw the flower—and certainly not our neighbors. Rather, we are to wait and to watch—and perhaps also to water—and to see how the flower breaks through the asphalt into glorious, resurrective blooms.

We must break free from scientific sight if the *novum* is ever to bloom. Music, for Bloch, awakens in us the ability to perceive differently—and not simply the ability, but the hunger, even the imperative.

---

53. Westhelle, "Scientific Sight," 344.

54. Inwood, "White Supremacy," 579–96; Vandiver, "The Radical Roots."

55. Here Bloch aligns himself with Marx and the Young Hegelians, materialists (opposed to idealists) who relied on an understanding of history as one not flowing from a static or eternal *Idea* or *Word*, but rather as material to the core. Material history, understood dialectically, is in constant tension, moving toward syntheses from theses and antitheses. Where Bloch will push back is in his mysticism. Though materialism does not exclude the possibility of spiritual speech (and for Bloch atheistic spiritual speech), it does remain skeptical of the mystic. Hope buried in music and art seemed weird and suspect to leading Marxists in Bloch's day, leaving Bloch often alone and alienated from various directions.

56. Westhelle, *The Church Event*, 125–35.

57. Westhelle, "Scientific Sight," 341–47.

"Listen to carrion — put your ear close, and hear the faint chattering of the songs that are to come."[58]

For Bloch, in music played and performed, the Spirit of Utopia somehow mystically arrives. This Spirit is not received by reading musical notes written upon a page. It is never understood through the eyes. Indeed, it shatters our lenses that we might perceive. It is understood/felt only with the senses of the homesick heart. When music is played, performed, it becomes. It is dynamic and alive. It encounters us. It enlivens our body. It infects and moves our flesh as joyful noise. It is an event, communal, never static.

Filling the Room with Sound: Musical Experiences as Sources of Utopian Surplus

So music transforms a whole space. It fills a room. It sings into emptiness. In so doing, it reinvents or at least *reshapes* a whole inhabited world. What Marx wished for, saying "philosophers have only hitherto interpreted history. The point, however, is to change it,"[59] Bloch experiences already, right now, as a fleeting event and as a premonition, in a space filled with a song.

This returns us to the question of hunger: the taste of a transformed room, a momentary utopian experience, is a taste that leaves Bloch hungrier for a better world. If this room can be changed, enlivened by sound and song and bodies and hearts, how wonderful the taste of a transformed world where all people can dance and where all will finally be able to eat.

Music and Melody Make Life Worth Living: They Bring Joy

We will return to music and performance below as we enter into conversation with José Esteban Muñoz. Yet for now it is important to mention one other aspect of Bloch's love and taste for music and music's utopian and presentimental potential. This aspect concerns hunger for actual food—a hunger that, as discussed above, is quite important and deeply linked to utopian desire.

"Bread without violin," Bloch often reminded his peers in the struggle, is a communistic vision that will never be worth its weight. Scientific

58. Berry, "Manifesto: The Mad Farmer," 14–15.
59. Marx, "Contribution to the Critique," 145.

socialism, Bloch would argue, did not always take this seriously into account. Many would denounce Bloch for his music and his mysticism, as well as for this criticism.[60] Still, Bloch never backed down. We can feed the whole world, but for Bloch, if we lose music, we forfeit our soul. Life without pleasure is no utopia. Equality without joy is communal misery. It is not worth living for. It is not worth dying for. One cannot live by bread alone. We need music, joy, culture, dance.[61] We need songs that summon utopias that have yet to be dreamed, dreams that aid our eternal becoming. Here Bloch finds resonance with Mikhail Bakunin: "freedom without Socialism is privilege and injustice, and . . . Socialism without freedom [and without song] is slavery and brutality."[62]

Utopian Surplus: Innovation Trained, Innovation Untrained

Before we avert our senses away from music and toward visual art, something must first be said of the creators of music themselves. The musical innovator, more than any, for Bloch, inhabited "the Front." And the Front is that space (which is in front of us) where the melodies of a hunger-worthy future leak through.[63]

Though clairvoyance had been lost with the emergence of scientific sight, there was still something in music, in the vibratory languages of the embodied heart, of the emotions, of invoked desire, that could conjure the Not Yet Conscious and a hunger for the Not Yet like no other mode of expression and participation. It follows, for Bloch, that the composer was the closest thing that the world had to a prophet. The composer played utopia, thereby planting utopia in the listener. The creation of music is prophetism. It

---

60. Plaice et al., "Translators' Preface," xxii; Bloch, *The Principle of Hope*, 1:87–91.

61. Bloch, *The Principle of Hope*, 1:243–44.

62. This text, from "Federalism, Socialism, Anti-Theologism," was delivered by Bakunin as a speech, called by the author a "Reasoned Proposal to the Central Committee of the League for Peace and Freedom," at the League's first congress held in Geneva, September 1867. In contrast to Marx's emphasis on the synthesis that should result from the thesis and antithesis, Bakunin taught that the thesis and antithesis (for example, in his Russian homeland slaves and masters, and any system which creates or perpetuates these roles) systemically must be smashed and obliterated so that there is no synthesis, but rather so that something new might spring up from the ashes. Bakunin, "Federalism, Socialism, Anti-Theologism"; Duncan, "True Liberty, True Equality, and True Fraternity."

63. Westhelle will pick up and utilize this term differently in Chapter 4. Bloch, *The Principle of Hope*, 1:200.

is messianic in its pull, creating hunger for the liberative. Once again: "music is the only subjective theurgy!"[64] In other words, the composer is one who gives birth to a clairaudience that serves the utopian function. In music, one does not have to dig. Utopian Surplus is at hand. It spills into us.

To be clear, contrary to the elitism of his time (to which Bloch is not immune), it is not the trained composer alone who holds such potent and creative capacities. So, as well, does the traveling minstrel—the one who travels from village to village with his songs. The composer plays utopia, creating new compositions, building on the past, sometimes reshaping conventions and rules, transgressing delineations and definitions; sometimes demolishing and rebuilding with the raw materials of the musical rubble. So, in a different manner, the traveling minstrel enacts, says Bloch, "the Innovation of the Untrained."[65] He creates out of nothing, out of emotion, perhaps, more than academic discipline, he is playing from the heart, for he (according to Bloch) had no rules to begin with.[66]

Each of these improvisers creates something full of surplus hope. Each creator has the possibility of instilling in her listeners a hope for what might yet be. Each of these gives a taste of another beautiful reality, creating hunger for what else might yet become.

Utopian Surplus: Feeding Hunger with Art

Primary as it is, music is not the only source of Utopian Surplus for Bloch. Visual art, like music, is also a way to instigate hunger for the Not Yet. Visual art enters the body through the eyes (and not as music through the ears and the vibrations of the body and its skin) and so visual art resonates with and awakens the body differently. Still, the images produced

64. Bloch, *The Spirit of Utopia*, 163.

65. Again, I am using Bloch's capitalization practices for Bloch's terms. Bloch, *The Spirit of Utopia*, 39.

66. Though Bloch here overlooks his own elitism in the assumption that the traveling musician is "untrained," he, perhaps because of his elitism, stumbles upon this important phrase. "The innovation of the untrained" deserves further thought precisely because it breaks away from an elitism that demands that creativity and hope come from the "trained" in elite ivory towers or exclusive institutions. This nod to proletarian creativity should be embraced—as it will be in Muñoz's praise of punk and queer culture, and as it should be in the realm of political and revolutionary hip-hop. Though Bloch here distinguishes between "true" and "false" folk songs, he would do better to let them remain subjectively judged as potential spaces of utopian surplus. Bloch, *The Spirit of Utopia*, 48.

by visual artists (as in all objects imagined and created in the presence of their absence) may offer to the person without a wishful image, (to the person unable to imagine), one possible shape for the projection of their own longing. Seeing the presented image and internalizing it, if the image syncs with her own hunger or desire for the Not Yet, the subject then holds that image as a memory.

Every image retained in memory is morphed into a different image. It becomes an object of the imagination grounded in the memory of its viewing. In the subject, this memory lives as an imaginative fantasy, no longer an object encountered outside of the body, but within. This image, begotten of the image observed, is now the hoper's own, even as it is inspired by another's creative work.

In this way, like music, art may also offer a glimpse or transport into another world, creating varied wishful-image-options for the one who hungers beyond. Like music, visual art may feed one's hunger for what could be, becoming a springboard into multiplicitous and previously unimagined possibilities. This form of imbibing art feeds cyclically back into *heimweh*, creating a hunger feedback loop, a loop which grows louder the longer one remains in proximity to art's Utopian Surplus.

Bloch's musings about visual art expand into the architectural realm, especially in his commentary on European cathedrals as elaborated in *The Spirit of Utopia*. There, it is in Gothic cathedrals that Bloch finds a deep well of surplus hopes and dreams.[67] In addition to their shape and their presentation of space, these buildings also allude to stories of faith which, although they hold the possibility of being corrupted by fascism, still often hold in themselves the feeling of a certain longing for something which is beyond.

Bloch notes, in a surprisingly polemical fashion, that at the center of a pyramid is a dead person, a lifeless body prepared for the underworld—in other words, at the center of the pyramid is death. This is the god of slave-holding empire. In contrast, Bloch lifts up, at the center of the cathedral, wherever there is a crucifixion (an image of the right now), there is also the body that is again alive. There is at the center of all of the bloodied bodies, still a glimpse of resurrection. There are vines in the woodwork. There are grapes carved into the altar. In other words, for Bloch, even in static materials, there is the feeling of growth, of liveliness, and of becoming. There is a

---

67. This especially so as he contrasts them to the pyramids of Egypt. Bloch, *The Spirit of Utopia*, 20.

yearning to live more fully wherever we look. Everything in the cathedral screams the secret desire of those who pray: the body hungers for resurrection. The body wants life. The images of a messiah, the apostolic confession about the resurrection of the body—these are wishful images and ideas, daydreams that, like music and art, feed hope. Bloch does not need to believe them to find their value. It is not the dogmas, but the hunger for a better life, the Utopian Surplus contained in the art, and the space, and the images, and even the spoken words, that Bloch wishes to imbibe. "The last shall be first" (Matt 20:16; Luke 13:30), "The tyrants shall be torn from their thrones" (my translation), "Now the whole group . . . were of one heart and soul, and no one claimed private ownership of any possessions, but everything they owned was held in common. With great power the apostles gave their testimony to the resurrection" (Acts 4:32–35). These holy words are filled with utopian surplus and so they should be tapped for the sake of hope, and for the sake of messianic longings among and within the hungry.

Utopian Surplus in Many Wells

Bloch's work is very much the product of this activity: mining history, art, theology, mythology, anything he can get his hands on, for Utopian Surplus, for traces of utopia, for residual hope. All of these might be utilized to feed hope and instigate hunger and *heimweh* today.[68] Indeed, in all of his encyclopedic tediousness, this is his primary objective: to drill into cultural expressions of generations now deceased, to find in them the sweet syrup that longs for a liberated world, a classless society, something better beyond what currently is, and to pull that syrup to the surface so that it may be tasted and so that it may feed hope, increasing the hunger and the *heimweh*, that resides within those who dream, or who would dream of a better life and a better world.[69]

68. Bloch, "Man as Possibility," 65.

69. In conversations about Bloch, I am often pointed by peers to Walter Benjamin. As noted early, Benjamin was one of the few scholars and friends from whom Bloch was never estranged. Apparently the two used hashish together. Benjamin, like Bloch, retained the spiritual and the messianic in his materialist hopes for this-worldly revolutionary activity. Benjamin held something of a deep reverence for Bloch, and the two obviously influenced one another. Whereas Benjamin (in short) looks back at the haunting cries and pains of the past, seeking to redeem history by amending the present, Bloch looks back through the same cries and conditions, but traces instead the emancipatory hopes that pulsed through those who cried out. For Bloch, we are not to redeem the pains

In his digging through German history, for example, in search of a German "heritage of hope," a task which he held like a heavy weight as he saw fascism rising around him, fascism which claimed that Bloch was no longer German himself, Bloch will comment: "Our German heritage in not Hansel and Gretel!" It is not blood and soil. The true German heritage, if there is one, is obvious: "it is the peasant's revolt!"[70] With Müntzer and the peasants, and with Bloch, the poor and the persecuted cry: *Omnia sunt communia!* This is the heart of Bloch's revolutionary hope.

In this section we explored briefly Bloch's conceptualization of Utopian Surplus. We also took a look at his conviction that music and musical creativity, as well as visual art and artists are primary sources in the search for good sites for the extraction of Utopian Surplus. We will say more about sources of Utopian Surplus below. Before we do, we will pause here to investigate, for Bloch, what *heimweh* is not, or should not be. What excess surplus should we avoid consuming? Which is contaminated? As has already been hinted at, there is certainly a hunger that is quite contrary to the peasants' cry, and a hunger that is better suppressed. The next section will explore a longing that is antifascist, and that intentionally avoids and abstains from fascist desires.

III. Dreaming Forward, Never Look Back: Suppressing Fascist Longing

Bloch, mining the surplus hopes and dreams of the living and of the dead, prides himself in his orientation toward the future, that which he calls (among other things) the Not Yet. But we must remember that the Not Yet is in no way promised. Sometimes becoming happens badly. This is why Bloch must become a refugee as he writes. We cannot simply hope aimlessly if we wish for something of the common and something of the good. So the question must be asked: How is the desire for a Not Yet home (*heimweh*) different from a desire for an Eden or for a time of fairy tales and castles?[71]

---

and oppressions of history, but rather to dream the messianic dreams of the oppressed and pained who lived before us. We are to amplify and augment those dreams and move toward their fruition. For Benjamin's approach, see Benjamin, "Theses on the Philosophy of History," 196–209.

70. Bloch, *The Principle of Hope*, 1:236.

71. Or we might ask: how is *heimweh* different from the longing nostalgia of the far right in the US, wishing to "Make America Great Again," and different from the Nazi party who longed for a return to an idealized "pure" and Arian past, "One People, One

To start, we should note that the problem for Bloch is not simply looking back in itself (again, this is an activity which fills volumes of his project). The problem includes making the idealized past into the wishful image. As mentioned above, this is what the propagators of blood and soil were doing. When one does this one does not imbibe the Utopian Surplus contained in the past, but rather eats the poison of the static image itself. We return to this point now.

The pasts toward which Bloch's fellow Germans were looking were themselves static images. As such they became snapshots of "purity," a poisonous nostalgia for what was, distorting hope into a conviction that what *was* is what *ought to be* now: Make Germany great again. Similar to the problem of scientific sight, this idealizing sight is a problem for Bloch, because for Bloch, again, history is never closed or still or static. Rather history, if one is to speak of it rightfully and faithfully, is always dynamic. To grasp what has been is to grasp it as becoming.[72] Every still life is not life itself, but a skin that was being shed along the way to the present becoming moment. To see history in an image is to miss the story. There is no essence. There is becoming. And a desire for the essential, especially as enhanced through the sciences of racial hierarchies and the white-supremacist mythologies discussed above, is quite literally to wish death (it is the *death wish*), to stop becoming, and to destroy true history.

Hyperaware in his time of rising human fascist tendencies toward backward glances and backward longing, this poisonous *heimweh* which is the *death wish*, Bloch will become hyper vigilant against more or less any past-oriented philosophies, as he understands them. All must be tested. Particularly, he takes objection to what he identifies as the backward gazing impulse in psychoanalytic discourse and clinical practice—particularly as he interacts with Freud and Jung.

Backward Glances in Freud

Freud, argued Bloch, looked into the unconscious, repressed dreams of sexual desire to understand behaviors and emotions in the present. The past held the key to understanding the right now. Understanding the present,

Country, One Leader"?

72. In addition, for Bloch, historicism can itself become an opiate—preventing desire for revolutionary change by instead making one drunk with images of the past. Bloch, "Man as Possibility," 61; Bloch, *The Principle of Hope*, 3:911.

Freud could help his bourgeois clients adjust better to capitalist society—to manage their desires (to adapt to reality) so that they might better become a useful part of the capitalist-industrialist machine. At best, Freud was a compassionate capitalist conformist and accommodationist. He did not desire freedom from the violence that capitalism inflicted on the individual and on the poor, yet he did want his clients to feel better, to have pleasure. For this reason, Freud was the new opiate of the people. He offered compassionate palliative care—even if only to the people who could afford it.[73]

It was not the repressed unconscious of the frustrated past that moved us alone, Bloch clarified in his own understandings. It was the Not Yet Conscious—the melody of the future. Bloch's preferred hunger desires toward the better and the utopian, toward a virgin land, and not a Fatherland. It is not born of the past, be it conscious or repressed.[74] Memories of banquets may make us desire to eat, but we hunger for the meal that is yet to come.[75]

If Freud speaks of the night dreams of the repressed teenager, dreaming of the unattained cheerleader or jock, night dreams ending in ejaculation, then Bloch speaks of daydreams, of waking hope, revolutionary dreams of the hungry oppressed, dreams that hold the power of giving birth to a new world and a different life.

Carl Jung: The Psychoanalytic Fascist

Jung, found on the other hand, in his backward glances into the imagined "primordial," something easily tapped into by the religious and spiritual of his time. He was an answer to Freud's seemingly unnecessary atheism. The problem with Jung, for Bloch, however, is that faith and spiritual experience for Jung (looking backwards) was understood as something of a return to an imagined emotional "pool [with] drives in every direction."[76] It is this

73. Bloch, *The Principle of Hope*, 1:91, 95, 99.

74. Bloch, *The Principle of Hope*, 1:157.

75. Bloch will come to apply a similar critique to Jung. "Freud the teacher is on the same plane as his perverted pupil on the crucial point: both understand the unconscious solely as something past in historical development, as something that has sunk down into the cellar and only exists there. . . . [T]hey in fact recognize no pre-consciousness of a New." All these understandings idolize the drives (they become something absolute and outside the body). . . . In this way an idolized libido arises, or will to power or primeval Dionysus, and more significantly these idols are made absolute." Bloch, *The Principle of Hope*, 1:64.

76. For Bloch, Jung understood the drives as aimless/impulsive. They aim at no

aimlessness that troubles Bloch the most. There is no object of desire, no clear object of hope. One still begins with pain, oppression, and absence. Yet without hunger for the Not Yet, without an image of what could be, without some version of the *omnia sunt communia*, this starting place easily breeds, rather than hunger for the common liberation of all creatures, hatred and violence instead. And so Bloch is compelled to declare Jung to be "the psychoanalytic fascist."[77] For Bloch, Jung desires into an imagined idealized past that is a will to nothingness, no direction, chaos. He, too, overlooks hunger, the daydream. His *heimweh* is pointed in the wrong direction. He, too trades Bloch's preconscious for Freud's unconscious, Bloch's presentiment for Freud's repression. He cuts off desire for a better world and a better life. He opts for *coping* instead of revolutionary *hoping*, and in another opiating move, escapes into the mystical.

Bloch, continuing the line of thought described above, asserts, again, that just as there is no static or still snapshot of history, so also there is neither an "essential man" nor an "essential self," as Jung would have it. Our essence is nowhere to be found. Our essence, if we choose to speak in such a way, is becoming. We cannot be ourselves or become ourselves. There is no such thing. We simply become. Each one becomes. It does not arrive. It is never defined. It is dynamic. We are not human beings. We are becoming human. We are becoming. "Who we are is not yet."[78]

By claiming religion as acceptable, (in contrast to the somewhat ambivalent Freud and the often hostile Marx and Engels) but directing religious sentiment toward the primordial, Jung means well, but misses the point entirely: glossolalia is not the catharsis of repressed or forgotten pasts. It is not

---

future goal and so lack the utopian impulse. For Bloch, Jung seeks reconnection not with a better future, but with the primeval, and this happens through religion/witchcraft/etc. "Jung's collective unconscious flows thicker in witch-crazes than in pure reason." Looking backwards, Jung falls among those who imagine the past and long for it as a goal—an impulse at the heart of the German fascism of his time: "Libido becomes archaic; blood and soil, Neanderthal man and Tertiary period leap out simultaneously to confront us." Freud's sublimations at least lead to society, but Jung's primeval return leads to "orgy." The point is that this enables capitalism to continue to destroy and use the proletariat. "The rapport of this Panic libido with German fascism is obvious; the consciousness of the C. G. Jung somnambulist is in no way suspended here. To fascism also, hatred of intelligence is, as Jung actually says, 'the only means of compensating for the damages of today's society'. Fascism too needs the death-cult of a dolled-up primeval age to obstruct the future, to establish barbarism and to block revolution." Bloch, *The Principle of Hope*, 1:61–64.

77. Bloch, *The Principle of Hope*, 56.

78. Bloch, *The Spirit of Utopia*, 202–3.

a return. It is not meant to be a wet dream ending in autoerotic explosion. Rather, religion is the cry of the oppressed creature[79]—a cry that, in community, is to be shared, in common, and by the Spirit becomes prophecy, the naming of an absence, and the calling into being of the new.

By turning to the unconscious/repressed desire to describe the present, Jung and Freud never discover the Not Yet Conscious, and so they never understand with Bloch the presentiment of the future. As Bloch was fond of saying, one cannot understand heliotropism by looking only toward the past.[80] If one does, one will miss the impulse of the Not Yet Conscious and the hungry becoming toward the Not Yet.

The Not Yet Conscious and Presentiment

The Not Yet Conscious and presentiment, Bloch believed, were not born of repressed desires, sexual or otherwise (like Freud's night dreams or Jung's spiritual regressions). On the contrary, each desired the new, the *novum*, the Not Yet. It was not a fascist longing for return to a Fatherland/Motherland, but a revolutionary project toward the becoming of a "virgin land."[81] Bloch's expectant emotions are the anticipation of birth, of creation and prophecy— they are the emotions of Advent, the deepest blue before the great dawn— they are hunger and *heimweh*. "Then let the daydreams grow really fuller, that is, clearer, less random, more familiar, more clearly understood and more mediated with the course of things. So that the wheat which is trying to ripen can be encouraged to grow and be harvested."[82]

Bloch opposed fascist nostalgia, "backward thinking," and "backward dreaming." This is clear on every page he writes. Yet, to reiterate, Bloch was in no way opposed to history, its telling or its interpretation. History remains, with music, with the arts, with religion and with innovation, an indispensable source, helpful in feeding the Not Yet Conscious. History—especially

---

79. "Religious suffering is at the same time an expression of real suffering and a protest against real suffering. Religion is the sigh of the oppressed creature, the sentiment of a heartless world, and the soul of soulless conditions. It is the opium of the people." Marx, "Contribution to the Critique," 54. Marx's mistake was that he thought religious longing should be rejected in its religious form. Bloch's correction is that religious longing has the possibility of enhancing and instigating the utopian in the individual. It holds power to move people into revolutionary activity.

80. Bloch, *The Principle of Hope*, 1:131–32.

81. Bloch, *The Principle of Hope*, 1:236.

82. Bloch, *The Principle of Hope*, 1:4.

the cries of history, the hopes and dreams yet unfulfilled, hold the possibility of augmenting daydreams of a better life now, the dreams for which Bloch worked and wrote and longed.

Contrary to what Bloch sees as the idealizing (making-static/immobile) impulse in fascist ideologies, Bloch looks back at no Golden Age, but only at dissatisfaction and its struggling hopes and dreams, only at becoming and the dreams that helped bodies to make history become. "Our heritage is the Peasants' Revolt!" Here we see: he looks back not to go back or to be "great again," but, rather, in order to hope and dream as the peasants hoped and dreamt, even as we hope and dream anew.

Bloch finds in the Exodus, in Jesus, in Joachim of Fiore, in the peasants, and ultimately in Marx (who he believes offers a concrete way forward), the same impulse: a world where all things are held in common, where each has according to her needs, and where all people are able to eat—and a world where "humanity and nature no longer see each other as strangers," but as friends.[83] The world will be new—and so will we. We will have become, even as we will still be becoming. Simply put, Bloch's looking back is looking back in order to dream forward, toward the dream of the classless banquet, which is the resurrection of the body.[84]

It is true: the impulse toward change always runs the risk of going awry. Bloch would be the first to say that the longings of the heart take terrible and even evil turns. Again, he was made a refugee by the *heimweh* of the Reich. However, *not hoping*, is an impossible task. Indeed, hope and hunger are what bring the body to life, make life worth living. Though, it seems, the question must be about life for all, not just for me. Said differently, hope must become collective. We must all be looped into one another. Self-preservation (which is willing to sacrifice the other) must become communal and hungry self-extension. For Bloch, this means some form of socialism.

---

83. The question of a kind world (as Alves will come to speak of it), and of one where humans are at home (for Bloch), is the question of a humanized world for Marx. Of course, in contemporary conversation, the "humanization" of the world must be re-examined. Certainly, it is in bending the earth into human service, that humans may eventually create a situation in which the earth for humans is uninhabitable. Today, our challenge is perhaps to speak less of "humanization," and more about responsibility, care, cohabitation, and the like. Bloch, *The Principle of Hope*, 3:919; Alves, *What Is Religion?*, 29.

84. Bloch, *The Principle of Hope*, 1:210, 236.

My fears and dreams must become a gathering of the hopes and dreams of all. And as we hope and dream together, we must remember. No past (glorified or not) is without its scapegoats and victims. Therefore, no past is to be idealized and longed for. On the contrary, we receive the dreams, the cries, the desires, the hunger for justice (often frustrated) echoing from the past. We hope and dream them anew. We dream them in the context of our pains and oppressions. And we look to where we might feed this hunger—music, art, places, spaces, faiths . . . so that we may not simply daydream, but really be moved. We search for Utopian Surplus, fuel and fodder for the struggle for what is just.

In section four, we explore an adaptation of this hope-extracting project in the work of José Esteban Muñoz.

IV. Muñoz and Bloch: The Art, the Awe, the Ecstasy

Bloch's concept and *use* of Utopian Surplus has curiously resurfaced in the last decade in the work of Cuban-American scholar José Esteban Muñoz (d. 2013).[85] A queer theorist, Muñoz adopts Bloch's method of seeking out and extracting utopian surplus, and builds upon Bloch's project, introducing into the conversation popular art which, for Muñoz, depicts (and evokes) "awe."[86]

Awe is an important emotional state for Muñoz. This is because awe transforms the present "Now," into something more mystical. When one is awed, one experiences a certain sense of enchantment. Awe gives a fleeting taste of something numinous. It is a foretaste, an at-handedness. It Blochian terms, it awakens or augments the Not Yet Conscious.

Said awe, or awed-ness, for Muñoz, is further an entering into what Muñoz calls "queer time."[87] *Queer* here refers to that which is undefinable or moving beyond definition, something that is marked by becoming.[88]

---

85. Muñoz's embrace of popular culture is an important advancement away from some of Bloch's unfortunate elitism as discussed above. Muñoz, *Cruising Utopia*, 1–15.

86. Muñoz, *Cruising Utopia*, 5, 14.

87. If this concept is of interest, it may be worth the reader's time to compare Muñoz's concept of "queer time" and utopia with Agamben's understanding of "messianic/operational time" and Nancy's description of "intoxication." The interplay between these three is quite enjoyable. Muñoz, *Cruising Utopia*, 25; Agamben, *The Time That* Remains; Nancy, *Intoxication*.

88. Queer theory, rejecting societal gender and sexual norms, embraces gender as fluid or becoming, challenging and transgressing normalized conceptual and behavioral

Queer time then, in subjective queer-experience, is time experienced out-side of the delineations of the body and simultaneously outside the confines of the chronological—even if it is experienced in the body and today. It is an experience of flux. Outside of art, such ecstasy may also be induced by the drug of the same name (to which Muñoz dedicates his brief concluding chapter).[89] Like Bloch, and Benjamin before him, Muñoz discovers, contrary to Marx, that a drug need not only be viewed as an opiate which furthers oppression. It might also foster even more vivid daydreams.[90]

In art, when art is received as such, such ecstasy, such a state of awe (or queer becoming) is conjoined with something of the artists' own dreams. "The utopian function is enacted by a certain surplus in the work that promises a futurity."[91] "A certain mode of nonbeing . . . is imminent, a thing that is present but not actually existing in the present tense."[92] Alves will call this the presence of an absence experienced as *saudade*,[93] similar to Bloch's *heimweh*, that, in this case, art presents.[94]

Such art-induced ecstatic moments of awe and queer-becoming give a sort of proof and taste of a potentially different time—Bloch's Not Yet, Mu-ñoz's queer future. The experiences themselves "open possibilities." The logic runs something like this: Another world exists. I've been there. I've tasted it.

---

structures. Here Muñoz applies this challenge to being itself. If "being" is normativity, "becoming" is the queer counterpoint.

89. Muñoz, *Cruising Utopia*, 185–89.

90. Bloch, *The Principle of Hope*, 1:88.

91. Note that by using "promise" here, Muñoz is not referring to a static image that serves as the image of salvation of a coming society or Reign. Rather "promise" is here used as it is with youth: "She holds a lot of promise!" That is to say, promise means open and plentiful possibilities, an open future, and not a closed history with a "promised" fulfillment point. Muñoz, *Cruising Utopia*, 7.

92. Muñoz uses Agamben's sense of *potentiality*. Muñoz, *Cruising Utopia*, 9.

93. "Translators with expertise in several languages say that there is no precise syn-onym for [*saudade*] in other languages. It is a feeling close to nostalgia. Nostalgia is pure sadness without an object. Nostalgia has no face. Whereas *saudade* is always *saudade* 'of' a scenario, a face, a scene, a time. The Brazilian poet Chico Buarque wrote a song about *saudade*, in which he says that '*saudade* is a piece of me wrenched out of me, *it's to straighten up the room of the son who just died.*' It is the presence of an absence." Alves, *Transparencies of Eternity*, 15. Disappointingly, as far as I know, Alves never makes men-tion of Bloch's *heimweh* in relation to his Brazilian Portuguese *saudade*. Certainly, this conversation would have drawn a deeper connection between the two.

94. For Muñoz (and for Muñoz's Warhol and O'Hara), "utopia exists in the quotidian. Both queer cultural workers are able to detect an opening and indeterminacy in what for many people is a locked-down dead commodity." Muñoz, *Cruising Utopia*, 9.

Therefore, another world could exist here and in this time. I have a taste for this. Times can change. I hunger for this. I will work toward the fulfillment of this hope.[95] Certainly this is not too far from Bloch's conception.

Stages and Communities: Rehearsing Our Becoming

Here Muñoz adds to Bloch's wells. Utopian Surplus, as we have said, is not for the individual alone. Art, music, theater, etc. all bring people together. "Scenes," cultured communities, form around objects which contain thick Utopian Surplus. Individuals build chosen families and develop new and becoming identities. This is true, especially for Muñoz, in "minoritarian communities."[96] Where individual dreams are instigated, and experimental becomings take place in a common space, there, dreams and becomings collide. There we can taste a world that is here, but Not Yet; for example, and for Muñoz, a world in which "queer youths of color actually get to grow up,"[97] where queer youth of color can *become.*

Such communities, Muñoz testifies from personal experience, allowed Muñoz to tap into, and eventually act upon his own queer desires, thereby helping him to become the queer person he was becoming throughout his life. For Muñoz, examples of such communities were found in clubs—in designated spaces, and at designated events. These were specifically found in performative spaces—in locations that, as a centerpiece, housed a stage—platforms, spaces of presentation, on which actors "performed" or "rehearsed their becoming."[98]

Here, from the stages, possible identities were offered to the crowd (even as each attendee offered the same), expressed, at once, both as performative and as open and becoming. As we create ourselves, as ourselves become, so we imagine the world we wish to create, the world we wish would become, that which we desire to be becoming and creating together.

95. Muñoz, *Cruising Utopia*, 14.

96. Muñoz, *Cruising Utopia*, 98.

97. Muñoz, *Cruising Utopia*, 96.

98. Muñoz, *Cruising Utopia*, 103, 111.

Queer Stages, Punk Stages, An Ideal of Imperfection
and the Rehearsal of Becoming

Muñoz does not speak of Bloch's "innovation of the untrained." Yet Muñoz does speak of "performative amateurism."[99] The ideal in performative
amateurism, says Muñoz, is imperfection. In other words, the ideal is to be
queer, to be becoming, to resist a defined ideal as delineated by a society or
a group—be that the society of the classical elites or the distastefully over-
produced mainstream pop and disco to which punk initially responded
with transgressive defiance.[100]

By performing in a way that is perceived as amateur, performers re-
fuse not only masters, but also mastery, says Muñoz.[101] In so doing, they
perform simultaneously their own non-conformity to definition and scientific sight (their own becoming queerness) as well as their own utopian
desire: a world with "no slaves and no masters."[102] Subjective becoming and
utopian longing, for Muñoz, here are linked. A freer spirit longs for a freer
space. "For many [punks and queer punks in the 1980s] the mosh pit was
not simply a closet [a place to hide, yet a place to safely be free]; it was a
utopian subcultural rehearsal space."[103] It was a place to rehearse becoming
and to feed desires for a more becoming world.

At punks shows, the imperfections (forgetting lyrics, deviation from
the song as it is recorded on an album, bad notes, turning the microphone
toward the crowd, etc.) themselves create an opening for those who are present to "fill in," similarly to how a child approaches a blank coloring page,
crayon in hand. Filling it in, it becomes her own. Here the crowd of becom-
ers may offer their own expressions, their own becoming voices, whispers,
screams, to the becoming of the living song, performed uniquely in that
moment in that space of becoming—the event, the stage. This is a far cry

99. Muñoz, *Cruising Utopia*, 103–6.

100. In this case, Muñoz's sense of punk is somewhat in line with Bloch's early resistance to a sort of plastified or watered-down German folk music, which he argues sucks
the spirit out of it—the spirit being the Spirit of Utopia. "It is the stillborn character of the
false folk song or popular song [to have been stripped away of the Spirit]. Singing abandoned the cry, the dance, and the incantation quite early." Bloch, *The Spirit of Utopia*, 48.

101. Muñoz, *Cruising Utopia*, 106.

102. Bloch, *The Principle of Hope*, 1:492, 496; Gibson, *A Punk Rock Flashback*; Miller,
Anarcho Punk Albums. This longtime battle cry became deeply embedded in the language and ethos of the punk movement, in general, and especially in the realm of anarcho punk.

103. Muñoz, *Cruising Utopia*, 111.

from the musical worlds experienced by Bloch! Becoming is "rehearsed" as it is performed. It is acted out even as it takes place and takes formation/reformation. Community and individuality become together.

Such experiences, like our other sources of Utopian Surplus, have the possibility of feeding our hunger. In the experience of this other world of becoming, in participating in it, we imagine how the world might become.[104]

V. Sass and Resistance

Surplus in the Sass Event: Acting Up,
Enacting and Reenacting

Bloch seeks to feed our hunger for the Not Yet with surplus hope, dreams and desires sometimes hidden, sometimes overflowing, from song and art, from innovators and instigators, and indeed from anything anticipatory with the impulse toward life that he can get his hands on. Muñoz finds Utopian Surplus on the stage, in the performative, and in the performers and communities who gather around them—in moments of awe and moments of ecstasy. Of course, other "scenes" also may serve as wells. Just a few examples follow.

M. Shawn Copeland's essay, "Wading Through Many Sorrows," is concerned with suffering and sorrow among Black and enslaved women. In her essay, Copeland finds hope not so much in performance or art, but rather in another fleeting event that does not so much involve performing or rehearsing becoming, as it does performing freedom—"acting out" and enacting liberation even as chains remain. In the narratives of enslaved Black women in America, Copeland recovers the concept and activity of *sass*.[105]

Sass is a term which takes its name from the West African sassy tree. It is said that tea from the tree's bark was once used to test for witches. If the person who drank the tea from the sassywood died upon drinking it, then that person, it was concluded, was a witch. If that person did not die, then that person was not. As a result, the term *sass* in an American

---

104. To my knowledge, this "rehearsal of becoming" in/on a performative utopian stage has not yet been picked up by much theology. We would certainly benefit by thinking about liturgy, protest, and even the category of "public church" as performative stages on which we rehearse our becoming or rehearse the hopes and dreams which we offer. We will return to this thought at the conclusion of this chapter.

105. Copeland, "Wading Through Many Sorrows," 122.

enslaved context, came to mean "giving the master a taste of his own poison,"[106] by sassing back.

Strong sass, when it was performed or enacted functioned in a number of ways. First, it was an assertion and naming of one's own identity against one's aggressor—one who was accustomed to naming and defining her. Secondly, as she was being attacked, assaulted, manipulated (in whatever way the slaveholder was exercising his literal ownership and control over her body), to say "No!" momentary though it was, disrupted the power dynamic that allowed for the slaveholder to abuse. Thirdly, enacting sass, being sassy, inverted shame. In being sassed, the shame intended to be placed on the enslaved person, was instead turned back onto the perpetrator. In response to feeling such shame, he would likely try to victim-blame or re-shame her, calling her crazy for "acting out" (meaning out of her designated place in society). We see that the sass event itself put the dominator, the powerful abuser, on the defensive, meaning power was disrupted for a moment. There was a brief eruption of emancipation, though it was quickly gone. Lastly, as sass was enacted, it was possible, then and there, that the abusive act would be averted. On occasion, it would at least defer rape or some other act of abuse that the slaveholder was intending to commit.[107]

Sass itself, affirms Copeland, is an act of faith. It is the enslaved women's faith, according to their own testimonies, that allowed them to stand up and talk back. In these testimonies, they also made a distinction: the Christianity of the South is most certainly not faith in the High God of the enslaved African people. The masters were sinning—if not in their "ownership," then at least in their "making us work on the Sabbath."[108] We will return to the elements of faith that underlie enslaved Black women's acts of rebellion in Chapter 3.

For now it is enough to note that in the *sass event*, there is enacted a role-reversal. There is a defiance of oppression. There is power regained, if only for a moment—indeed, only for a moment—by the enslaved. There is an act of self-definition, a *becoming* that involves the will of one who has been defined by an oppressive society against her will, by North American scientific sight. In sass, she becomes, breaks through the delineations

---

106. Copeland, "Wading Through Many Sorrows," 121–23.

107. Copeland, "Wading Through Many Sorrows," 124.

108. Mary Prince believed God would judge the slave master for making an enslaved person work on the Sabbath, even as she initially struggled with her understanding of slavery as an institution. Crawford, *Hope in the Holler*, 29.

of identity that have been imposed upon her. The world is not completely changed because of it. However, in the act, in the presence of the holy No! both she and the oppressor and all who are gathered in that place, get a foretaste, a taste, and an inkling of what might yet be—indeed, what ought to be. There emerges a presentiment. Such acts of defiance and sass are shot through with Utopian Surplus, and serve as wells of hope, summoning the Not Yet, every time they are remembered, enacted, or reenacted.

Occupying Hope: Direct Action as Public Sass Event

Something such as *sass*, a brief act of defiance that, though fleeting, transfigures the room from the world as it is into a liberated moment of ought, serves also as a carrier of Utopian Surplus as it enters the public sphere. This is especially helpful in thinking about public protest and the creative imagination that defiance against oppression is known to instigate. At their symbolic best, public actions, direct actions, protests, demonstrations, (whether they win demands or not), have the power to demonstrate, in gathering, that vision for which those who gather hope. The gathering itself becomes a taste for that which those gathered desire. The chant "show me what democracy looks like / this is what democracy looks like," lands poorly if one hears it chanted as protesters are gassed, arrested, or brutalized by police. For that actually is not what democracy looks like. Such action is the image of suppression and silencing of voices by state-sanctioned force.

However, if the chant is received as referring to those gathered in protest—those who neither employ, nor have invited any police, none to restrain or punish cries of pain and cries of desire for a better world—then the chant takes on a prescient truth. It, too, becomes a presentiment. That is to say, those gathered, for a moment, become something of a snapshot of that for which those gathered hope. Alves will have more to add to this discussion in Chapter 2.

One example remarked on by Angela Davis in her book of interviews, *Freedom is a Constant Struggle,* is the Occupy movement as it took place in the US. As a participant in the movement in Chicago, myself, her words ring true to my experience and certainly many others'.

Eventually Occupy died down. It activated many who were never activated before. It provided a popular framework in polarizing the 99% from the 1%. Yet it did not "win." Ultimately, the world remains unjust, the people dispersed from their space of solidaritous songs and cries. Davis explains,

"Many people assume that because the encampments are gone and nothing tangible was produced, that there was no outcome, but when we think about the impact of these imaginative and innovative actions and these moments where people learned how to be together without the scaffolding of the state, when they learned to solve problems without succumbing to the impulse of calling the police, that should serve as a true inspiration for the work that we will do in the future to build . . . transnational solidarities." After all, she concludes, "Don't we want to be able to imagine the expansion of freedom and justice in the world?"[109]

Davis indicates what direct actions (done in community) can be. They can be moments of Utopian Surplus, public *sass* events, encasements of the ought-to-become. These small, localized, collective expressions of solidarity can become, for those who hope in this way, a sacramental taste for solidaritous communities worldwide—like Occupy, like Black Lives Matter at Fergusson and all over the world, like the kids of Sandy Hook, and so on. For those with hearts that hunger, these tastes of a new order, of the classless reign, of a banquet, become fuel for the long construction of the new table at which all will be able to eat—a foretaste of the feast to come. With Utopian Surplus, these feed our hunger for a liberated tomorrow. Perhaps this brings us to church.

Returning to Church?

According to Tillich, a symbol is more than a sign. A sign points us toward a thing. A symbol both points to and participates in that toward which it points.[110] In this sense, a community of hope is more than a sign. It, too, is a symbol. It points toward the banquet, toward the *omnia sunt communia*, as it is also a part of its becoming. In Bloch's language, it is a space where one might receive the melody of the future. The melody does not simply point to the future. It leaks in from the time/space about which the community dreams and dances, and toward which the community seeks to move.

The community that sasses back in the face of oppression, the community that gathers around a desire for God's reign (a world where the last become first and all are finally able to eat), the community that learns to function without police and without the scaffolding of state, the community who shares a meal in which no one is ever turned away, the

109. Davis, *Freedom Is a Constant Struggle*, 145.
110. Tillich, *Dynamics of Faith*, 47.

community which gathers and shares stories and art overflowing with Utopian Surplus: such communities as these are communities which just might become bearers and instigators of hope, pointing to and participating in the Not Yet. Here the Spirit of Utopia may be stirred. Here, from pain and from the absences that fill our lives, we may dream together. Here the Spirit might swell.

Such communities feed their own hunger, as in an escalating feedback loop. As they are able, they struggle for liberative justice with hearts full of desiring love. And when they do, those who observe from elsewhere, from outside of the community, may begin to hope for their own communities, their own contexts. Such communities feed the hunger of those who dream in similar directions and shout out from spaces of similar pain. A church, if it becomes a community that is full of Utopian Surplus, if it becomes a Utopian Surplus community, will participate in that messianic dream toward which it points.

Alves, to whom we will turn shortly, will call such communities *aperitif communities*.[111] Different from an appetizer which is designed to make one less hungry, an *aperitif*, when consumed, is meant to give one joy and pleasure in tasting, but also to make one *hungrier*—that is, to desire even more. It is meant not to suppress hunger, but to prepare one for the feast to come. An *aperitif community*, likewise, gives pleasure to those who gather, even as it evokes the body, the senses, the emotions to name what is absent, to desire what is Not Yet, and to daydream, hungry for a liberated world.[112] It points to and participates in hope's object, even as it hopes. And hope feeds hope. It is contagious. That is how Utopian Surplus works.

VI. Lost in Promises

Utopian Surplus: Food and Fuel for Hope All Around Us

In his preface to Bloch's essay "Man on his Own," Moltmann writes, as a preamble *to Bloch's work (!)*, that there is an atheism that is for Christ's sake—the iconoclastic impulse—an atheism that is the destruction of every image and a crucifixion of any God that would block the only truly religious feeling—an agitation of the heart toward the horizon of the promised

111. Alves, *Tomorrow's Child*, 202.

112. Alves, *The Poet, The Warrior, The Prophet*, 31.

and resurrected future.[113] Here is the religious affect: *not*, "It is well with my soul," but rather, "God's Gonna Trouble the Water";[114] not "God is here!," alone, but God or God's kingdom is "present as promise."[115]

As Luther spoke of a theologian of the cross, rather than of a "theology of the cross," so Moltmann, in his early years, spoke of a theologian of hope more than he did eschatology. Hope became *the* point—hope grounded in promise, evidenced in resurrection, lived in mission. Revelation was for Moltmann no longer an apocalypse or an unveiling, but the unveiling of the promise itself. Mission was not so much catechetical as it was the dispensing of, and infecting the world with, hope.

Lost Hope All Around Us

Moltmann's intention was good. Indeed, it changed theological and ecclesial worlds. Yet, the promise itself becomes a new limitation, does it not? Is not the promise its own "idol," arresting the gaze, attempting to contain or control the hopes that may be found in wells all around us—beyond promise, without promise?

Answer: *Yes.*

In restricting hope to Promise (and to Christian faith) theologies of promise miss the richness offered by Bloch's other wells of utopian surplus: art, music, politics, all of the places of innovation and creative acts of love which bring to the receiver a new clairaudience. Instead, with Moltmann and those who promise, the Christian seems to be left only with the stuff of the Christian tradition. As much as Moltmann seeks to transform or renew the faith theologically, in restricting hope itself to the Christian God's promises, the Christian future remains as closed as its canon.

Perhaps with such a view the church can sing, "my hope is built on nothing less than Jesus' blood and his righteousness," but it would be better if it was fed by much, much more. Bloch reminds us that surplus hope is hidden nearby and all around us. The Reign of God is within and among us—it does not simply exist as a promise! It is in art and music, on stages, in queer clubs and punk clubs, where people gather and dance, gather and shout, gather

---

113. See Moltmann's introductory remarks in Bloch, *Man on His Own*, 27–28.

114. Moltmann will develop this iconoclast affect later in Moltmann, *The Crucified God*.

115. Moltmann, *Theology of Hope*, 78.

in sass, and in rebellion, and in the transgression of oppressive norms and repressive regimes—and perhaps it is even in the church.

Lost Human Dreams and the Authority of Pain

"Christian hope alone is realistic?"[116] So claims the theologian of promise. Yet this is a rather arrogant thing to say—especially by one who mined Bloch himself, a Jew and an atheist, for materials to build his own Christian theology of hope. "Christian": is this the limit of God? Of hope? It should not be so.

It is not worth gaining a promise if, promise in hand, we negate all other hope. It is not worth gaining a promise if we forget how to dream. It is not worth dreaming if we leave buried the nourishing and liberative dreams of old, waiting for us at hand, so close we can literally touch them.

Indeed, when dreams are traded for an imposed or "handed down" promise (1 Cor 11:23), when the dreams are not our own—then dreams become contingent upon an authority, a magisterium, a charismatic leader, the stewards of the promise, to tell us, to teach us, to inform us how to hope and how to behave in accord with the vision of the promise. When this happens, the imposition of a *promise* over and against a *daydream* becomes an oppressive act, restricting a hoper's hope, robbing the subject of subjective hunger for the Not Yet, and exchanging it for an obsession with another person's dream. *Heimweh* for a home is rewarded with a cage.

As Bloch has shown, daydreams are born from something lacking.[117] Absence and pain are the beginning of hopes and dreams for a better life. To exchange these very personal dreams of the hungry, of the frustrated, of the oppressed, with a promise delivered by a man in a robe, even if the dream claims to be liberating, is quite literally to disempower the dreamer—and worse, in the name of care and concern for "the Poor." "When the people are being beaten with a stick, they are not much happier if it is called 'the People's Stick,'"[118] and in the same way, when people are forced to adhere and conform to another person's vision, they are not much happier if it is called "the truth," or "the true Christian hope," or even "the Kingdom of God."

---

116. Moltmann, *Theology of Hope*, 14.

117. Bloch, *The Principle of Hope*, 1:76.

118. Bakunin, *Statism and Anarchy*, 23.

Lost Freedom of Faith to Doubt and Despair

This brings us back to our first questions. *Where might we look for hope outside of promise? Where might we find hope for an agnostic church and for those of us who find it hard to believe?* If we demand that hope be sourced from God's promises (presuming that they are God's), it follows that we end up also requiring a person, a church, a community, or a believer, *to believe*—either in God or in the promises themselves, whatever psychological effort that takes on the believer's part. If this is the case, we may perhaps come to say something awful about the "sin of despair,"[119] as did Moltmann in his theology of promise, and as did so many theologians of old.

If our task is to foster hope, to feed hunger for the Not Yet, then certainly shaming the feeling of despair is quite counterproductive. Indeed, it is from the places of pain and absence that we first feel hunger for the banquet. If a promise becomes a source of shame or an inducer of guilt, set against, in contrast to, or as better than, our own sources of utopian hunger, then it becomes a distortion of hope and a hope suppressant. It is false. And it should be subject to scrutiny and rejection. Faith that finds sin, alone, in doubt and despair has no place in a community of hope. It is a hindrance to the hunger drive that gives birth to hope itself.

An Unpromising Hope

As we step outside the imposed promises of Moltmann, something is gained. *Where do we look for hope outside of promise? Where do we find hope for an agnostic church and for those of us who find it hard to believe?* For Bloch the answer is simple: all around us, in the many receptacles and repositories and events which contain Utopian Surplus. Utopian Surplus does not hold *promises*. It contains, rather, hopes and dreams.

Outside of promise, we find freedom to dream. To dream from our hunger, to dream from our pain, to have our hunger, our *heimweh* fed by the hopes and dreams of those who have gone on before us. Outside of promise, inside Utopian Surplus, we need not believe. We need not even *trust!* Belief and trust: these are not the grounds of hope. With Utopian Surplus, there is no promise "lorded over" us (Matt 20:25), no promise demanding faithful allegiance or accusing us of *sin*.

119. Moltmann, *Theology of Hope*, 7–10.

Hope feeds hope. Our hopes are fed, not dictated, by surplus hopes and dreams. Freed from promise, we need not conform, but, rather, *create*.

The iconoclastic impulse: it is perhaps time to turn this impulse toward the promise. Freed from its restrictive confines, we might find hope anew: a hope without a promise, an unpromising hope. Freed from the confines of promise, we might taste the hungry hopes all around us.

CHAPTER TWO

Hope in the Key of *Saudade*

Dreaming the Messiah's Dreams

SAUDADE: THIS IS THE emotion that runs through Rubem Alves' theological and poetic work. Perhaps he never spoke of it as clearly as he did in the introduction to his small devotional booklet, *Transparencies in Eternity.* What a fitting place this is in which to articulate the importance of his saudadic to project. Here Alves speaks with the hindsight of one who has spent nearly forty years writing and reflecting on human desire, on the human spirit, and on human words about God:

> *Saudade* is a word I often use. I believe it is the foundation of my poetic and religious thinking. Translators with expertise in several languages say there is no precise synonym for it in other languages. It is a feeling close to nostalgia. But it is not nostalgia. Nostalgia is pure sadness without an object. Nostalgia has no face. Whereas *saudade* is always *saudade* "of" a scenario, a face, a scene, a time. The Brazilian poet Chico Buarque wrote a song about *saudade*, in which he says that "*saudade* is a piece of me wrenched out of me, *it's to straighten up the room of the son who just died.*" It is the presence of an absence.[1]

Longing remembrance, dreams of a garden, the desire for dry bones to dance and sing: every word that Alves comes to utter is shot through with this emotion. Like Bloch's *heimweh*, Alves' *saudade* is also the emotional ground for his understanding and articulation of hope. Hope, for Alves, is felt as longing, in the body, before it can ever be spoken about. It involves both hunger and sadness, the "presence of an absence," memories

1. Alves, *Transparencies of Eternity*, 15.

of pasts, as well as anticipations of that which is Not Yet, that which exists only as a far off, distant melody.[2]

Like Bloch's *heimweh*, Alves *saudade* is grounded in his own story of exile, displacement, and persecution—and his own spiritual journey, whether or not the spiritual necessarily implied a belief or devotion toward a god (as in Bloch, such an identification seemed superficial and unimportant compared to the spiritual and historical depths that might be plunged in search of hope, and in hopes that hope might hope again).

This chapter will highlight four ways in which Alves grasped for and articulated *hope* in a saudadic key. Alves spoke of his own work as variations on recurring themes. Rather than a chronology (which might wrongly imply a linear evolution in Alves' thought), I will attempt to pull out some of these threads in Alves' work which run through it from its beginnings. These threads will help us to think about hope and to think about hope *without promise*. Indeed, our questions remain: *Where might we look for hope outside of promise? Where might we find hope for an agnostic church and for those of us who find it hard to believe?*

The first section, "Making and Keeping Life Human," will take a cue from Alves' early dissertation work on the project of the "humanization" of the world, and the language of "Messianic Humanism" he desired for a church who hopes for liberation and the recreation of the world. The second section will highlight his reflections on community as *aperitif*—as source of hunger and desire for a better, more human world. The third section, "Of Dead Men and Dance Halls," will address one of the threads that became most distinct when Alves moved into the worlds of psychoanalysis and theopoetics. This involves deepened theopoetic talk about desire, projection, and resurrection as they pertain to the work of the church and *aperitif* communities. The fourth section, "Drinking and Dreaming Messianic

---

2. It should be noted that *saudade* is a commonly used word in Portuguese—in Portugal as well as in Alves' native Brazil. There are literally cafes that bear the name. Claudio Carvalhaes notes that Alves' particular use of *saudade* in relation to religious sentiment is probably most influenced by the work of Feuerbach. Feuerbach, Carvalhaes argues, believes that religion is a projection of something lacking in the human soul onto the object of religious affection. This, Carvalhaes, says is why Alves is constantly found quoting Paul Válery, "What would be of us without the help of that which does not exist?" As Carvalhaes also notes, "Alves was also influenced by Augustine, Calvin and Zwingli, mixing an understanding of the sacrament of the eucharist as the presence of an absence." Indeed, both "absences" present something for Alves. Each induces the longing that he will identify as *saudades*, and as religious sentiment. Carvalhaes, "About A-Mazing Rubem Alves," 309–10.

Dreams," will complement Bloch's work on Utopian Surplus, and contextualize it for eucharistic denominations. Dreams will be an important key for us, as dreams have not so much to do with belief as they have to do with desire. Lastly, we will look briefly at Alves' agnostic-spiritual approach to religious hope, leaving the reader with a few of his words regarding the altars we build for the warming of our souls.

I. Making and Keeping Life Human: Universal Resurrection as Memory, Task, and Hope

To Make and to Keep Life Human in the World

A Theology of Human Hope, Alves' doctoral dissertation, was originally titled *Towards a Theology of Liberation: an Exploration of the Encounter Between the Languages of Humanistic Messianism and Messianic Humanism*.[3] Alves' foundational question, around which the dissertation is built, is the following: "What does it take to make and to keep life human in the world?"[4] Though he famously complained about being confined unhappily by the parameters of this required assignment, the work as well as this question, in spite of his protestations, would remain for Alves the

---

3. According to a legend told to me by Vítor Westhelle, the leadership at Harper & Row (Alves' first publisher) thought it too dangerously controversial to publish a book with a title that spoke of "liberation," so they chose the safer title, incorporating *hope*. This legend has been oft repeated in theopoetic and Alvesian circles. In 1971, two years after Alves' work, however, Gustavo Gutierrez published his classic text, *A Theology of Liberation*. James Cone's *Black Theology and Black Power*, also published by Harper & Row, was released in 1969. Though its title did not include "liberation," this was a central theme of the book, written after its namesake *Black Power*, which was published by Stokely Carmichael in 1967. Carmichael, and to a lesser degree, Cone, clearly denounced pacifism and encouraged revolution. Linhares is probably most correct, noting that "the term *liberation* was considered to be too Marxist at the time."

Despite later critiques by liberationist purists, Alves' early book has often earned him a title as a "grandparent" of Latin American liberation theologies, and sometimes liberation theologies, in general. According to Raimundo Barreto, who relays a story perhaps more congruent with the publishers' official narrative, "in light of the attention being dispensed to the theology of hope in academic circles at the time, and of the fact that Alves' work engaged and challenged Jurgen Moltmann's understanding of hope in his well acclaimed Theology of Hope . . . , Alves' publisher decided to go with the more marketable title *A Theology of Human Hope*." Raimundo Barreto, "Rubem Alves," 49; Linhares Junior, "Nevertheless," 101.

4. Alves, *A Theology of Human Hope*, 35, 55.

springboard into a conversation and a task which Alves would never abandon throughout his life.[5]

Brief Contextual Remarks: A Theology of Human Hope

In 1967 and 1968, Alves wrote his dissertation from Princeton Theological Seminary in the United States. This was not his plan, but here he was, attempting to write. How did he arrive at Princeton?

In 1964, after he had completed his master's thesis, *A Theological Interpretation of the Meaning of the Revolution in Brasil* at Union Theological Seminary in New York, Alves had returned home to Brazil.[6] Yet upon his return there was no happy reunion. "Between his masters and doctoral degrees, the 1964 Brazilian *coup d'état* [which was backed by the US and its military, had] wrested control of the government from the [democratically] elected leadership and placed it in the hands of a military regime that lasted until 1985."[7] The new regime, sniffing out alleged communists and radicals, and other so-called dangerous enemies of the now police-state, needed scapegoats. As a result, Alves, along with six others, had been offered up by the Presbyterian Church of Brazil (his own church!) to the regime. "There were more than forty accusations," Alves recalls

> that we preached that Jesus had had sexual relations with a prostitute, that we rejoiced when our children wrote hate phrases against Americans on milk cans donated by them (during the 'Food for Peace' program years), that we were financed by funds from the Soviet Union. The positive side of the document was that it was so virulent, that not even the most obtuse could believe that we were guilty of so many crimes. But that was precisely the tragedy: the people in the church, brothers, pastors and elders, did not have a minimum of ethical sense, and were so willing to denounce us."[8]

5. After his dissertation had been published for the world to read, Alves apologized for his "boring" work: "I apologize for having written such a dull book. I did not want to, for I'm not that way. If I wrote this way it was because I was forced to do so, in the name of academic scholarship. It is thought that truth is something cold and even a funny way of writing was invented: always impersonal, as if the writer did not exist, thereby making the text look like it was written by everybody and by nobody. And it was this coldness that forbade beauty and humor from surfacing in scientific texts. Knowledge, you see, must be something serious, without taste." Linhares Junior, "Nevertheless," 236.

6. Alves, "A Theological Interpretation."

7. Keefe-Perry, *Way to Water*, 40–41.

8. Linhares Junior, "Nevertheless," 260–61.

Quickly, Alves was forced into hiding. The Freemasons helped Alves both to hide as well as to escape from his home country and back into the United States. The Presbyterian Church, USA, helped secure him a place at Princeton, where he would become a PhD student and a refugee.[9] Here, in exile, full of *saudades*, Alves tells us what he sees.

A World Waking Up

The world is "coming to," Alves says. In the US, Black communities and churches have shifted in emphasis from a struggle for integration to a struggle for Black liberation and Black Power. In the Global South, people are claiming the name "Third World," saying "We are neither the East nor the West! We are a Third World!" We are our own. Women are beginning to demand not only equal rights, but also equal power—liberation. Even students, seemingly privileged, often from the middle or even upper classes, are beginning to resist, wanting no more to be "well rounded for the workforce," or "another cog in a machine."[10]

Black Power, Third World Resistance, Women's Liberation, Student Movements: What do these movements of bodies have in common? Each group, in its own new self-awareness, has come *not* wanting to be passive recipients of history, relegated to the background. Each group desires no wealthy, white, or first world charity. This struggle is not about "stuff."[11] Rather, these, The World Proletariat[12] share in common *a new mind*, an awakened awareness, a new and common consciousness that desires precisely this: *to be creators and authors of their own history, their own future!*[13]

9. Keefe-Perry, "A Song for Rubem."

10. Alves, *A Theology of Human Hope*, 9.

11. "This basic, negation, therefore, is not born out of the slave's envy for the 'things' of the masters. It does not envisage an inversion of the world whereby the affluent will be plundered by the envious masses which will then become rich. The central issue is not 'things,' but freedom to create history. This is why a society which creates and perpetuates man as a reflexive animal is rejected by this consciousness." Alves, *A Theology of Human Hope*, 12.

12. Alves, *A Theology of Human Hope*, 5.

13. For Alves, "true" freedom is the ability and power to create one's own future, to create one's own possibilities of being. In this space of freedom, one is no longer a "means" for the growth/profit of a present system or ruler. Rather the free subject (the one who can truly hope) sees to it that society is recreated for the sake of humankind's (and the earth's) happiness. Here we may hear an echo of Bloch: for the freely creative subject, hope moves beyond self-preservation to self-extension—that is, the humanization, the

Dissatisfied with the world as it is, these groups all proclaim, together with Alves, "What is cannot be true!"[14] They recognize that they are unhappy, and that they have been made objects of history rather than creators and subjects. They have been "lorded over" (Matt 20:25; Luke 22:25), colonized, subjugated, denied, or enslaved. Their bodies feel the pain of oppression and depression, and yet the time of silencing is over. Recognizing the presence of an absence, they speak. They name their desire for that which is not present. And in turn they seek *power* to make that for which they dream into a material reality. As these voices arise and speak, Alves begins to think about language.

With what language does (or might) the World Proletariat speak toward a new future? What frame might be constructed with which to speak of hope, with which to create hope? What language might we use not only to analyze and describe "the world as it is," alone, but also to move bodies in the world in order *to change it*? What language will feed this history-creating project of making and keeping life human in the world? On the other hand, how do we also avoid passivity, hopelessness, and non-action? How might we avoid what Alves calls, "Bringing history to an end?"[15]

In his dissertation, Alves offers two languages to his readers as languages of hope. These are *Humanistic Messianism* and *Messianic Humanism*. Alves describes the first, simultaneously calling communities of faith

---

"making kind" of an unkind world. This cannot happen without power. Freedom takes agency and agency is made possible by power, so that one might participate in "the creative act." Such power and ability, for Alves, is what contributes to a person's or people's "full humanity." This means that even as one comes to "humanize" the world, one, in the process, is "becoming human" in a new way.

As noted above, *freedom*, for Alves, is neither the ability to "have" nor the openness to "having" more of the stuff produced by capitalist structures. Having freedom does not equal having products. Neither is *freedom* demonstrated when oppressed or marginal communities are allowed (or coerced) to become absorbed into or complicit with hegemonic systems, be those systems capitalist or socialist. Assimilation is *not freedom* just as integration is not power and inclusion, and inclusion, when it is not incorporation into a body, becomes tokenism or, worse, "blackface."

Further, gaining "rights" here and there from those in power does not mean one has power. If the oppressed remain powerless, integration and assimilation must be understood as a reconfiguration or reconstruction of the chains of oppression, and not the solution, not freedom. Inclusion is not a New Creation. It is simply a renewed slave relation to the same old oligarchy of masters.

For this analysis, Alves relies heavily on the post-colonial work of Frantz Fanon. Alves, *A Theology of Human Hope*, 169–70; Fanon, *The Wretched of the Earth*.

14. Alves, *Tomorrow's Child*, 83, 112, 137.

15. Alves, *A Theology of Human Hope*, 25.

and hope to participate in the creation of the second. Following is a brief description of each.

Humanistic Messianism[16]

Humanism Messianism, Alves identifies, is one option in the search for a language to be used for speaking of and participating in the history-making project of "making and keeping life human in the world." Humanistic Messianism is easy to identify in various secular movements for justice and liberation. It is also easy to recognize in various contemporary theologies.

Pithy slogans and imperatives such as "Be the change you wish to see in the world!" and "We are the ones we have been waiting for!" as well as, perhaps, St. Teresa's "Christ has no body now but yours"; these are all examples of Humanistic Messianism today. Said simply, Humanist Messianism indicates that humans are the messiah. We have come to save ourselves. We are the answer to our prayers. Again, we are the ones (we are the *messiahs*) we've been waiting for.

Hope, argues Alves, among the Humanistic Messianists seems most often to emerge in the individual when the individual is acting in a hopeful or liberative way. "Humanistic Messianism hopes because it acts."[17] That is, according to early Alves, when we act, when we behave as "the answer we've been waiting for," somehow, as a byproduct of our activity, we receive a new sense of what is presently possible—hope is generated in and through hopeful activity.[18] For many who have been active in society or in politics, especially as a young person, especially if change has been achieved, this is obvious and self-evident. *We hope because change is possible! We know because we have made it! We are making it!* But what happens when we become tired? When we cannot act? When we become burnt out? When we have lost our ability? Is hope lost? What if we are exiled? What if we are in hiding, for example, at Princeton Theological Seminary?

---

16. In his notes, Alves thanks Professor Paul Lehmann for the phrase, "humanistic messianism." Lehmann, *Ideology and Incarnation*; Alves, *A Theology of Human Hope*, 171.

17. Alves, *A Theology of Human Hope*, 142.

18. Here Alves is somewhat lacking in his analysis. Where this may be true, it seems to be also an incomplete critique. Clearly Alves is setting up Humanistic Messianism in order to praise its counterpart.

Inadequacies of Humanistic Messianism

From experience, Alves finds the language and logic of Humanistic Messianism risky for the project of making and keeping life human. Revolutions go badly. Communities rally for change and end up with only a slightly modified, still oppressive status quo. Radicals stand up valiantly to fight the system only to find that their swords cannot pierce the thick skin of capitalism, of militarism, of technologism—of *the world as it is* at any given moment. The fight is fierce, but the dragon remains un-slain.[19] If we are the answer, it seems that the answer was incorrect—and so, perhaps, was the question.

The risk of Humanistic Messianism is the risk of becoming disillusioned and hopeless, either resigning to the world as it is, becoming a domesticated or "happy slave,"[20] or becoming delusional and naïve, like Don Quixote, flailing at windmills, changing nothing, dreaming naively about what *might be*.[21] Hope is lost at the smallest disappointment—and even more at the largest. The movement fizzles as boundary-defying revolutions evolve into border-building conservatisms, becoming an imitation and adaptation of the last unjust and corrupt regime.[22] In the end, the once-hopeful-masses trade desire for "acceptance." We learn to sleep, coming to believe that the world is as it always must be. But in our restful state, we forget how to dream. Desires dissipate. Hope's fire is extinguished. History comes to an end.[23]

Messianic Humanism

So how do we keep the dream alive? How does a community continue to gather around the presence of an absence, not with resignation and defeat, but with desire to create that which is absent, to move our bodies into a new future, a new horizon? How do we keep the future open, not as an infinite abyss, but as a horizon of possibilities for the fulfillment of the desires of the human body to be at home in a beautiful and kind world?

19. Alves, *Tomorrow's Child*, 97.

20. Alves, *A Theology of Human Hope*, 116, 145.

21. Alves, *What Is Religion?*, 48.

22. Alves, *Tomorrow's Child*, 184.

23. Alves, *A Theology of Human Hope*, 25; Alves, *Tomorrow's Child*, 113.

Alves offers as a language and a logic another possibility: *Messianic Humanism*. Later in his career Alves will do more to "create a language." He will begin to fulfill the imperative he placed upon the church when he takes up the project of theopoetics. But in 1968 he has not yet arrived at poetry.[24] Here, in *A Theology of Human Hope*, Messianic Humanism serves as Humanistic Messianism's alternative language and logic. In contrast to Humanistic Messianism, Messianic Humanism, argues Alves, speaks of humans *not as gods or messiahs*, but rather of *God as a humanist*.[25] This con-

24. Messianic Humanism for Alves existed at this time more as a project than as a reality—though no doubt it was surfacing among his peers in the movements in Brazil. Still, his dissertation called for the creation and deepening of such language. That is, in his initial works, he offers more of a prolegomenon than the product itself. Yet, already in the dissertation, Alves's understanding of the And Yet is emerging. We will touch on this in our section on the And Yet, below. Alves, *A Theology of Human Hope*, 87.

25. Following the logic laid out in *A Theology of Human Hope*, when God creates the New (in an in-breaking disruption of quotidian expectation and limitations), it will not, in distinction to revolutions that have led to further oppression, be a reworking or reconfiguration of the same old oppressive systems. From outside of history, Alves holds early on, God can "redo" history in a completely new way. God has more materials to work with than we can imagine.

God is a humanist. This is the revelation, Alves claims, that came to him when he was at seminary in Brazil. Suddenly, breaking free from his strict, conservative, and body-denying Calvinist world, the world which taught him that "God was a giant, never shutting-eye that sees me under my sheets," Alves was made to read the bible with a new heart. To reiterate what we have said above, Alves came to hope in a God that did not want Alves to suffer, and a God who did not smile when Alves whipped himself. It is not insignificant to say at this juncture that as Alves' writings and later poetics would take on healing qualities for his readers (themselves, many of them, also recovering from religious trauma) certainly every word Alves wrote was also a step in *his* recovery from his own previously inhabited abusive religious environment. One gets the sense that every word he writes, he also needs to hear, and indeed wishes deeply to believe.

From the world of the all-seeing eye who demanded the church's obedient evangelization for the saving of souls, Alves and his friends came upon a new mission. God's mission, in which the church is called to participate, is about bringing humans to a better state of living here on earth, today. Inspired partly by Bonhoeffer, Alves was able to say that God's good gifts of joy were meant for our happiness. Indeed, God's gifts really were *for us*.

Later in life, Alves will outright reject any portrayal of God in the bible that contradicts this fundamental belief, calling it awful and simply "bad." For example, in *Transparencies*: "Christmas is a poem. In this poem God is revealed as a child. The grownup God is awful: grave, serious, never laughing, never sleeping, with eyes lacking eyebrows and always open, never forgetting anything, and making a list of everything in the accounting book that will be opened at the last judgement. The grownup God generates fear. There is no love in this God. This God has nothing in common with a child: a child is forgetful, laughing, playful, an eternal beginning. It is not for nothing

viction (that God is a humanist) will become more explicit and pronounced in Alves throughout his life and career. Yet for now, God, as a humanist, is understood by Alves as a God who desires humans to have pleasure and to have abundant life—and to have them together, both at the same time. Here a brief detour into Alves' later work will help us to understand this important thread in the work at hand.

Absence and Abjection: The Breast Named Eden

In his later work, especially in *The Poet, The Warrior, The Prophet,* a book that will reflect both his poetic and his psychoanalytical training, Alves will come to say that God desires (or even that *God is the desire*) to return to a place which is like the place of the breast.[26] The memory of the breast, asserts Alves, as each of us holds this memory unconsciously, is the embodied memory upon which we build our utopian and eschatological visions: the garden, the playground, the paradise, the banquet, the reign, the city of God, the land of milk and honey, and so on. Why? Because the breast is the first place at which we arrived, having come out of the womb sucking at the void, in faithful anticipation of the milk of life. Having arrived, it was the first place that the infant experienced both pleasure and life-giving sustenance all at once, in one place, in one taste and swallow. This is Eden, says Alves! This is paradise, the land of honey, of milk.[27]

---

that the Child Jesus runs away from the grownup God. I prefer the child God. In the lap of the child God, I can sleep peacefully." Alves, *A Theology of Human Hope,* 98; Alves, "From Paradise to the Desert," 288; Alves, *I Believe,* 27–42, 52; Alves, *Ostra feliz,* 189–90; Alves, *Transparencies of Eternity,* 38.

26. Alves, *The Poet, The Warrior, The Prophet,* 70–77.

27. Alves will come to take for granted that the human condition begins in abjection, the "being split in two" feeling/awareness that emerges when the infant is separated from the mother's breast. Additionally, the breast is that location that the body learned ethics for the first time: *What is good is pleasurable (it "tastes good") and it gives my body life. Both at the same time!* This subjective ethics, grounded in the utopian nipple, is of course reminiscent of a Nietzschean ethic—quite literally, what is good is a "matter of taste." Indeed, Nietzsche will be a companion for Alves throughout his writing career, making at least cameo appearances in every lengthy work that Alves creates. In the presence of an absence, the infant imagines that which it desires—life and beauty. And so begins the struggle for a world that makes the estranged human more at home. It cries out. The word (the first word) is formed because of the Void. It is spoken as desire. Alves will also say, "Our Soul is a Void! But where is God's home if not over the Void?" "God is hunger, God is love—same thing!" Alves, *The Poet, The Warrior, The Prophet,* 27–28.

Shortly following this Edenic moment, of course, perhaps by mother being absent or tired, perhaps by mother refusing, will occur the first moment in which the infant is denied milk. Here the infant will come to experience *something lacking*. She feels the presence of an absent breast, an absent parent, a void (abjection). In the presence of the absent breast, the infant imagines the breast. The memory produces the image again and projects it into the future as a fantasy of what *could be again* because *it was once before*. Seeing this future possibility and desiring it, the infant calls out, cries, *hopes!*[28] She hopes for the breast's return. She cries out, desiring nourishment and pleasure in one place, at once.

Life and beauty, pleasure and a fed body, all at the same time, a world that is friendly and kind to the body—society that becomes again the breast—this is what, Alves says, God desires for humans. This is what it means for God to be a humanist. God wants us to feel pleasure and to be fed: this is the feast of victory for our God, the ground of our eschatological imaginings. This is Messianic Humanism.

And Yet: Memory and Hope

In *A Theology of Human Hope*, Alves has yet to mention the breast. His gaze does not yet reach back in that particular direction. Yet he does look to the "historic" past, seeking there wells of hope for the imagination and desire of that which might yet be. This "looking back" is not the task of Alves alone. Pastorally, he reminds his readers that this is a communal task, and that it, particularly, is the work of Christian community.

In the language and logic of Messianic Humanism, a language which speaks of God as ultimately a humanist, one comes to understand that God desires liberative change *for us*.[29] Understood this way, every call to repentance or *metanoia* discovered in scriptures is not meant to serve as a restriction on or a depletion of the human spirit or body. Rather, such calls are invitations to become liberated into more abundant life. But how can this be so? Has not the church taught us just the opposite?

---

28. Though Alves does not use the term "abjection," it is helpful to locate it as a Freudian/Lacanian concept. It has been used extensively in the Christian theological world similarly by both Julia Kristeva and Margaret Kamitsuka. See Kamitsuka, "Sex in Heaven?"; Kristeva, *This Incredible Need*.

29. Alves, "From Paradise," 288; Alves, *Ostra feliz*, 189–90.

The church has taught just the opposite, says Alves. And the church has been wrong. From this error, the church ought to repent so that the church and, more importantly, the people who gather as church and as churches, might more fully live.[30] The God of which Alves speaks, he maintains, is the God that is revealed in the Bible.[31] Clearly this humanistic God is seen in the countless stories of what Alves will call *the And Yet*.[32]

What's more—and here is a significant shift from the "low anthropology" of Alves' religion of origin—God wants this because, in addition to God being a humanist, God is also the *suffering servant*, the messiah who longs and cries out for resurrection. As such, God is not the *suffering servant* in the Hebrew Bible alone.[33] Rather, God still suffers in and through the poor and oppressed today.[34] Said differently, not only is God a humanist who desires resurrection for any who bear any cross today, but God is also *embodied* in the bodies of those who suffer now,[35] those whom later theologians will call the crucified people, the tortured flesh of God, and so on.[36] God is a *humanist* and God is *human* in and through those who suffer.

Further, lest we get the wrong idea, God does not become embodied in the suffering oppressed because God loves suffering. On the contrary! God is not a sadist. Rather, God loves our human flesh and therefore God desires, in and through us, to feel good, ecstatic, and even pleasured.[37] We should be assured, then, that when hope—that when defiance and resistance (indeed, the urge toward resurrection) well up in us as expressions of *desire* for human happiness and as the negation of the negative in society that the desire for happiness demands—that there we have *in us* a sacred impulse grounded in, fueled by, co-felt, and co-desired with God. God's dreams for resurrection are our own. God desires with us desires for liberation. Moved

---

30. For a full discussion by Alves, see Alves, *Protestantism and Repression*.

31. Alves, *I Believe*, 12.

32. We will speak more of Alves' concept of God and the *And Yet* below.

33. Alves, *A Theology of Human Hope*, 114–16.

34. "Where is God to be found? Wherever man is suffering. . . . This is why the biblical symbols of the Suffering Servant, in whom the desire for salvation is born, becomes the Messiah, the power that dissolves the old and creates the new." Alves, *Tomorrow's Child*, 111, 118.

35. Alves, *A Theology of Human Hope*, 111.

36. Jon Sobrino credits Ellacuria for being among the first to introduce this concept into popular usage. Sobrino, *No Salvation Outside*, 3–8; Ellacuría, *El Pueblo Crucificado*.

37. Alves, *I Believe*, 37–42.

by desire, then, we seek God's reign and its justice (Matt 6:33). Moved by hope, we seek to "break every chain" (Acts 12:7).

If Humanistic Messianism *hopes because it acts*, says Alves, Messianic Humanism, *acts because it hopes*! And it hopes and dreams with the *suffering servant*, the messiah within, among, and beyond us, divine, human and humanizing.[38]

And Yet Communities: Looking Back to Gaze Ahead

Yet, perhaps the question remains: *How do we know God's gifts are for us?* How can we trust that Alves is correct about the Bible? For Alves, the answer is simple. We know God is *for us* because we remember and retell and dig up the stories from scripture that testify to this truth about God. And how are we able to do this? We are able to do this primarily because of the stewardship of the scribes and of the church—because these stories have been kept and passed down by communities of hope who for centuries have translated, transcribed, and tended to these holy documents, even in the times when it seemed that no church leadership was actually reading them! Communities of hope, churches, are the curators and keepers of the memory and of the telling of *And Yet*.[39]

Of course, not every sacred story is a story of the *And Yet*. And yet for Alves this seems not to be an issue. This is because the *And Yet* is Alves' own canon within the canon. The *And Yet* is what makes the scriptures holy for him. To borrow a phrase from Luther, the scriptures are the dirty, filthy manger that nonetheless holds the *And Yet*.[40]

So what does this mean? Specifically, for Alves, the *And Yet* is described as something of an unexpected interruption or interjection. It is embodied in events or moments where liberative transformation has taken place, signifying that such events might still take place once again in history, opening history, despite history's apparent closed-ness and rigidity. They are, to reference again Alves' later work, memories of a

---

38. Alves, *A Theology of Human Hope*, 142.

39. In Alves, community is often presented as an ideal community, the church as it could/should be. This stands in contrast to his own accounts of being a pastor in conservative Presbyterian congregations in Brazil, and certainly against his experience of betrayal mentioned above. Alves, *Ostra feliz*, 13–14.

40 Famously, in his preface to the Old Testament, Luther refers to the scriptures as "the swaddling clothes and the manger in which Christ lies." Luther, *Basic Theological Writings*, 98.

breast-appearing-in-the-void, moments in the past which create desires in the present, desires for a pleasurable and nourishing future.

In communities of faith, *And Yet* stories include the following: The Hebrew people were held in captivity, Pharaoh's army was closing in; Abram and Sarai were without child, Daniel was in the lion's den; Lazarus was dead and gone for a few days, and there was a stink; Paul and Silas were locked in jail. Bondage, militarism, oppression and persecution, fear of extinction, the captivity of the tomb, the shackles and chains of empire: every bit of reality screamed that this is how the world is and this is how it will end. Every observed moment proclaimed that there was no hope to be had. There was no hope . . . The tomb is sealed . . . *And Yet!* For young Alves, these are the stories of Christian hope and faith.[41]

Remembering what God had done, one recalls a God who liberates God's people—who desires liberation and life *for us*. Remembering a God who liberates, one might come to hope in what God is perhaps about to do. In so doing, one might come to know a God who desires God's people to be fully alive. Even if liberation is not at hand, the memory of the *And Yet* may yet serve as a mountain top from which the person of faith might see the Promised Land, even if only from a distance.

Above and Beyond, And Yet

In these stories, one may also come to know a God who exists "beyond" history, and, so to speak "beyond and above reality."[42] That is, when reality has dictated: *This is how the world is!*, the God who is *And Yet*, who exists *beyond* history may reach into history in order to disrupt and change history, transgressing reality, making it turn from what simply *is*, into what *ought to be*. Stories of divine action, liberation taking place in spaces of impossible oppression and cruelty: because these have happened beyond us and in spite of us, we might believe that they can happen among us, in human society, once again.[43]

Messianic Humanism allows for a hope grounded in the memory of historical experience, and allows hopers and dreamers to keep hoping and dreaming, to live by hope and not by sight, to hope against hope. *And Yet* has taken place. God is messiah, human, and humanist. God is

41. Alves, "Confessions," 186; Puleo, "Rubem Alves," 190–91.

42. Alves, *A Theology of Human Hope*, 122.

43. Alves, *A Theology of Human Hope*, 122–23.

with us, within the suffering, in our struggle, desiring that we be fully alive, desiring that we should be free to write history together with God, to dream our own destiny, to live the desires of our flesh for a kind, new, pleasurable, and resurrected world.

A Not Yet Language

As mentioned, Alves ends *A Theology of Human Hope* with a call to communities of faith to develop this language, to bring to voice Messianic Humanism in a way that, perhaps, only communities of faith might be able to do. This language, he warns, must remain always open to the critique of Humanistic Messianism, and to the critique of anyone who shares the project of keeping history open. It is to be formed in dialogue with those who share the task of making and keeping life human.[44]

Nonetheless, he says, this language should be spoken in the dialect of the community of faith, authentic to its memory and stories. And it should add something. It should not simply "copy" Humanistic Messianism, substituting some words here and there to make it sound religious.[45] At the same time, it must discard the trappings of theological language accumulated over centuries (when necessary) wherever that language oppresses rather than instigates desire for human participation in the creation of a better and more human world. This means change: change for much of Alves' own "right doctrine" Presbyterian tradition is Brazil, and change for much of Christianity.

Though *A Theology of Human Hope* issues the call, I believe that Alves' later work is the constantly evolving response to his own commissioning. Alves' life will be devoted to the creation of a language that seeks to, as one colleague put it "[lead] us [into] deserts, and [invite] us to become gardeners and planters of hope."[46]

---

44. Alves, *A Theology of Human Hope*, 159–68.

45. This is a common occurrence in faith organizing. An organizer, perhaps with little thought about faith or theology, offers a faith leader talking points, which the faith leader then "Christianizes." This leads to a speech feeling shallow and religious folk feeling used. Alves calls for a deeper language, from the depths of faith and the pain caused by the political and societal situations of our days.

46. Gill, "The Ecumenical Movement."

Still: A Need to Believe?

Paul Tillich will remind us into many eternities that faith that is faithful is ever changing and always *dynamic*.[47] Especially in *A Theology of Human Hope*, Alves is in many ways (as per his own complaints) forced to make an argument—and to do so against his open, dynamic, and becoming nature.[48] In the dissertation, Alves claims to prefer Messianic Humanism over Humanistic Messianism. That is his argument, his thesis, his "unique contribution" to the academy. Yet anyone who spends any amount of time in Alves' other works knows that Alves is always more fluid, certainly more complex, and always less certain. Sometimes an atheist, sometimes a Presbyterian, sometimes an ardent liberationist, sometimes an agnostic poet looking out at the sea, Alves' journey is full of turbulence, belief, estrangement, disbelief, desire, antagonism to dogma, poetry about Christ's incarnation, doubt, and, of course, always *saudades*. Alves' argument for Messianic Humanism ultimately cannot hold up either for him or for us. Why? Because it still requires that we believe—that we believe in Daniel and the lion's den, that we believe in the stories of the *And Yet*. Beautiful as those stories are, we are asking for hope in our unbelief, for *hope without promise*, an unpromising hope, hope that desires *the And Yet*, certainly, but may have yet to have experienced it or committed it to belief.

As we unravel more threads from Alves' words about hope, this is what we will be seeking out. Where are the threads in which Alves conveys a way to hope without belief? What do they look like? In them, does Alves still make use of the *And Yet*? Can a community, gathered around the presence of an absence, hope even if they've come to approach the scriptures with a hermeneutic of suspicion—even if they do not believe? The short answer is that Alves comes to believe that they can. The following sections will explore how.

As we explore Alves' "variations on a theme,"[49] pulling threads and avoiding a forced chronology, Alves will provide us with priceless resources, gifts from a teacher, which will aid us in our pursuit of an *unpromising hope* for those of us who find it difficult to believe.

---

47. Tillich, *Dynamics of Faith*, 55–57.

48. Barros, *Sobre deuses*, 9.

49. Alves, *The Poet, The Warrior, The Prophet*, 141.

II. "I Don't Know What I Believe, but I Believe in the Community": The Creative Negations and Prophetic Function of an Aperitif Community

"What is insane is not [the bird's] painful, clumsy, efforts to fly, but rather the hand that broke its wings."—Rubem Alves[50]

Maintaining Dissatisfaction and Desire

William James, who has been utilized quite often by recovery communities such as Alcoholic Anonymous, distinguishes between two kinds of spiritual experience/awakening. One is akin to the punctiliar conversion experience: in a moment the whole world is changed and the scales fall from the eyes. This was Saul/Paul's experience. The other is what James calls a spiritual experience of an "educational variety." It takes place slowly, over time, and is most noticeable when one looks back, after time spent growing and learning in community.[51]

Each of these spiritual reconfigurations solves/salves the problem of anomie (of a world that has lost meaning or has become senseless) in its own way. It reconstructs a way of behaving, which in turn reconstructs a way of thinking and feeling and interacting with the world (or vice-versa). Spiritual persons experience a "psychic change" which allows them to function in the world anew, as something of a New Being. The person will stay in and continue to recover, says the program, but success is contingent upon the "maintenance of the spiritual experience."[52] This maintenance takes place through prayer, meetings, service to others, and fellowship. One must remember and relive through memory one's experience regularly if one wishes to recover. One must maintain the conversion if one wishes to keep up and to progress in this salvific, life-saving work.

50. Alves, *Tomorrow's Child*, 100.

51. W., *Alcoholics Anonymous*, 53.

52. W., *Alcoholics Anonymous*, 85.

Hope and a Dialectics of Freedom

Early on, for Alves, *hope* emerges as desire and presentiment within the framework of a "dialectics of freedom."[53] The dialectics for Alves involve (a) the renunciation of what is, (b) desire for what might be, and (c) as possible, a creative act.[54] Renunciation and imagination themselves in this scheme appear to be two sides of the same coin: when one is imagining what could be, one is simultaneously imagining the end or the transformation of what currently is. When one is renouncing what is, one is already summoning a desire for what is Not Yet. "The urge to destroy is also a creative urge."[55]

Moving beyond the *And Yet*, understood in this framework, echoing a strategy akin to that of recovery communities, communities of hope could do well to serve the cause of hope by providing spaces for such maintenance of one's conversion experience to world deconstructing/recreating desires. In such a community of hope, one could assert both one's own confessed dissatisfaction with the oppressions and repressions of the world, and sing with longing for resurrection, rebellion, revolution, and so on. Without such a community, without accountability, it becomes easy to give

53. I personally wish that Alves would not have used the term "dialectics." In the shadow of Marx's use, it easily becomes confusing and unnecessary. Yet Alves uses it, and his use evolves with time.

54. Alves' "dialectics of freedom," in *A Theology of Human Hope* and in *Tomorrow's Child* (the path by which freedom might arrive) consists of three basic movements. It begins, *first*, in the naming and renunciation of what is (the economy, militarism, and technologism) as detrimental to the human body; *second*, the negation of the negative and the desire for the "resurrection of the body"; and *third*, the creative act. Alves, clearly following Bloch, emphasizes the importance of the body and its hunger for life. Whereas Bloch rejects Freud's *libido* in exchange for *hunger* as a primary drive in humans, however, Alves will pick up both hunger and the libido. No desire is disqualified. No type of hunger is preferable. It is all from the body that wishes for life. Each is a gift from (or expression of) God. Though the creative act may not yet be possible, we may possibly move toward it, slowly, via acts of renunciation, protestation, and the fostering of creative and resurrective desire, by paying attention to our bodies' pain and to its wishes—to use the Blochian concept, by leaving wells of Utopian Surplus full and around so that future generations might drink and dream. These hungers and desires for pleasure and life within us are the messianic impulses in our bodies. They hold in them a presentiment of the Reign about which Jesus speaks: the banquet, the playground, the place of pleasure and joy for all. Even where they are powerless today, they may remain "seeds" planted for tomorrow's fruition: to give birth to "tomorrow's child." Alves, *A Theology of Human Hope*, 101–5; Alves, *Tomorrow's Child*, 202.

55. Bakunin, "The Reaction."

up, to assimilate, or as Alves might say, simply to become domesticated.[56] Without a community of hope, one will too easily revert back to passivity, and perhaps to the re-colonization of the mind.

If the recovery community is to help us "to accept the things we cannot change,"[57] by adjusting to "life on life's terms,"[58] the community of hope, on the contrary, is to help us to negate what is, and to dream from our deepest depths what might become.[59] The house of prayer for all people becomes for us, then, the house of longing desire for what could be—the house of *saudades*. Indeed, this is how Alves sees the ideal church: the community of those longing in the same direction for the Garden of God, a community of those who dream the same dreams.[60] Indeed, it is for these communities that Alves composes prayers of longing remembrance and desire.[61]

And yet, beyond renunciations and negations, and beyond the maintenance of desire via spoken word or prayer or song, Alves offers us something more, perhaps something deeper. This is because Alves knows that hope, that renunciation, that *saudades* live in our body long before we have words. Our body knows them when we do not. They appear at the first presence of our first absence, in our first fantasy for the return of the breast. And if we are to attend to these in their manifold forms, we must move beyond the limits of language and logic alone.

The Ethical-Prophetic Function of Magic

In *Tomorrow's Child: Imagination, Creativity, and the Rebirth of Culture*, Alves, as an extension of his "making life human" project, moves beyond *humanization* to speak also of *personality*. Here Alves claims that *personality* is that which begins the first time a child screams "No!" To return to the language of Alves' early dialectics, that is, *personality* begins when a child first comes to negate the negative—to renounce that which stands

---

56. Alves, *Tomorrow's Child*, 133; Alves, *A Theology of Human Hope*, 158.

57. W., *Twelve Steps*, 41.

58. W., *Alcoholics Anonymous*, 417.

59. Alves, *Tomorrow's Child*, 202–3.

60. "Saint Augustine said that a people is 'an assemblage of reasonable beings, bound together by a common agreement as to the objects of their love . . .' In our language: a people are those who dream the same dreams." Alves, "Theopoetics," 169.

61. Alves, *I Believe*, 17–28.

between the child and her imagined object of pleasure and sustenance (we remember, yet again, the breast).

Magic, play, and utopia, are all expressions of *personality*, of what we might call *creative negation* (the negation of the negative born alongside a hope/longing for that which we imagine and desire). Such negation and desire are the assertion of one's humanhood (one's personality) in a world that would make or deem one less than human, that would leave one hungry and wanting. Magic, play, and utopian visions all express a rejection of the *is* of suffering and a desire and hunger for a summoned and imagined *ought*. And in each case, such desires (not too different from the infant's) are born from impotence.[62] They are born from impotence, yet we humans participate in them, nonetheless. Why?

Alves argues that magical acts (a rain dance, a fertility ritual, a fast for peace, or communal prayer for that matter) are not to be judged by their outward effects (the arrival of rain, the achievement of peace, an answered prayer, etc.). When we judge these acts as good or bad, successful or unsuccessful based on such criteria, we actually miss the mark.

Although magicians and prayer warriors may intend such effects, and rejoice at their occasional fruition, Alves argues that magic's function (despite the magician's intent) is *not* actually to change things. On the contrary, Alves argues. Magic knows it is impotent. However, imagination uses magic in order to act out, beyond words, the world as it should be. That is, the *function* of magical acts is not magical results. Rather, the function of magical acts is ethical and prophetic. It projects a "should/could" into the horizon of the future. It does this by acting it out on a sacred stage. Magic says, in gestures and movements with props and with passion: "I desire this, even though the world is not this way." In so doing, magic declares judgment on the world and affirms the magical community's desire to live. With desire, from impotence, magic "speaks at the same moment of the necessity and the impossibility of the creative act."[63]

When we say, in churches, "receive our prayer," if we follow Alves' line of thought, what we are saying in these moments is "Yes! This prayer is true!" It is true in the sense that—*amen!*—you should not be sick. It is true in the sense—*alleluia!*—that this is not the way the world should be. It is true—*abracadabra!*—in the sense that sickness should be no more. Amen: "and so it is." We would better interpret this as Amen: "And so it should

---

62. "Magic is a flower that grows only in impotence." Alves, *Tomorrow's Child*, 81.

63. Alves, *Tomorrow's Child*, 84.

be." Our prayers are ethically true. They are true according to desire. They are true in that they judge and transgress reality (the world as it is). They are ethical and prophetic.

Like magic, the function of prayer is also ethical and prophetic.[64] Whether the prayers are intended to change the world by each community who prays (or not), the prayers nonetheless testify: the world is not as it should be. And testifying, desire is affirmed or perhaps stoked within both for destruction and recreation. This is important for our question of an unpromising hope for those who find it difficult to believe: In praying these prayers, one need not believe in a god or in a promise for the prayers to be true. Again, they are *true* to us when we, too, come to desire their prophetic *ought*.

> If magical [or prayerful!] behavior seems senseless, it is because it represents the object one aspires to [or prays for] without actually creating it. But when we move beyond this superficial level into its unarticulated meaning we hear something quite different. The absurdity of magic [and prayer] is really the absurdity of the situation that demands it, by making the real act of creation impossible and so reducing man to impotence.[65]

> What is insane is not [the bird's] painful, clumsy, efforts to fly, but rather the hand that broke its wings.[66]

Reality breaks our wings. And our prayers and our liturgies are judgment against it.

The Ethical-Prophetic Function of Play: Universal Resurrection

Play is not a means or a tool. It does not summon spirits or power or even peace. Play has long been understood as a thing that is good, as it is pleasurable in itself. When children play, Alves believes, however, empires should tremble. Why? Because when children play, something about reality is brought to light. In one instant, a child is the mailman, then a fairy, then a

---

64. "Like magic, prayer is the cry of the oppressed creature. It is a refusal to accept the cruelty of facts as final, a hope that human values can bend invisible necessity, a wager made on the pleasure principle as opposed to the reality principle." Alves, *Protestantism and Repression*, 113.

65. Alves, *Tomorrow's Child*, 82.

66. Alves, *Tomorrow's Child*, 100.

fire-truck. In the next we are cops and robbers—we shoot-up one another, but then the play does not end. We simply hit reset. We start again. Alves claimed, "Children's play ends with the universal resurrection of the dead. Adult's play ends with universal burial. Whereas the resurrection is the paradigm of the world of children, the world of adults creates the cross."[67] Incidentally, this understanding would become key for Alves' interpretation of Jesus' call for his followers to repent and to become like children.[68]

Like magic, play offers judgment of what is. It also, then, exposes something about reality that is so often forgotten: that the rules can be changed mid-game, that what *is* does not *have to be*. Our roles in life and in society need not remain permanent or unchanging. Similarly to communities and events that hold Utopian Surplus, of which we spoke in Chapter 1, *play* may serve as a foretaste and instigation toward the possible. We will return to this conversation in just a moment.

For now, regarding play, it is enough to keep in mind that play may *intend* only to have fun, but like magic, it's role and its *function* is prophetic. It is an expression of creative desire, outside the bounds of the "grown up" world of domesticated and conforming individuals. Play summons the possible by acting out the impossible in the here and now, making it palpable.

The Ethical-Prophetic Function of Utopia

Utopias and utopian dreamers were harshly renounced by Marx and Engels more or less as heresies—as they are today in many capitalist and socialist circles. As we spoke of in Chapter 1, Bloch was subject to such ridicule, as was Alves—and each from their own circle of co-conspirators and peers!"[69] Aside from a once every three decades John Lennon song, *dreamers* are the butt of jokes, declared to be "unrealistic" or "illusory hopers."[70] Christian pastors in the Lutheran tradition, at their ordinations, are charged to "make no occasion" for such hope.[71] It is regarded as dangerous or at least as *false*.

---

67. Alves, *Tomorrow's Child*, 100.

68. Alves, *Ostra feliz*, 13–14.

69. Bloch, *The Principle of Hope*, 1:xxi–xxii; Puleo, "Rubem Alves," 189; Linhares Junior, "Nevertheless," 120.

70. *Imagine* was first produced in 1971, two years after *A Theology of Human Hope* was published.

71. For a detailed treatment of the development of the rite and the insertion of this charge, "So discipline yourself in life and teaching . . . giving no occasion for . . . illusory hope," see Nelson, "Lutheran Ordination," 207–20.

Yet, Engels evaluated utopian dreams only by one standard: *Will these bring the proletarian revolt?*[72] Will they bring an end to the misery of capitalism? Such "scientific" socialism did not understand the prophetic function held within the magical, prayerful, utopian imagination. Freud, too, tried to move his clients away from "unrealistic" dreams, away from the "illusory." The goal of therapy, in the end, is to develop a human who is better adjusted and better able to interact with reality. Here Alves' critiques echo those of Bloch's.

Yet, for Alves, each of these (Marx, Engels, Freud) misses the point. "To say that a vision is utopian," he corrects these giants, "reveals almost nothing about the vision itself, but definitely [does unveil] the logic of the system that passes this judgement. And since the vision emerges from the very experience of the absurdity of the system, by declaring it to be utopian the system unwittingly confesses the need for its own extinction."[73] By declaring a beautiful, just, utopian desire as "unrealistic," a judgment is cast on reality itself as it stands. This judgment is a form of renunciation, and renunciation is the first movement in Alves' dialectics. Yet, "the tragedy of utopia," Alves admits, "is the tragedy of the cross. [Ultimately] the creators are put to death because of their vision."[74]

More than Maintenance—Sustenance: An Aperitif Community

When we see the rebel who resists say No to reality . . . it is likely we will hear the verdict society passes upon [the rebel]: misfit—insane, neurotic, heretic. But do not believe! What is actually happening is that personality is affirming the priority of its values against the brute factualness of a world that conspires against the aspirations of the heart. It is not for society to say what forms of life are sane or insane. Life itself must say whether society is sane or not. And if life finds that society conspires against it, there is no course of action left but resistance and rebellion.[75]

For Alves, church, communities of hope—perhaps better articulated as "what Alves wishes to be church"[76]—are in the same family as communities

72. Engels, *Socialism Utopian*, 41.
73. Alves, *Tomorrow's Child*, 119.
74. Alves, *Tomorrow's Child*, 119.
75. Alves, *Tomorrow's Child*, 129.
76. For Alves, even that which exists only in potentiality (that is, for Alves, only

of magic and play and utopia. We've already touched on this is thinking about the kinship between magic and prayers. In communities of hope, the community gathers around pain, the presence of an absence. We gather around displeasure and *something lacking*. Historically, at the baptismal font, this community had rejected what *is*, renouncing that which it identified as sin, the devil, and even the grave. The ethical and prophetic function, if one enters the experience from such an angle, is palpable. One feels "not at home in the world." One seeks to create a new world. The community is removed from the breast and imagines the garden.

What's more, is that the first communities of Christians (if we may take the risk of setting to the side the Hebrew Bible for a moment) were formed around a rebellious messiah—Jesus of Nazareth, chief of reality's transgressors. And he is not alone in the Bible, for in the Bible, against the norms and ethics-for-maintaining-reality, "villains become heroes and heroes become villains."[77] Jesus is no exception. Jesus spends his ministry speaking and eating with the oppressed and the insane. The tax collectors and prostitutes would enter God's Kingdom *first*, he said. As a result of such activity, Jesus was declared insane, himself. He was unrealistic, transgressive, and a *dreamer*—an enemy to those who conform to and maintain defined *normalcy*. This is why they killed him. Dreams about change, creative negation, are a threat to the status quo. Nonetheless, the crowds, the poor, the hungry who came to be fed in the thousands: these people's hope did not dissipate with the erection of a Roman cross. Their hope was not placed in this world, in reality as it is—even if it was born because of it. In fact, "their existential condition is what [created] the need and possibility of rebellion [in the first place]."[78] Jesus was killed, as was John before him. Dreamers, each of them spoke clearly and passionately of a world which would no longer be governed by the Caesars and "the sons of the gods" who ruled over Rome. Be transformed, they pleaded: for the reign of God is near. And the church, even in the messiah's absence, still gathers, desiring such a reign today.

As in the world of magical wishes, the church does not only desire, but also acts. In this community of hope, there is prayer, there is ritual, and there is public protest: the renunciation of Rome, a pledge of allegiance

---

according to *desire*) still exists as a prayer. It is for *aperitif communities* that he encourages his readers to pray. Alves, *I Believe*, 78.

77. Alves, *Tomorrow's Child*, 130.

78. Alves, *Tomorrow's Child*, 131.

to the messiah's Reign. In other words, the church participates in varied forms of ethical and prophetic function, affirming (with or without *And Yet* stories, with or without belief) that the *right now* is inhuman and in need of resurrective transformation.

Here, within the role of ethical and prophetic function, *And Yet* stories move beyond that which is believed of the past in order to stoke the flame of hope for tomorrow. Regardless of whether they are historically *true* or *not true*, such stories testify to that which the community believes *should become*. This is a beautiful leap. And it is helpful for those of us who are seeking an *unpromising hope*, those of us who find it difficult to believe. We will say it once again, differently: stories of *the And Yet* need not be true in the historic sense (they need not be grounded in a historical occurrence) in order to be true in the ethical and prophetic sense. There need not be a *was* or an *is* in order to be an *ought*.

Eucharistic Magic

In the community's role as ethical and prophetic, the supper, too, may take on new meanings. Just as the community acts out Jesus' supper, making sure each and everyone in the room who desires to eat will be fed; so, in the act of feeding those who hunger, does the community act out, in gestures and movements, the reign and the banquet about which Jesus preached. Here, at the table, we get a taste of a world where all people are able to eat. We are performing that which we hope the world will become. Such moments, movements, and gestures, such events, as we mentioned in Chapter 1, are what Alves called aperitif moments. The communities who made occasion for such moments, he called aperitif communities.[79]

Aperitif

An aperitif, says Alves, is something that is taken before a meal—in preparation for the feast. Yet, the aperitif is not an appetizer. An appetizer, as everyone knows, is meant to lessen one's hunger—to make one less hungry while one waits. An aperitif is different. It, too, is taken before a meal. Yet it is not meant to fill one up. On the contrary, an aperitif is meant both,

---

79. "The community of hope is an aperitif of what is to come." Alves, *Tomorrow's Child*, 201.

(a) to give one pleasure, and (b) to make one hungrier! This is just what a community of hope ought to be: an aperitif community, a foretaste of (and an instigation of hunger for) the feast to come. An aperitif community is a hunger stimulant.[80]

Without a Need to Believe

Such communities, be they churches or gatherings of another form, just might give hope to the hopeless, whatever our dogma, no matter each one's confessed beliefs. The taste, the aperitif offered, is not grounded in theological constructs or intellectual ascents. Not at all. Rather, it is grounded in the senses, in the body, in the bones. Instigated, the body longs. It is filled with *saudades.*

This is what Alves meant by aperitif community. It has an ethical and prophetic function, indeed. Yet we mustn't forget that ethics, for Alves, are always a return to the breast—a saudadic longing for being at home in the world, a kind world, where our communities might find pleasure and suste- nance all at the same time.[81] Is this utopian desire? Yes. Of course it is! May it make us hungry. May it feed our hunger. Alves would wish this for us, so that it might move us into the dialectic of renunciation, desire, and creativity. The aperitif community: to embrace with desire such a community is to bear wit- ness to a faith and a hope palatable and digestible and *unpromising* for those who don't know if we believe, even as we "believe in community."

III. Of Dead Men and Dance Halls: Presenting the Abyss that Bones Might Dance

"I wish theology were about that: words that make visible dreams, and then, when they are pronounced, they could transform the valley of dry bones into a crowd of children."—Rubem Alves[82]

---

80. Alves, *Tomorrow's Child*, 201.

81. "Religion is to society what dreams are to the individual. If this is true, then we are profoundly mistaken when we classify it as a form of false consciousness or sickness. *Religion reveals the logic of the heart, the dynamics of the 'pleasure principle' as it struggles to transform the inhuman chaos around it into an* 'ordo amoris.'" Alves, "Confessions," 190; "The purpose of everything we do, from play to politics, is the recovery of the lost garden." Alves, *The Poet, The Warrior, The Prophet*, 131.

82 Quoted in Cervantes-Ortiz, "A Theology of Human Joy," 20.

Our next, and penultimate thread, which we will unravel in this section, will move us in a slightly different, albeit related direction as we continue to be led by our questions: *Where might we look for hope outside of promise? Where might we find hope for an agnostic church and for those of us who find it hard to believe?* How might we speak of an *unpromising hope?*

Here we will move away from Rubem Alves the grandparent of liberation theologies. We will focus more intensely on Rubem Alves the grandparent of *theopoetics*. To be certain, they are each the same person. However, when Alves moves in his writing toward poetry and away from his first "dialectics," it becomes clear that he holds nearest to himself something different than he had at first, even as he remains engaged in the project of human liberation and human hope.

Studying War No More: Creating Ambiguity
and Deconstructing Fundamentalisms

Less than ten years after *A Theology of Human Hope*, received by reviewers in Latin America as well as in the United States as something pivotal, a watershed book, a passionate changer of conversations, a radical voice for liberation in the name of God,[83] Alves had come *not* to be so enthusiastic himself.

He began to question his constructs. Had he exchanged one fundamentalism, the strict Calvinism of his youth, for another: radical revolutionary Christianity? Had he exchanged one dualistic worldview for yet another? Alves' answer to himself was, "Yes." The liberation movements made sense of the world to him. This was their appeal! They gave him manageable categories for understanding and acting in the world. They allowed him to live and move in meaningful ways. But they also made the theological other the enemy (a tactic he had seen utilized by his faith communities of origin to divide and to oppress) and, in the end, didn't actually create the qualitatively New. In Alves' experience, faithful revolutionary fervor ended in a new and still oppressive status quo. And the people of Brazil, says Alves, were crushed. Once again, they had no hope. Alves' anomie returned.[84]

83. Alves, *A Theology of Human Hope*, vii–xiv.

84. Alves, "From Paradise," 300–2.

Making Life Human: Adding Nuance

In the midst of this deconstruction, Alves' mission, though changing frame, still retained a similar imperative. We still need a new language and logic which will help us "to make and to keep life human in the world." However, before we humanize the world, Alves adds, we need to bring the living dead, the people, the proletarian dry bones back to life. We have to find a way to restore in the people a will to live. "And if people are going to struggle and to fight it is necessary for them to be rocked back to life from their oblivion, and this happens when they are able to dream again."[85] "Whoever is joyful and loves beauty fights better."[86] If pushed, it is clear to me that Alves would say that being rocked back from oblivion is in fact *more important* to him than "to struggle and even to fight." This is partially because any moment and any bit of joy in life always holds the possibility of serving as an *aperitif*—and therefore as an entrance into his dialectics of negation, desire, and creation. Hope feeds hope which feeds the possibility of rebellious action. This is also partially because Alves became uncertain about the possibility of building an actually new society. Perhaps it would be more honest, he would say, to consider ourselves as *in exile*, planting trees for future generations, trees whose fruit we will personally never taste or see. Indeed, Alves came to think of himself as an *exile* theologian.[87] Nonetheless, in spite of the death that surrounds us, we should still strive to dance and to become more fully alive, Alves argued.[88] And theopoetics, he believed, was one way we could become midwives of hope: helping new hope, nourishing hope, to be born. It was one path, he saw, toward the resurrective work of filling a dancehall with once dry and dead bones. So Alves gradually makes his turn toward theopoetics. On the way, Alves looks back to the faith of his youth.

Protestantism and Repression, Religion and Desire

In the early 1980s, after having earlier rejected his faith of origin and, then in turn, having rejected the self-identified "dualism" or "new

85. Alves, "Theopoetics," 170.

86. Alves, *I Believe*, 9.

87. "We must live by the love of what we will never see. This is the secret of discipline." Alves, *Tomorrow's Child*, 204.

88. Carvalhaes, "About A-Mazing Rubem," 315.

fundamentalism" expressed in his liberationist faith, Alves decided to take a detour. He would revisit that fundamentalism of his youth as an academic task, and he would write a bit of an alternative to these dueling dualisms. The first task he tackled in his book, *Protestantism and Repression*. The second emerged subtly in *What is Religion?*

What Is Religion?

In his 1981/1984 (Portuguese/English) work *What is Religion?*, Alves offers a presentation of religion that is both anti-dogmatic, as well as un-dogmatic, to the core. Here, for Alves, faith and hope are nearly one in the same. Hope, again, has to do with desire. Yet there is a departure from Alves' first works.

In 1972, Alves held that hope "is the presentiment that imagination is more real and reality less real than it looks. It is the hunch that the overwhelming brutality of facts that oppress and repress is not the last word. It is the suspicion that Reality is much more complex than realism wants us to believe; that the frontiers of the possible are not determined by the limits of the actual, and that in a miraculous and unexpected way life is preparing the creative event which will open the way to freedom and resurrection."[89] In this sense of *hope*, there is in Alves a conviction and even a defiance tied to emotion—and still something (if only traces) of belief.

Further, faith here is to be moved (emotionally and physically) by such convicted, believing, and defiant hope: "Hope is to hear the melody of the future, and faith is to dance to it."[90] There is something contained in faith of premonition, conviction, and rebellion.

But in *What is Religion?*, faith for Alves appears to become less of a convicted *belief*, and more of a desiring *risk*:

> And the reader, perplexed, in search of a final certainty asks, "But does God exist? Does life have a meaning? Does the universe have a face? Is death my sister?" to which the religious soul could only reply: "I do not know. But I ardently desire that it be true. And I make the leap unreservedly. For it is more beautiful to risk on the side of hope than to have certainty on the side of a cold and senseless universe."[91]

89. Alves, *Tomorrow's Child*, 194.
90. Alves, *Tomorrow's Child*, 195.
91. Alves, *What Is Religion?*, 90.

"It is more beautiful to *risk* on the side of hope than to be certain on the side of a cold and senseless world." It is subtle, but by the 1980s, as he slowly trades in the theological for the theopoetical, *presentiment* for the moment (the not quite certain hunch) becomes outweighed by *the wager* (that which we bet on—and live by—not because we fear risking hell with Pascal, but simply because we wish the contents of faith to be true, because to us it is beautiful).[92] Belief in gods is traded for the desire that a god might exist and that the world might be kind. "Prayer is the sacred name that we utter before the Void."[93]

In *Protestantism and Repression,* after hundreds of pages of describing what Alves sees as the problem with fundamentalism in Brazil, Alves finally concludes, "Is there a way out? I don't know. [It seems to me that] those who already possess the truth [those who claim to be certain] are destined to become inquisitors. Those who have only doubts are predestined to tolerance and perhaps to burning at the stake. That is why I see only one way out. We must consciously and deliberately reject truth and certainty before they take possession of us. We must make our own the sentiments of Lessing: [choose striving toward truth and never truth itself]."[94]

Alves becomes anti-dogmatic and poetic not because of a disdain for theological constructs. They had helped him survive some very difficult years. Rather, he becomes anti-dogmatic because in his experience, rigid theological constructs were quite literally harmful to the bodies of believers, and became weapons in the hands of corrupt (and even well-meaning) authorities.[95] Ultimately, they led not to freedom, but instead became the opium den of the enslaved. They encouraged that even the most persecuted become "saved" and thereby better adjusted to the feeling of their chains, believing that their prize was in the blessed beyond.

Heimweh and *Saudades*

"What does it take to make and to keep life human in the world?" This was Alves' first question in his *Theology of Human Hope.* But as he picks up theopoetics, his question takes on a different shape. Yet it remains a question

92. Alves, *What Is Religion?*, 80–90.

93. Alves, "Theopoetics," 168.

94. Alves, *Protestantism and Repression,* 206.

95. Alves, *Protestantism and Repression,* 195–99.

about how. How do we rock the dry bones back to some sort of life?[96] In other words, Alves moves from needing a language and a logic, and even a dialectics for *changing the world*, to something quite different. The question shifts focus from the object of hope (changing the world or creating the world for which we are longing) to the subject of hope (bringing the hoper to life). As the shift takes place, the question becomes again (as Bloch would say) about hunger or *heimweh*.[97] For Alves this also means that, in a renewed way, but as it was all along, *hope* becomes about internally born desire, hunger, the erotic, and of course all kinds of *saudades*.[98] That is, hope remains about the expectant emotions—and it becomes about what effect these emotions might have upon a person or upon a people.

Theopoetics

Especially through the 1980s, and still in his 2010 book of religious reflections, *Transparencies in Eternity*, Alves turned to poets and mystics as his theological sources. As stated early, this was not so much a chronological evolution, as it was a recurring theme—and, above all, he returned to the body. Why?

All theology, Alves often said, was heresy. It was the making of an idol. It is webs we spin over the void, words we use to pave over the abyss to cure our anomie and to live day to day. This is not all bad. But Alves' project remains about the dry bones, the poor, the villagers, and (perhaps to a lesser degree), all who have lost hope. Covering the void may help us to cope with our death, make it less painful, add cushions to our coffins, but it will not "rock us" back to life.

A Dead Man and a Resurrected People

To explain the theopoetic task, Alves uses a story of Gabriel Garcia Marquez. Like Alves, I shall recall the story from memory. Unlike Alves, I will recall Alves' version.

---

96. Alves, "Theopoetics," 170.

97. Bloch, *The Principle of Hope*, 1:11.

98. For further conversation on Alves' full embrace of the erotic, see Regis, *A Magia Erótico*; Cervantes-Ortiz, "A Theology."

There was once a small village, a fishing village. One day in the village a youngster saw in the mist, in the distance, a mysterious object floating. As the object came closer, others from the village gathered: "What could it be?" Sadly, as it neared, it became clear what they had on their hands: it was a body of someone who was deceased.

There was only one thing to do with a dead body in this village: they had to bury it. It was the tradition in that village that the women would prepare the body for burial. So they took the body to the place of preparation and began their work.

Usually there is an etiquette around death (Alves says): "Ahhh! Good old Mrs. Smith! She was a fine ____." "She would always____," "We'll miss her____," "Too soon . . . Too soon . . ." "Alas . . ." And so on.

But something odd happened around this particular death. They did not know the man. There was no etiquette to dictate the conversation, there were no words with which to cover the body. This body was unknown—undressed. It was a blank slate.

And so the women began to wonder: "What large hands! Perhaps he was a warrior! Or a musician! I wonder how it felt when he caressed!" Some blushed. And then another: "He is so tall! If he lived here, he would often hit his head!" Some laughed. As the women inside the preparation area came to life, filled with imaginings, the men outside seemed to be jealous! What were the women imagining? Is it this dead man who makes them blush and laugh?

Their jealousies caused them, too, to imagine. They thought of the adventures they had never had, the lovers they had never loved. And so before long, the whole town was imagining, dreaming, telling stories of wonder and awe—all about this dead man that they had never known. Before long the face of each sad person was transfigured, flush. Before long the presence of the dead man had that town resurrected. And even after the dead man was buried, his memory remained—and the memory, quite often, was enough to bring a spring to the step of a tired villager.[99]

The work of the theologian—the theopoet, says Alves, is the work of the dead man, the dead woman, the dead person. The work of the theopoet is not to interpret dreams, but to instigate them. But how? By presenting the villagers with the dead man, with an opening, with the void. Our soul is the void, the place where the Spirit dwells. And it is in the face of an absence that desire emerges. Whereas theology covers with words, fills the

---

99. Alves, "Theopoetics," 170.

void (and sometimes provides comfort and meaning), poetry, says Alves, is meant to open it back up.

"My reading is a non-reading, my texts, pre-texts: empty word-cages with open doors, with the purpose of creating the void for the Word which cannot be said, but only heard. What matters is not what I say but the words that you hear, coming out of your forgotten depths . . . One must forget in order to remember." One must unlearn to learn anew.[100]

The void, for Alves, in addition to being ripe with varied theological meanings, an important quality for theopoetry, also represents the beginning of human experience itself—or at least the beginning of what Alves called personality. Remember? The void is among the first experiences of the infant, having been born. She comes out of the womb, into an unknown world, and there she sucks into the abyss, into the Void. She does not understand the world she enters. She has no name for the void, yet in her body, in her bones, she knows to grasp desperately with hunger for the place of pleasure and sustenance at the same time. She knows—not with her mind, but with her body—she desires the place the breast.

Theopoetics, when it works rightly, is that which makes us suck into the air again, to reimagine a place of nourishment and joy. We blush in anticipation. The color returns to our face. The imagination itself moves us to life, even if the object of our hope has not yet arrived.

Without a Need to Believe

Where might we look for hope outside of promise? Where might we find hope for an agnostic church and for those of us who find it hard to believe? Here is certainly a space of hope and longing which has no need for us to believe. Indeed, this hope is a hope that was born before we were able to believe! This is the hope to which Alves, the theopoetic Alves, would have us return. It is a hope that is born again when we scrape the paint from our existence to see what is underneath,[101] when we unlearn the words with which we have covered our desires, our hungers, our gods.[102] It is the hope that can be

---

100. Alves, *The Poet, The Warrior, The Prophet*, 17–18.

101. Alves uses countless metaphors in attempts to speak of the ways both language and logic "cover up" that which is truly essential. Among his metaphors are spider webs spun over the abyss, and layers of paint covering a wall. Alves, *Transparencies of Eternity*, 28–29.

102. "And if it is true that 'in the beginning was the Word,' it must be added that the

born again and born again (that can become!) when we have come to stare out again into the face of the abyss.[103]

IV. Drinking and Dreaming Messianic Dreams

To a large degree, this section of our second chapter returns us to the primary concept of our first chapter—that of Blochian Utopian Surplus. From Bloch, we learned to dig into everything we could, hoping to find buried around us

---

Word was uttered because of hunger. God is hunger, God is love: it is the same thing. These are metaphorical ways of pointing to the same longed for object, which must become one with the body." Alves, *The Poet, The Warrior, The Prophet*, 78.

103. Callid Keefe-Perry has written and spoken on theopoetics widely in the last several years. When this book was written he was co-chair of the Arts, Religion, and Culture group (ARC) of the American Academy of Religion—a group started by Paul Tillich, among others. A point that Keefe-Perry likes to make in his teaching and speaking is that theopoetics can be interpreted in at least two basic ways: (1) as poetry about the divine, and (2) as "building," "arting," or *creating* God. Silas Krabbe, in turn has distinguished between these two types, calling one *theopoiesis*, and another *theopoetics*.

Although we are avoiding a chronology, it seems to be important at this juncture to make one note about Alves' development. Early in his life, and perhaps into his academic career, Alves had a "belief" in God. There was theological scaffolding that aided him in his belief. We've touched on this already above. He would at that time in his life find theology to be more and more a theopoetics of the second type (poetry about the divine). Yet as he aged (and indeed already near the mid-late 1970s), I think Alves shifted more to the first type, to the idea of "building" God.

In his autobiographical reflections, and even in *What is Religion?*, Alves understands that if, in the face of the Void, as we experience it and as it is exposed to us, we desire; if over the face of the deep we speak our deepest want, for Alves that word becomes *the Word*—or better, *the Poem*. Therefore when we speak of God we speak of "our secret desire" (for this idea, Alves credits Wittgenstein). And "what hidden treasure is not religious?," Alves would ask, "And what intimate confession of love is not pregnant with gods?" (*What is Religion*, 4–5). What poem/word/desire spoken from our depths does not want to become flesh?

Silas Krabbe, in his *A Beautiful Bricolage*, attempts to label Alves in the *theopoiesis* camp, and not the *theopoetic*. Although I'd love to argue against this point, I'd like even more to offer that I think these classifications are fruitless. Moreover, they are *certainly* against Alves' own spirit. I believe they would disturb him. Remember, Alves does not know if he believes in God. Yet the fire from the altars he builds warm his face (*Ostra feliz*, 187). This is Alves—eternally an agnostic in his poetry, an atheist to the fundamentalists. To the militant liberationists, he's just a magician. And yet to those who love him, he is a prophet—one who whistles sweet melodies while sweeping the clutter from the Void, so that the "dry bones become a crowd" of laughing, playing, poeticizing, prophesying, fighting, dancing children!

For the uses of poiesis and poetics, see Krabbe, *A Beautiful Bricolage*; Wipf and Stock, "Theopoetics - An Interview."

the hopes and dreams of the ones who dreamt and created the things (the poetry, the art, the scriptures, the sweet music, etc.) we were mining. We sought to uncover buried hope, lying there, nearby, all around us, knowing that hope feeds hope and that our hope is hunger and hungry. Alves would add: and such hope is good to be eaten. Indeed, it is aperitif!

Entrails and the Future

In very ancient days, it is said (by Alves), that the diviners or the prophets of old would perform a very important service for the people in their town or in their tribe. You see, anxious people would come to the diviner, frightened, and so also curious about the future.

Seeing that they were anxious, the diviner had compassion, and, according to custom, she would make a small sacrifice. After making the sacrifice, it is said, that the diviner would then take the entrails of the sacrifice, and the diviner would arrange them, and the diviner would then lift the cup up to the heavens and, perhaps, take a sip.

And eating the entrails, and drinking the blood, the Diviner would become able to see the future. And this was comforting: to know how the crops or how the wars or how the marriage would turn out. One could eat and drink and see the future. And it was comforting.[104]

The First Christians

The first Christians, who appeared only a couple thousand years ago, had a slightly different approach. According to many of them, no one could really know what the future holds. It was "unseen." It was "a thief in the night." "A dim mirror," "a foggy looking glass." These are the images the Christian scriptures call to mind about the future. We can't really know it. And whatever we do know is pretty fuzzy. And if it isn't fuzzy, it seems safe today, it's probably a metaphor.

Yet, in the midst of all of their unknowingness, in the midst of life's unpredictability, in the midst of an oppressive empire that persecuted them, these Christians, who couldn't see the future, still got together and shared a cup. They ate the body of Christ, and shared in the blood of this "sacrificial lamb."

---

104. Alves, *The Poet, The Warrior, The Prophet*, 139.

And even though this cup did not reveal the future, it did it seems (and perhaps it still does), contain something of a *surplus*. Because for those Christians, in the chalice and in the bread there were infused hopes and dreams—waiting there to be shared by those who gathered. When they ate, they couldn't see the future, but they did have something even better. Why? Because, eating and drinking of the messiah, they would begin to dream the messiah's dreams.[105]

Jesus Dreaming

"Blessed are the poor in spirit," they dreamt. "Blessed are those who mourn." "Blessed are the meek." "And those who hunger." "And those who thirst for justice." "Blessed are the merciful. And the peacemakers. And the pure of heart." "Blessed are the persecuted and the oppressed!" "For the last shall be first." "For the lowly shall be lifted." "For every tyrant shall be removed from every throne." "Blessed are you! For the reign of God—the reign of God and not this horrible, oppressive empire that persecutes you—is near!" "And soon and very soon, all people will be able to eat." These are the dreams of the Messiah. These are Jesus' radical messianic dreams. These are the dreams that those first Christians ate and drank and dreamt together. At least this is one way that we can think about it.

When we eat and when we drink, we may not see the future, but perhaps we will begin to dream Jesus' messianic dreams. Let us not hold this gift from Alves lightly. It is incredibly important.

Without a Need to Believe

These ideas are Blochian, and then also Alvesian, through and through. Jesus' dreams, and the reign about which Jesus preached are saturated with Utopian Surplus—and not just his dreams in the form of parables or proverbs or words. Communities of hope receive these hopes and dreams sacramentally! Indeed we "eat the entrails of the Victim,"[106] says Alves! We gather around the presence of his absence. Yet at the same time, we eat and drink him. And in so doing, we "are what we eat."[107] We become as we ingest. Jesus' dreams

---

105. Alves, *The Poet, The Warrior, The Prophet*, 139.

106. Alves, *The Poet, The Warrior, The Prophet*, 129, 131, 138.

107. Alves, *The Poet, The Warrior, The Prophet*, 86.

become infused with our own. We begin to dream the Victim's anti-Roman, pro-garden dreams in our context and in our communities.[108]

One need not believe in a god or in a Son in order to believe and love and dream Jesus' dreams. One needs only to like their taste, to eat, and to become with them. Perhaps this is our most delicious find in Alves as we seek an *unpromising hope* for agnostic churches and for those of us who find it hard to believe.

Perhaps this also makes us guilty of the ebonite heresy, saying simply that Jesus was a human who dreamt good dreams. That is fine. Let us be heretics. There are many worse things we could be: conquistadores, inquisitors, exclusive fundamentalists. All of the right and proper knowledge in the world does not help one to dream Jesus' dreams. And all of the right and proper knowledge will not change that which is unjust the way a dream might move us into becoming and into becoming together.

V. Altar to an Unknown God

I don't know the moment when Alves stopped belonging to a church. He was involved in starting a new Presbyterian denomination in Brazil. He stayed active in theological communities and academies and in the World Council of Churches. But by 2010, he was clear that the church did not hold any doctrine or other religious thing which he would readily claim as his own. And he seemed never to have found (or founded) the community that would hold it.[109]

Yet there is one mention. There is a short three or four pages in *Transparencies of Eternity*, in a reflection titled "Outside Beauty There is No Salvation," where Alves speaks about the local radio station playing sacred songs all day in Brazil throughout one Good Friday. He was moved by the music. It took hold of him. He wept. And he concluded that this is what the church holds that is for him worth keeping: *beauty*, that which moves the soul and brings one to tears. I am a Christian because of the beauty, he says. "Outside beauty there is no salvation."[110]

108. "Inside the Void, a universe slowly makes itself visible: dreams. What is not . . . And they are beautiful: a Garden . . . The same Garden which lives in the entrails of the Victim. And they blow with the Wind, and in the graveyard, life appears. A flower in the desert. The secret of messianic hope." Alves, *The Poet, The Warrior, The Prophet*, 140.

109. In other interviews, however, Alves claims to be "very much a Protestant." Puleo, "Rubem Alves," 193.

110. Alves, *Transparencies of Eternity*, 119.

The Bible holds mysteries when one is a child. It is mystical, a window through which to see and imagine an already mystical world. It opens up more mystery, wonder, awe. I think this is how Alves saw things. As one grows, the canon becomes not a window, but "closed," not a door to mystery but a border wall, keeping out the heretics and bad guys. Orthodoxy, Right Doctrine Protestantism, and the like, make one "safe," "protected," "saved," wrapped up in bandages and balm. But in the safety, the Void is lost. Beauty is replaced by certainty. Desire is subdued, domesticated, and sublimated. What is meant to keep one alive, robs one of life. One must become re-exposed to the dangerous sun if one wishes to grow again. "Lazarus," calls the messianic dreamer, "come out of there."

This is the point of the Gothic cathedral, says Alves (knowingly or unknowingly alluding to Ernst Bloch's same point).[111] It is empty space. It brings us back to the Void. No words. No theologies. Just a return to the face of the deep—the birthplace of the personality, negation, desire, the first holy "I want," the first hope.

> I was being asked a zillion questions by four Folha journalists, and also some others, while at the theater. From one of these listeners came to me this question: "Do you believe in God?" As the question was vague, I asked, "Which God?" The person did not understand. So I explained: "There are many gods, each with the face and heart of the one who holds that god inside her chest. The God of Saint Francis was not the God of Torquemada. Francis used the fire of his God to warm the soul. Torquemada used the fire of his God to barbecue heretics on bonfires for the amusement of the people." As the person could not clarify the matter, I went ahead and confessed. "I don't know if I believe in God. But I know I'm a builder of altars." I build my altars with poetry and music. The altars must be beautiful. I build them before a deep, dark and silent abyss. The fires I light in them illuminate my face and warm me. Yet the abyss remains the same: dark, cold, silent.[112]

The aperitif community, the dead man presented by the theopoet, the sacramental dreaming of liberative messianic dreams: these are all sources of hope for those of us who find it difficult to believe in a promise and for those of us who find it difficult to believe.

111. For Bloch's original usage, see Bloch, *The Spirit of Utopia*, 24–30.

112. Alves, *Ostra feliz*, 187. Endless thanks to Angelica Tostes who helped me with translating some idioms in this passage which were unknown to me.

CHAPTER THREE

Hope in the Key of *the Holler*

A Countercultural Passion for the Possible

WHAT IS *THE HOLLER?* It "is the primal cry of pain, abuse, violence, separation. It is a soul-piercing shrill of the African ancestors that demands the recognition and appreciation of their humanity. *The Holler* is a refusal to be silenced in a world that denied their very existence as women. *The Holler* is the renunciation of racialized and genderized violence perpetrated against them generation after generation. *The Holler* is a cry to God to 'come see about me,' one of your children."[1] *The Holler:* this is the emotional space within which A. Elaine Brown Crawford writes and retrieves historic and contemporary Black women's' narratives of survival, striving, and *hope.* Indeed, it is the space which instigates her to write of hope in the first place.[2]

The Holler is also a term which has long been used to describe the shouts of enslaved people on plantations as they communicated with one another across vast fields.[3] *The Holler* may refer to the low point of a valley, out of which it is difficult to climb. In this sense, to be "in the holler," is to be "stuck between a rock and a hard place," a seemingly *hopeless* situation. Blues singers "holler," transforming agony into voice, commensuration, and solidarity.[4] *The Holler* is the space of oppression and stuckness. And yet it is also the sound that is made in defiant, desiring, resisting

1. Crawford, *Hope in the Holler*, xii.

2. Crawford speaks not only of the abuses endured by black women in general, but also speaks of enduring abuse herself. Crawford, phone interview with Thomas Gaulke, June 19, 2019.

3. Browne, "Some Notes on the Southern 'Holler,'" 73–77.

4. Wald, *The Blues*, 14–15.

hopefulness, with potentially liberative longing that the pain might stop, that what *is* might be transformed or reconfigured, that something else, a new reality, will perhaps become.

For Crawford, this *Holler*, these spaces of subjective and/or collective pain and longing, with all the agony contained therein are, nonetheless, "the wellspring of hope."[5] In and through *the Holler*, there emerges the very real presence of a "passion for the possible in this life,"[6] and a passion for that which is possible *right now*.[7]

Approaching *the Holler*

This chapter will differ slightly from the previous two chapters for two primary reasons. First, unlike our other primary authors from other chapters, A. Elaine Brown Crawford is alive and active in ministry. Second, and also unlike those authors, as of yet, Crawford's work is not as widely published. Spending less time producing academic publications, Crawford has dedicated much more time to living out and leading ministries of hope and passion in the world and through the church. Because of this second difference, though inspired by Crawford's work, this chapter will not be dedicated to Crawford alone, but rather it will engage her work *Hope in the Holler* as it intersects with (and proceeds from the context of) other Black, Womanist, and Black Feminist thinkers and activists. We will spend a moment with Fanon, followed by James Cone, as Fanon influenced Cone's "Manichaeism." Cone influenced especially early waves of womanism, directly or indirectly through his teaching, and it was often to his work, including the Manichaeistic element, that Black women scholars responded with critique and re-creation.[8] From Cone, we will move to Delores Williams and Emilie Townes. At last we will circle back around to Crawford's *Hope in the Holler*.

In our journey into these authors, then, we will highlight four somewhat distinct responses to our questions: *Where might we look for hope outside of promise? Where might we find hope for an agnostic church and for those of us who find it hard to believe?* These responses will include the hope of liberation (and even hope for martyrdom in the name of liberation) in Cone; followed by the hope of Delores Williams, a Hagarian hope which will inquire

5. Crawford, *Hope in the Holler*, xiii.

6. Crawford, *Hope in the Holler*, 15.

7. Crawford, phone interview with Thomas Gaulke, June 19, 2019.

8. Mitchem, *Introducing Womanist Theology*, 41–45.

"What if God does not always liberate?" We will then also turn to the *ornery* hope proposed by Emilie Townes, a hope that simultaneously emerges from, and fuels, counter-hegemonic memory and creativity, before we conclude the chapter by returning to Crawford, examining her vision for a womanist hope in *the Holler*, a vision at which she arrives through the study of various narratives of enslaved and freed mothers in the faith.

I. Which Side Are You On? Hope against a Dehumanizing Oppressor (A Manichean Hope: Fanon to Cone)

Though Moltmann wrote of *hope* theologically in 1967, claiming inspiration primarily in Ernst Bloch and in the student movements of his day,[9] and though Alves initially served as somewhat of a revolutionary/radical "response," to Moltmann in Latin America with his *Theology of Human Hope* (1968/9),[10] followed more systematically (and with a clear Marxist frame) by Gustavo Gutierrez (1973),[11] certainly just as important as all three to liberative theological thought in the US, and especially to Black Liberation Theologies and the *praxis* which informed them, was Frantz Fanon's work, *The Wretched of the Earth*, published prior to all of these, in 1963.

As liberation theologies and theologies of *hope* and *promise* developed, many turned to biblical motifs such as the God of the Exodus, and the church as a "pilgrim-" or "exodus- *people*," those who are on a journey together toward God's promised liberated/fulfilled/holy future. The Roman Catholic Church, as well as the Protestants picked up and utilized this renewed imagery. The exodus was understandably a primary motif in Bloch, who, as mentioned in Chapter 1, was a Jewish refugee, and who migrated away from the rising fascism in his own homeland—that is, who, in a sense, had an exodus of his own.[12] The motif was, in turn, strong in Moltmann, as he borrowed from Bloch.

9. Moltmann, *Theology of Hope*; Bloch, *Man on His Own*.

10. Alves, *A Theology of Human Hope*; Anderson, "Alves," 358–59.

11. Gutiérrez, *Teología de la liberación*.

12. Interestingly, this impulse in Moltmann, who latches onto the "Pilgrim Church" a term also utilized and lifted up by Vatican II, may have been first introduced to Moltmann by Bloch, a Jew, whose own concept of pilgrimage and exodus had to do with escaping very real persecution and certain death had he stayed in Germany. He made the crossing to various sanctuary countries, including, eventually, the US. Vine Deloria's and Baldwin's critique stand in contrast. The crossing of the European colonizers led to the subjugation and slavery of Deloria's and Baldwin's ancestors. This was no salvation.

Under this motif, generally, God calls God's chosen oppressed to pass through the troubled waters, out of bondage, toward the promise/expectation of freedom and becoming. As it was already a central biblical narrative, this motif was naturally widely accepted into newer theologies of hope or liberation, even as the motif itself took on significant scrutiny from native scholars such as Vine Deloria Jr., whose *God is Red* would be published in 1974; and from African American scholars such as James Baldwin, who repeatedly lifted up the corollary between the Hebrew people's "crossing" in order to possess a land and the Anglo-Saxon crossing of the Atlantic which seemed to be inextricably enmeshed with the myth of American Exceptionalism (not to mention the crossing of the Atlantic slave trade). As in the crossing of the exodus, so the crossing into the Americas lead to the conquering, territorialization, and possession of a "New World," by a "chosen people." Here was the New Jerusalem and the City on a Hill.[13] These highlighted that the biblical account of the exodus, though apparently liberative to the "chosen," bore witness not only to the deliverance of the chosen people through the Red Sea (a liberative element in the narrative, to be sure), but also by way of the spilled red blood of indigenous people and tribes, let alone the Egyptians (as emphasized by Robert Allen Warrior), many of whom were slaughtered at the command of YHWH, and even enslaved, as the chosen ones took, by force, ethnic *others* into their own *possession*, reintroducing slavery's chains, even as their own chains were shaken. These chosen people of YHWH justified their own slave-keeping and ethnic cleansing through a territorial and theological claim to a so-called Promised Land/territory (the *promise* itself overshadowing and

---

It was death and degradation. The kidnapping and human trafficking of Africans by Europeans/Americans and the subsequent crossing of the Atlantic were the first steps in the dehumanizing chattelization of the same. Do we discard the motif? It has no doubt been powerful for Jews like Bloch, escaping certain death, and others who have migrated toward something of freedom. Contextually, the exodus may speak liberatively. This appears to be true of its utilization by Black Christians (and especially King) in the work of Civil Rights and liberative organizing, a point Kelly Brown Douglas and other womanists continue to make today, noting enslaved people's utilization of texts holds the possibility of turning once-oppressive texts into tools of freedom. Among critiques to the utilization of the exodus motif, Robert Warrior and Delores Williams stand out, especially in response to Cone, as cited and expanded upon below. I wish not to make a strong argument here, but to note the complexity and to call for caution and discernment by preachers as each preaches to a unique context. Bloch, *The Principle of Hope*, 1:7; Moltmann, *Theology of Hope*, 268; Paul VI, *Lumen Gentium*; Grant, "Womanist Theology," 280; Douglas, *Stand Your Ground*, 163–64.

13. Baldwin, "From Nationalism," 15.

ethically outweighing any moral or mandate not to kill).[14] Delores Williams will famously pick up and expand this critique, speaking to the person of the enslaved Hagar as the embodiment of the faith of an historically enslaved people. She does this in her work *Sisters in the Wilderness*, first published in 1993,[15] to which we will return later in this chapter. Womanist scholar Kelly Brown Douglas has offered quite recently one of the more thorough and in-depth theological critiques of American Exceptionalism as it is tied to migration, conquering, colonization, Anglo-Saxon mythology, slavery, the emergence of whiteness, "white space," and territorial racism. Today, she says, all of this is embodied in "stand your ground culture," a concept which is reflected in the title of her book of the same name.[16]

Fanon

Frantz Fanon, professedly anti-Christian (in agreement with Baldwin in this particular sentiment), wishes not to engage this theological image or motif (either *the promise* or the *migration/crossing of the exodus*). Neither does he have any urge to transform or redeem it. The danger of its misuse is apparent. Fanon has no desire whatsoever to salvage Christian theologies. For Fanon, for the sake of the world's *wretched* and oppressed, the church, a mighty fortress of colonization and enslavement, is better off destroyed.[17]

That said, Fanon will champion one messianic imperative, one which proceeded famously from the lips of Christ himself in the gospels. For in the revolutionary work of decolonization, Fanon will insist, again and again, that "the minimum demand is that *the last become first* (Luke 13:30; Matt 20:16)."[18] Of course, Fanon has no obsession with theology. The theological is not his world. This messianic saying simply "works" for him. It rings true, despite its trappings. Fanon's concern is primarily with society's actors and institutional reinforcers: the police, the military, and the psychological and

---

14. Deloria, *God Is Red*; Warrior, "Canaanites, Cowboys, and Indians."

15. Williams, *Sisters in the Wilderness*, 15–33.

16. Douglas, *Stand Your Ground*.

17. "The Church [is a propagator of the Manichaeism itself] in the colonies [the Church] is a white man's Church, a foreigners' Church. It does not call the colonized to the ways of God, but to the ways of the white man, to the ways of the master, the ways of the oppressor. And as we know, in this story many are called but few are chosen." Fanon, *The Wretched of the Earth*, 7.

18. Fanon, *The Wretched of the Earth*, 10.

physical violence that these enact in order to maintain and keep in place *the world as it is* and *the people as they are* so that they might remain *just the way that they are* (colonized, exploited, left for dead, and so on).[19]

In other words, Fanon's concern with the church is limited to his de-colonial institutional critique which extends to all of these institutions in general (as it also extends to other pacifying communal religious activities and social configurations. For, example, Fanon equally hates tribal dancing and localized exorcism rites.[20]). That is, Fanon is concerned with the church insofar as the churches have been an indispensable tool in the colonial proj-ect, used with skilled precision for the maintenance of hegemony and the reinforcement of a docile, submissive, colonized mind, namely the produc-tion of the "happy slave," and the non-revolting masses.[21]

The colonization of the mind, aided by colonial Christian values, says Fanon, is a colonization that makes the whole body sick, as it simul-taneously also makes oppressed communities suffer more, and sometimes even glorifies suffering. The church, the colonizer's religious institution, contrary to Jesus' words, certainly does not bless the poor or the meek. It does not lift the lowly or exalt the humbled. The last do not become first in the church. On the contrary, the church keeps the oppressed pressed down even more, erasing any hope for change and even demonizing the messianic impulse and desire, even demonizing a hunger for justice (Matt 5:6), a thirst that the last might become first. Instead, rebellion is preached about as if it were a sin.[22]

Fanon's attention is also fixed on the physical violence of the colonizer and the violence reproduced as an extension of that violence, as well as the counter to and transformation of that violence (via armed revolution)

19. Fanon, *The Wretched of the Earth*, 16, 182.

20. Even local and indigenous religions, dancing and exorcism, Fanon argues, cause a "release" in the religious practitioner who would otherwise have been building up tension to use against the oppressor. Fanon recommends no such release, no such ca-tharsis. He wants (in this particular passage) tension that is waiting to burst against the colonizer in order that independence and power might be won. Fanon, *The Wretched of the Earth*, 18–20.

21. Fanon critiqued the image of the "happy slave," as it circulated especially in white propaganda, as well as in the US in Tom Plays and minstrel shows. For a fuller treatment, see Jackson, *Scripting*, 10.

22. Ta-Nehisi Coates has reiterated this critique recently, emphasizing that a Chris-tian understanding of redemption has often quickly explained away (justifying as God's divine plan) the real pain of real people who, Coates argues, were not redeemed, but died suffering. Coates, *Between the World*, 70.

into an independent nation where, again, *the last* (read: the *colonized*) *shall be first*, and where the subjugated peoples become free to define and lead themselves, create their own culture, and build their own nation, symbols, and perhaps, as desired, even a new religion. Naturally, then, Fanon is concerned with Black Power and Black empowerment as *the* pathway to freedom; and he is concerned with empowerment *by any means necessary.*[23] This, again, includes revolutionary violence. For Fanon, this violence is the only real means available. Only violence will pave the way to freedom and power. There is no reasoning with brute, oppressive, colonizing rulers. Only struggle will win, armed struggle, a violence to counter the perpetual violence of the colonizer which is daily imposed and implemented through armed soldiers, incarceration, and police.

The Unifying Potential of a Manichaeistic Worldview

This classic text (prefaced by the likes of Jean Paul Sartre and Homi Bhabha) took on a life of its own after its publication, inspiring and augmenting liberative and revolutionary movements worldwide, including and especially the Black Panthers in the US, who regarded it as something of a bible. Both its call for the last to become first, as well as its embrace of *any means* (which had tactically been a taboo idea, especially in the US during early movements for desegregation and Black Civil Rights) offered a framework and a fire for the revolutionary spirit as it was already being stoked worldwide in the 1960s and 1970s.[24]

Perhaps most notable in Fanon's *Wretched of the Earth*, is Fanon's own relative (if cautious) comfort embracing a dualistic worldview. This worldview, indeed, is the one that had named Fanon himself as *colonized*, a worldview which clearly sought both to dehumanize him, and to reinforce the subjugation of his people by the colonizer. This, of course, Fanon stated himself. Nonetheless, it is not the dualism (which Fanon aptly refers to as Manichaeism) that Fanon loves. He does not. Fanon notes these damages, time and again. Both society and the human spirit are diminished by this polarizing heresy. Colonial Manichaeism reduces the colonized to enemies, "bad guys," "poisoners of values," "threats," and ultimately animals.

23. "By any means necessary," of course, later became a famous rallying cry for Malcom X and the movement that he came to represent. See X and Starr, *By Any Means Necessary*; Myers, *Malcolm X*.

24. Harris, "Revolutionary Black Nationalism."

Anyone who is not "us" is the evil other. It is dehumanizing to the end.[25] This is to be sure, even for Fanon.

However, knowing this truth, the fact remains for Fanon that this Manichaeistic world is the world as it is. It is the world which Fanon received by birth, and the one he must struggle within. Choosing not to believe in it will not make it magically go away. This dualism categorizes and kills, yes. However, and this is what Fanon appreciates, in embracing this Manichaeistic outlook, the colonized people do actually gain one thing. What they gain is the opportunity to be *the colonized*. That is, as *the colonized* becomes the name of a once multiplicitous people, so there emerges an identity of *the colonized*. With a common identity, *the colonized* have a better chance at unifying, at uniting against the colonizer, at overthrowing him: *The colonized, unite!*

In receiving and adopting this imposed label, the colonized are given a name with which they might rise up and assert their humanity against those who would rob them of it and in turn create a world where their lives are truly valued.[26] To adapt a phrase made famous by Audre Lorde, Fanon takes the colonizer's tools and *does* turn them back on the colonizer in order to dismantle the colonizer's house.[27] The fight for liberation is a fight for the humanization of the colonized, and a more humane world for the colonized. In a world that turns one into an animal, even a caged animal, and even a caged work horse, this is not simply counter-cultural, but, rather, revolutionary work.

> We must remember in any case that a colonized people is not just a dominated people. Under the German occupation, the French remained human beings. In Algeria there is not simply domination, but the decision, literally, to occupy nothing else but a territory. The Algerians, the women dressed in haiks, the palm groves, and the camels form a landscape, the *natural* backdrop for the French presence.
>
> A hostile, ungovernable, and fundamentally rebellious Nature is in fact synonymous in the colonies with the bush, the mosquitoes, the natives, and disease. Colonization has succeeded once this untamed Nature has been brought under control. Cutting

25. "Because it is a systematized negation of the other, a frenzied determination to deny the other any attribute of humanity, colonialism forces the colonized to constantly ask the question: 'Who am I in reality?'" Fanon, *The Wretched of the Earth*, 182.

26. Fanon, *The Wretched of the Earth*, 10.

27. Lorde, *The Master's Tools*, 16–21.

railroads through the bush, draining swamps, and ignoring the political and economic existence of the native population are in fact one and the same thing.[28]

Colonization turns humans into landscape. Into animals. Into subhuman background characters in a movie that is about someone else, a movie which they will never direct, play a lead role in, and for which they will never receive compensation. Yet, says Fanon, "the colonized . . . roar with laughter every time they hear themselves called an animal by the other. For they know they are not animals. And at the very moment when they discover their humanity, they begin to sharpen their weapons to secure its victory."[29] Again: for Fanon, "weapons" is very seldom a figure of speech.

Cone's Adoption of a Manichean Worldview

James Cone was directly influenced by the Black Panther Party's revolutionary organizing, and Kwame Ture's work *Black Power*, both of which made frequent use of Fanon, and were influential social and political forces at the time that Cone was writing.[30] So it is no surprise that Cone, with Fanon and Ture, comes to denounce the white church as complicit in each of the ways that Fanon affirms, concluding, albeit christologically, that "through Christ [and not the white man's Christ] the poor man is offered freedom now to rebel against that which makes him other than human."[31]

Though the work of Fanon and the work of Cone disagree regarding theological language,[32] the aim of their work for their own given contexts was congruent: revolutionary activity that leads to the humanization and the development of their own subjugated people, especially Black colonized or historically enslaved people, into authors and masters of their own destiny, free from white power, white violence, and colonial oppression, free to build a new society. Black Power begins as "freedom now to rebel against that which makes" black and colonized people other or less than human.[33]

28. Fanon, *The Wretched of the Earth*, 182.

29. Fanon, *The Wretched of the Earth*, 8.

30. Zeilig, "The Influence"; Ture and Hamilton, *Black Power*, xix.

31. Cone, *Black Theology*, 131.

32. As noted just above, religion is one of the master's tools in colonized northern Africa which was not suitable for Fanon. Christianity especially was a colonial tool, justifying and aiding colonial rule and violence. It is corrupted to the core.

33. Cone, *Black Theology*, 131.

Cone's work will echo Fanon's colonizer/colonized Manichaeistic dualism. Theologically, this will include a true church versus a false church (a Rebellion church versus the pacifying white and pacifying black Christians), and, of course, Black Americans versus white/oppressor Americans. Cone, like Fanon, can easily relate that the latter is dualism thrust upon him by a legacy of enslavement and exploitation against Black people in the US from its founding. For Cone, however, to embrace American Manichaeism (as Fanon embraces colonial Manichaeism) means to embrace the possibility of Black unity for Black Power and liberation.

Unlike Fanon, Cone does not presume that revolutionary violence is *the only way* to Black liberation and power. However, Cone also does not believe that the choice is between violence and non-violence, as is often assumed in popular conversation. This dichotomy is quite misleading. For example, though the Rev. Dr. Martin Luther King Jr. was dubbed "nonviolent," as was his movement, violence was not absent from the movement's activities. The violence simply came from another source—not from the nonviolent protestors, but from their opponents. Violence was regularly utilized by authorities and individuals to injure civil rights leaders and ultimately to murder King himself.[34]

Though King's troops did not resort to retaliatory violence, some nonetheless asked the question which would become important to Cone. For Cone this question is a question about *tactics* in the work of social change. Will we win by violent revolt? Will we be crushed? Or do we use the oppressor's violence to expose the oppressor's evil so as to invoke moral disgust and shatter the nation's apathy? For Cone, the latter was the choice King made in his various non-violent direct actions. These actions, public and publicized, served to expose the nation to the actual extreme violence of the "civil servants" and police, those who were employed by power to *enforce* power.

One does not need to dig too deeply to retrieve this nation's memories of fire hoses and police dogs turned upon peaceful marchers and children. In fact, as I write this, one need only turn on the news. Of course, just as such images evoked compassion and outrage only for a few in King's time, so today a significant portion of the nation is *not* disturbed by images and

34. King's rhetoric remained ultimately anti-violence, but of course the point here is that violence was not only used against the civil rights marchers. The violence used against them was used also to create moral outrage in their favor. As King was forced by Malcom X and others to think beyond these tactics, he nonetheless insisted faithfulness to nonviolent direct action as faithfulness to Christ. King, "Where Do We Go From Here?"

videos of police murdering Black teenagers, police gassing and beating protestors, or ICE agents detaining migrants and immigrant children, many of
whom are dying in cages as I write.

Violence or non-violence? Cone shifts the question. He asks, instead,
whose violence are we to choose? Non-violent direct action, for Cone,
chooses the violence of the oppressor, and resists non-violently by utilizing
the oppressors' violence as ammunition against the oppressor's character
and authority. Yet, choosing the oppressors' violence (adopting a non-violent tactic for resistance), one must then also ask: is exposing the oppressor's violence enough? Cone asks this question with Malcom X.

The pressing moral question at hand for Cone is Black liberation, and
not the morality of violence. In this frame, the question of violence is better
understood as one of tactics for achieving Black liberation. What will work
for the achievement of this ethical goal? Cone leaves this tactical question
unanswered for the US context and the struggle for Black Power, even as
he sympathizes with the so-called rioters and the Panthers, the Panthers
themselves never launching an all-out revolt.[35]

Liberative Work and Total Liberation are Distinct:
To Rebel Is to Assert One's Humanity

A hasty reading of Cone may cause his readers to hastily affirm that, for
Cone, there exists only the oppressor and the oppressed. The liberator God
stands squarely on the side of the oppressed. The oppressor makes hell on
earth for the oppressed, and so God will return this favor on behalf of the
oppressed. In such a reading, this is the *promise*. This is the *hope*.

Indeed, is this not what *liberation* theology means? Hope for a revolutionary reorientation of the spheres? If not the new heavens, at least the
new earth? The new society? The beloved community? Christ destroys

---

35. Cone writes, with further nuance "It is the fact that most whites seem to overlook
... the fact that violence already exists. The Christian does not decide between violence
and nonviolence, evil and good. [The Christian] decides between the less and the greater
evil. [The Christian] must ponder whether [violent] revolutionary activity is less or more
deplorable than the violence perpetuated by the system. There are no absolute rules
with which [the Christian] can decide the answer with certainty. But [the Christian]
must make a choice. If [the Christian] decides to take the "nonviolent" way, then [that
Christian] is saying that revolutionary violence is more detrimental to man in the long
run than systemic violence. But if the system is evil, then revolutionary violence is both
justified and necessary." Cone, *Black Theology*, 143.

the gates of Hell even as Christ destroys the oppressor's rod? Sometimes. But not quite always. And not necessarily always in Cone. As suggested, the above reading is a bit hasty. Here it is important for us to slow down and to make a distinction which will move us into the next section of this chapter. There we will engage Delores Williams, Emilie Townes, and A. Elaine Brown Crawford.

Two Threads in Cone: Humanizing the World and Humanity Now

In the liberation tradition, there are almost always two threads running by one another, often so intertwined that at times it is quite difficult to see them both. Cone is no exception. Yet, pulled from the same sweater, these threads are different, and they often run toward divergent ends.

Cone (with Alves, whom we discussed in the previous chapter), makes an important distinction. It is a distinction about *hope*. Black Power . . . is an expression of hope," Cone says. However,

> [it is] not hope that whites will change the structure of oppression, but hope in the humanity of black people. If there is any expression of despair In Black Power, it is despair regarding white intentions, white promises to change the oppressive structure. Black people know that freedom is not a gift from white society, but is, rather, the self-affirmation of one's existence as a person, a person with certain innate rights to say No and Yes, despite the consequences. . . . To point out the futility of black rebellion is to miss the point.[36]

To point out the futility of black rebellion is to miss the point. Such a statement defies the common and sweeping caricaturization often imposed upon liberation theologies from the outside, as described above. To rebel is to assert one's humanity. To rise up, to assert that Black Lives Matter, to use a contemporary phrase, this is the "prophetic function" (to borrow from Alves' categories discussed in Chapter 2) of Cone's rebellion. It asserts one's humanity even in the midst of dehumanizing conditions.[37] It functions to humanize, or to assert humanity. It proclaims, "Black Lives Matter!" even if the larger world screams back, sneering, that it believes otherwise. It asserts the *truth* of Black humanity, dignity, and worth, even though society and its

36. Cone, *Black Theology*, 29.

37. Sadly, those who wished to silence Cone, the Panthers, and Black voices, in general, portrayed protestors and rioters not as humans asserting their humanity, but rather as animals. This practice continues today.

institutions remain largely built upon the *untruth* of racist lies. This *truth*, of dignity, of worth, for Cone, has divine, and therefore theological, origins. Asserting one's worth is an expression of hope in the truth and liberative intent of God. Cone further clarifies:

> Having tasted freedom through an identification with God's intention for humanity, [Black and poor people] will stop at nothing in expressing their distaste for white power. . . . [T]ruth, despite democracy, can never be measured in numbers. . . . The rebellion in the cities, then, [including the various race riots taking place while Cone was writing, and to which he was writing] is not a conscious organized attempt of black people to take over; [but] it is an attempt to say Yes to truth [the *truth* of Black humanity] and No to untruth even in death. The question, then, is not whether black people are prepared to die—the riots testify to that—but whether whites are prepared to kill them. Unfortunately, it seems that the answer has been given through the riots as well. But this willingness of black people to die is not despair, it is hope, not in white people, but in their own dignity, grounded in God himself. This willingness to die for human dignity is not novel. Indeed, it stands at the heart of Christianity.[38]

Cone finds hope demonstrated, lived out and performed in public, in the willingness of a Black person to die in order to assert, against the dehumanizing forces in the world, the full humanity of all Black people, and the full humanity of the one who would make such a martyr's sacrifice. This *full humanity*, for Cone, is theologically a gift of *grace*. It is grounded in a God who identifies with the oppressed and poor in this world, and who names the oppressed and downtrodden as God's own. Beyond identification, God's creative energy is also *in*, with and through the one who would rebel. God is working in/through the person who asserts her own humanity against the evil forces of degradative oppression.

This is where the second thread is divergent from the first. In this thread, hope's *object* is not necessarily full liberation for Black people. Neither, in this thread, is hope's object white adaptation or white willingness to change. It is not found in a successful revolution or revolutionary outcome (even if revolt were enacted through the help of God).

Rather, Cone's hope, at least in this brief passage, is simply grounded in the *truth* of Black humanity and worth, a *truth* that must be asserted against the lie of white power and white supremacy. This *truth* is expressed

38. Cone, *Black Theology*, 30.

in the language of the oppressed: rebellion and rising up. Such activities, in themselves are resurrective truths.[39] They are the crucified rising. Yet they also may result in crucifixion. Nonetheless, the call to discipleship has consequences. The Christian's life, even without words, should answer this question: "Whose side are you on?"

Or: Revolution and Prophecy

So, these are the two threads we find in Cone: one is missiological. The fulfillment of God's work, the *missio dei* on earth. This missiological thread is embodied in the deliverance of the oppressed into a state of freedom and flourishing, a Promised Land scenario, whatever form that may take. The second thread is akin to the theological concept of *justification*: one is a child of God by gift and by grace. Tillich spoke it as an imperative: "Accept the fact that you are accepted."[40] Black humanity is full and *true* right now. "I am somebody."[41] Freedom Now! It is the assertion that Black Lives Matter and are valued and are truly and fully human to God who abides in and with Black bodies here and now and always. To violate Black life is to desecrate the *Imago Dei*.[42] This is divine truth, even if the world does not acknowledge it. Speaking this truth may or may not have liberative effects. Indeed, just the opposite may result. In such a case, the second thread takes on the Christian tradition of the martyrs and the prophets, who speak God's truth whatever the consequences, even unto death. And perhaps the blood of these martyrs will still be the seed of an uprising, revolutionary community called church.

Though Cone and Fanon inhabit different worlds in terms of language and theology, these two threads run through each: (a) the world must be changed in a revolutionary way so that it affirms the humanity of the oppressed (it must be *humanized*); and (b) the humanity of the oppressed is already full and total, by virtue of their existence as humans, whether we call that full-humanity *grace* or *gift* or simply a fundamental

39. King often cited quotation, "A riot is the language of the unheard," was included in one of the first speeches he delivered when people booed as he advocated (as he had from the start) non-violent direct action. King, "The Other America."

40. Tillich, "You Are Accepted," 153–63.

41. This declaration and affirmation was often recited at the start of Rainbow/PUSH meetings in Chicago. Modood, "Catching Up."

42. Cone, *A Black Theology of Liberation*, 95–99.

human *truth* which should be a *human right*. If this "gift" is "accepted" it will lead to a pursuit of power, freedom, and self-assertion. As we turn, soon, to a few womanist theologians, the first thread is the thread which will be most directly challenged, as will the martyr's impulse in the second thread: death in the name of fully living.

Ecclesia Militans

Though these threads run side by side, there certainly remains in Cone a rather clear doctrinal assertion or belief: God does identify with the oppressed, and with the poor Black communities in the US. What God desires for, in, and through these communities, is the liberation, the uprising, and the resurrection of these communities. This is "God's intent."[43] In the US, this means Christ is a Christ who is manifest in, and fighting alongside, the revolutionary in the work of Black Power and liberation. And so, if there is a *promise*, it is this: to do the work of liberation, to participate in revolutionary activity, is to participate in the will, the work, and the true Church of God. All else, so to speak, is "fake" Christianity. It is false. It neither understands nor embraces what Jesus' revolutionary faith is truly about. "The [true] Church," for Cone, "is that people called into being by the power and love of God to share in his revolutionary activity for the liberation of [humankind]," and nothing else.[44] God stands with Black Power. Which side are you on?

A Need to Believe?

Might all of this mean something for those of us who are in search of an *unpromising* hope, a hope which is uncertain, a hope for those of us who find it difficult to believe? Of all things, perhaps, belief in a God who desires (and even facilitates!) liberation is much more difficult to stand upon than belief in a God who promises an other-worldly heaven for God's *elect*. Stories of "seeing the light at the end of the tunnel," after all, are much more common than stories of a truly liberated or genuinely liberating people. Are they not?

43. Cone, *Black Theology*, 30.
44. Cone, *Black Theology*, 65.

What if we fail to believe in a liberative end? After all, have we ever seen one? Certainly St. Thomas is not the only one among us allowed the sentiment of untrust and the desire to touch. What if we, too, wish to take part in his early Christian confession: "Unless I see the mark of the nails in his hands, and put my finger in the mark of the nails and my hand in his side, I will not believe (John 20:25)?" Unless I am touched by the Resurrection and the Life, I will not believe that the resurrective *does* or *is able to* take place in this world. I will not believe that uprising is possible when empire swings its sword or erects its cross.

Secondly, on the off chance that we can manage to grasp the subtilty of Cone's second thread, still: What if it is too difficult, too painful, too much of a risk, what if it requires more strength than we have at the moment, for us to fully, and without wavering, believe in our own *humanity*, to stand up and to inquire or to demand "Freedom Now!" "I Am a Human!" "I Am Somebody!" "Ain't I a Woman?" as Fanon, Ture, Cone, Harriet Tubman, and Sojourner Truth (exceptional heroes and overcomers in a long history of genocide) might encourage of us? What if self-assertion *is* martyrdom for us, as Cone affirmed might be the case, and that is not a risk we are willing to take? What if we wish to survive to feed our kids, to fight another day?

What might we find of hope outside the context of such belief, or such conviction and fervor? What might we find of hope outside the context of such certainty that a liberative situation awaits as sacred strength within on the one hand, or as a liberated world, nearby, on the other? To these questions, various womanist theologians and Black feminists have offered manifold and varied responses and convictions. To just a few of these responses, we turn now. And as we turn to these questions, they engage us in our own: *Where might we look for hope outside of promise (an unpromising hope)? Where might we find hope for an agnostic church and for those of us who find it hard to believe?*

II. "I Am Somebody!" / "Ain't I A Woman?":
Womanist Hope and the Assertion of Humanity

"I Don't Know About All That Liberation Stuff, But What I Do Know is That God'll Get Me Through Today!" Hope Without Promise of a Liberator God: Delores Williams' Hagar Spirituality in the Wilderness for Survival and Quality of Life

> "Black theology's starting point—the Black experience—does not include Black women's experience, [however] womanist theology begins with Black women's story of struggle. Womanist theology reflects at least two aspects of that story: first, the complexity of Black women's oppression and second, Black women's resolute efforts to survive and be free from that oppression."—Kelly Brown Douglas[45]

Delores Williams' now classic *Sisters in the Wilderness*, grounds itself in the unique and layered experiences of pain, oppression, and life-sustaining faith experienced and expressed by many Black women in the US throughout US history. It grounds itself, also, in a skeptical, albeit often mutually edifying, relationship with Black Liberation Theologies (and especially with Cone). Williams also brings to the work a critical engagement with white theologies, and a critical engagement with both white and African American churches.

Womanist critique, and womanism as an academic enterprise and movement is, and was from its beginnings, a movement born of a unique necessity. It is the result both of Black women's' marginalization in movements for Black people,[46] as well as the anti-Black racism and classism that permeates and permeated white feminism, white feminist action and organization, and various movements for women's liberation and women's rights.[47]

If Black Power was truly for all Black people, then why were the women of the movement still marginalized, relegated to be "behind the scenes," and treated as less-than? If feminism was really for all women, then why were black women marginalized and silenced in movement spaces as well as in the academy? Further, why did white women get to define and set the standards for what is feminine and what is womanly? Why were black women taken less seriously, if they were listened to at all? These are

---

45. Douglas, "Womanist Theology," 292.

46. Williams, *Sisters in the Wilderness*, 209.

47. Williams, *Sisters in the Wilderness*, 178–98.

foundational womanist questions, and foundational questions in womanist theologies.[48] The term *womanist* itself is famously credited to Alice Walker. Walker's writings have been largely picked up as a primary part of the womanist canon. While Walker is explicitly *not* a professed Christian, her deep spirituality, a current that runs through her literary works, provides a rich spiritual and theological source for theologians across the spiritual and religious spectrum, whatever their professed faith or dogmatic persuasions. This is Walker's definition of *womanist*:

WOMANIST

1. From womanish. (Opp. of "girlish," i.e. frivolous, irresponsible, not serious.) A black feminist or feminist of color. From the black folk expression of mothers to female children, "you acting womanish," i.e., like a woman. Usually referring to outrageous, audacious, courageous or willful behavior. Wanting to know more and in greater depth than is considered "good" for one. Interested in grown up doings. Acting grown up. Being grown up. Interchangeable with another black folk expression: "You trying to be grown." Responsible. In charge. Serious.

2. Also: A woman who loves other women, sexually and/or nonsexually. Appreciates and prefers women's culture, women's emotional flexibility (values tears as natural counterbalance of laughter), and women's strength. Sometimes loves individual men, sexually and/or nonsexually. Committed to survival and wholeness of entire people, male and female. Not a separatist, except periodically, for health. Traditionally a universalist, as in: "Mama, why are we brown, pink, and yellow, and our cousins are white, beige and black?" Ans. "Well, you know the colored race is just like a flower garden, with every color flower represented." Traditionally capable, as in: "Mama, I'm walking to Canada and I'm taking you and a bunch of other slaves with me." Reply: "It wouldn't be the first time."

3. Loves music. Loves dance. Loves the moon. Loves the Spirit. Loves love and food and roundness. Loves struggle. Loves the Folk. Loves herself. Regardless.

4. Womanist is to feminist as purple is to lavender.[49]

48. Williams, "Womanist Theology"; Grant, *White Women's Christ*"; Grant, "Womanist Theology"; Mitchem, *Introducing Womanist Theology*; hooks, *Teaching to Transgress*, 93; Townes, *Womanist Ethics*, 79.

49. Walker, "Womanist," xi–xii.

William's Two Theological Strands

A Christian Womanist theologian, and a descendent of enslaved women in the US, Williams delves into African American history, faith, and the biblical texts, in search of a faith closer to home and truer to her own body. Here Williams comes to locate two major strands in Black Theology and Black biblical interpretation in general.[50]

Intentionally, Williams searches for sources beyond the relatively new liberation theologies, published out of seminaries and academic institutions, into the wider tradition of the Black church, especially in African American preaching and biblical interpretation.[51] The first strand Williams identifies as a "male liberation theology" (most readily represented academically by Cone), a theology which appeals to the god of the exodus motif, as discussed above; and the second, a Hagar-centered theology of *survival* bolstered and augmented by personal and communal *testimony* about a God who "gets Hagar through," day by day, one day at a time.[52] Williams also refers to these strands as, first, "the liberation tradition," and, second, the "survival/quality-of-life tradition."

It is this second type of theology, this second strand, which Williams prefers as *truer* to Black women's' experiences. Embracing a Hagar theology, Williams, also, in a sense, embraces and prays the prayers of Hagar, and so also the prayers of those everywhere who've been abused and enslaved, the Hagars of the world, facing or enduring the wilderness, facing or enduring the master's household. Williams asks the question which serves also to name the enormous theological elephant in the room in a time when liberation theologies have gained a prominent voice: *What if God doesn't always liberate?*

Survival as Salvific Event

"God's response to Hagar in the Hebrew testament is not liberation," Williams proposes, beginning to respond to her own question, "Rather God participates in Hagar's and her child's survival."[53] Again, *survival* is a key

---

50. Note that these are distinct from the two threads we identified in Cone.

51. For Williams' understanding of liberative "appropriation" (her usage), see Williams, *Sisters in the Wilderness*, 6.

52. Williams, *Sisters in the Wilderness*, 2–4.

53. Williams, *Sisters in the Wilderness*, 5.

word here, and it should not take excessive subtly to realize that *liberation* and *survival* are two very different things. Nonetheless, for Williams, achieving or perpetuating survival (sans the Promised Land) is in itself something *salvific*.

God *saves* Hagar by ensuring her *survival*. And God does this twice: first, when Hagar was a runaway slave, and second, when she was made to experience homelessness. Hagar is encouraged by God to endure slavery a little longer. In doing so, she will achieve *salvation* from *certain death*. Such *salvation*, however, means a return to the master's quarters in order to *survive*. The master's home was arguably more hospitable than the lonely desert. Yet it was still enslavement. However, in this case, Hagar's humanity, to return to an earlier theme (which we've called Cone's "second thread") is asserted by her choice (*and* God's instruction for her): *to live*, to stay alive, to have some quality of life, even if it is not the best. Hagar's humanity is affirmed in God's call for her *survival* rather than in a call for her to die in the desert in some fantastical, heroic, self-sacrificing name of freedom and liberation. Life and *living*, not martyrdom, is the soteriological vocation of Hagar.[54]

When seen through William's particular womanist-survivalist-ethical lens, such dying-for the love or cause of freedom is no longer quite so laudable or even good. On the contrary, such a martyr's death, certainly noble in the eyes of Cone or of King, is something of a waste. That is, seen through William's womanist-survivalist-(theo-ethical) lens, such sacrifice is not at all glorious, but, rather, the image and apex of unjust murder of the oppressed by the oppressor. Such sacrifice amounts to "being sacrificed" by oppressive power under the illusion that we are giving of ourselves in the name of struggling *against* such oppression. The Ministry of Dying-For is Orwellian doublespeak. Such sacrifice, seen critically through this lens, does not lead to increased human worth or a fuller, deeper humanity for the martyr. On the contrary: a deceased poor or black freedom-fighter is simply another body to count in an ongoing and systematic government-funded genocide.[55] It is, when seen through the eyes of Hagar, dehumanization to the extreme: the elimination of humanity, the sacrifice of yet another Beloved Son. For Williams, there is neither liberation nor glory

---

54. Williams, *Sisters in the Wilderness*, 15–33.

55. Williams, *Sisters in the Wilderness*, 130–35.

in this or any death. What is good, faithful and just is for black bodies to survive and, when possible, to thrive.[56]

As stated, for Williams, this second (Hagar) tradition is truer to contemporary Black women's experiences. It is also more consistent than the first with the actual lived history of Black women within the spiritual context of "Slave Christianity." Utilized by Kelly Brown Douglas, Slave Christianity, as a term, stands in contrast to *slave-holding* or *Platonized* Christianity.[57] The latter was utilized by whites historically to justify their slave-holding.[58] While both *slave* and *slave-holding* Christianities utilized the bible, the particular utilizations employed by each was necessarily directed toward radically divergent ends.

Enslaved Black folks' interpretation of the bible made of the bible and the biblical narratives, for themselves, a life preserver, an implement for survival, for staying afloat, as well as a carrier of a spark of hope for liberation and a fuller life. If not always the case, says Williams, this was at least true much of the time. Slave-holding Christians, on the other hand, often prayerful and pious, though they were, commonly reduced Christianity into a doctrine about the salvation of the human soul, making this-worldly life irrelevant in contrast to the ultimate and eternal question: "Have you accepted Jesus as Lord and Savior [in order to salvage your otherwise doomed immortal soul]?" If one's answer to this question was "Yes! I am saved!" says, Douglas, it made no difference whatsoever whether or not one owned slaves in this life (or was enslaved in this life, for that matter), because the only thing that mattered is that one's eternal soul had been entrusted to God's care, "by grace," despite one's evil acts or circumstances.[59]

"I'm Just Going to Take It One Day at a Time!" From "FREEDOM NOW!" to Survival Today

Black women's faith, enslaved women's faith, Hagar's faith, Williams contends, was and is about responding to black women's everyday needs and experiences. This faith did not and does not pretend to respond to

56. Williams, *Sisters in the Wilderness*, 20–22.

57. Douglas, *The Black Christ*, 20–29.

58. Harriot Jacobs made a similar distinction between the "Religion of the South" and Christianity itself. Likewise, Sojourner Truth spoke of "the religion of Jesus" as opposed to "the religion of America." Crawford, *Hope in the Holler*, 29.

59. Douglas, *The Black Christ*, 20–29; Williams, *Sisters in the Wilderness*, 6.

a hopeless situation with promises of liberation that will likely never be achieved. "Make a way out of no way?" Perhaps. But, says Williams, let's be real: "God does not always liberate."[60] And who knows? *Perhaps God does not liberate at all.* Perhaps full freedom, total equality for all people, everywhere, will never arrive. Perhaps it is a false promise and a false hope. Perhaps it is a fairy tale. Perhaps its pursuit is like chasing the wind. Yet, for Williams, full liberation on the horizon or not, faith in God is not fruitless. For Hagar, for Williams' forebears, for historically enslaved peoples, faith presents the possibility of "survival and quality of life" today, every day, one day at a time.[61] This faith agrees with Cone, that Black folks are fully human and divinely beloved. Yet it does not demand conformity either to a hope for rebellion or a call for martyrdom. Instead, it is a call to survival and quality of life. During times of genocidal white oppression, "endurance [itself is] an act of defiance, a revolutionary act."[62]

Survivalist Revaluations and Humanizations

There is an additional function of faith for Williams. As women were enslaved and devalued, a devaluation testified to by the institution of slavery every day, their own faith testified otherwise. The worth of the faithful was not a worth produced by a slaveholding religion or a slave economy. On the contrary, the faith of the enslaved provided them with counter-slavery values, and values that rejected a slave-holding Christianity.[63] Beyond the white, colonial values that Fanon so detested and criticized in the colonizing churches of North Africa, Williams found, at least in the US, that "Black people [using the same biblical stories and some similar traditions, still] did not adopt the white Christianity of their white oppressors. Instead, they developed a black faith tradition that exposes the 'hypocrisy' of white Christianity and affirms the very sacred value of the black body,"[64] while simultaneously affirming the worth of these faithful women as beloved children of God.[65]

60. Williams, *Sisters in the Wilderness*, 196–99.
61. Williams, *Sisters in the Wilderness*, 5–8.
62. Williams, *Sisters in the Wilderness*, 237.
63. Douglas, *What's Faith Got*, 222.
64. Douglas, *What's Faith Got*, 217.
65. Williams, *Sisters in the Wilderness*, 5–8.

Although Williams questions the reality of the revolutionarily liberating God of Cone and the Manichean sacrificial-liberational impulse of Fanon's and Cone's revolutionary fervor, she nonetheless clings to an image or an idea of God: God who is strength, God who is sustainer, God who is a rock in a weary land, and so on. She casts doubt on the Liberator but not so much on God. Indeed, her work concludes with something of a *confession:*

> The greatest truth of black women's survival and quality-of-life struggle is that they have worked without hesitation and with all the energy they could muster. Many of them, like Hagar, have demonstrated great courage as they resisted oppression and as they went into the wide, wide world to make a living for themselves and their children. They depended upon their strength and upon each other. But in the final analysis, the message is clear: they trusted the end to God. Every important event in the stories of Hagar and black women turns on this trust.[66]

Trust Williams leaves us with—and, of all things, *trust in God*. Williams, to a large degree, rejects what we have identified as the first thread in Cone, and what she sees as the liberator strand in Black Theology. Yet she will not give up Cone's second thread, which is very much related to her Hagar strand: In God is affirmed each one's full humanity. The difference? The humanity received from God which is embraced by Hagar-believers causes them to desire survival and quality of life for themselves and for their children, a quality very seldom won through revolution. On the contrary, the full humanity received from God, which is embraced by those standing in Cone's tradition, causes them to rebel, to revolt, and to riot, and sometimes to give their own lives for the greater cause of liberation and Black Power. Williams desires no martyrs. One more dead is far too many. Each agrees and clings to the promise and gift of full humanity and the Divine worth of Black people and Black bodies.

Still, a Need to Believe?

At first glance, we might be skeptical of Williams. Perhaps we should be. How can her God, the God who facilitates survival and quality of life through a faith that *trusts* interact with those of us who find it difficult to believe (or, indeed, to trust)?

---

66. Williams, *Sisters in the Wilderness*, 239.

It is clear that, in terms of a void in "belief" in any god or *promise* at all, Williams is of little or even no help. She reveals to us very little personal agnosticism or even doubt in the reality of the Divine. She presents and passes as a theist. "Trust in God," is her book's aspirational ending. Nonetheless, in her rejection of the statically liberative god (but a god who might yet liberate somewhere at some time, maybe, if the time is right), Williams does offer up an option for faith which seems to have some comfort with embracing a certain uncertainty and unpredictability. This comfort with uncertainty places her loosely outside of the certainty of a *promise*—even if not incredibly far outside. Hope's object, being primarily "survival" and "quality of life" is less of an aspiration toward utopian existence, and more of an impulse to live, a *heliotropic impulse* if we may borrow a phrase from Bloch, a growing toward that which gives life and keeps one qualitatively warmer.[67]

William's faith is *unpromising*, in our positive use of *unpromising*, regarding the coming of a Reign, or the realization of total liberation and freedom, contrary to liberation-oriented theologies of promise, even as it does "hold promise" for those who, day by day, rely on faith and one another to survive. All the Hagars who remain in captivity, with Williams, hope perhaps not for a Promised Land or a New Jerusalem, but, once again, simply for survival and quality of life for themselves and for their children. Here, the old stanza, "strength for today and bright hope for tomorrow," becomes simply "strength for today, one day at a time." It is an *unpromising hope*, yet, nevertheless, it holds promise for those who trust in it, and for them, testifies Williams, that it is enough.

III. Hope Havens: Carving out Pockets of Humans Becoming and Fostering Resurrective Spaces in an Irredeemably Hellish World

If I would've started this chapter differently, it would've been with these words: As a number of white and Latin American theologians were talking, for a moment, about *humanizing the world* and European socialists were talking about seizing the means of production, Black people (and Black women) quite often were considered *to be the means of production*. Accordingly, they were also often not even considered to be human. Black bodies "were sold

67. Bloch, *The Principle of Hope*, 1:131–32.

next to mules," Kelly Brown Douglas reminds those of us prone to historical amnesia or erasure, and "to conceive of a body as chattel is to place it on the same level as tractors and rakes and farm animals."[68] People, humans, bodies were means, tools, implements for production. This cannot be emphasized enough. Slavery was culturally and legislatively accepted as "normal." White-skinned, Bible-toting, churchgoing, Christian slave owners participated in and perpetuated this system, generally believing that what they were doing what was right, just, or at least *necessary*.[69]

The end of legal slavery in the US certainly was not the end of white control and white desires to control. As Douglas notes, "The black body as chattel [is only the beginning. It] is that which all other racially stereo-typical perceptions of the black body are built upon."[70] Though the en-slavement of black Africans in no longer permitted, these perceptions and stereotypes, built upon a foundational practice and collective memory of captivity and exploitation (subconscious though it may remain for some), continue to be perpetuated, as well as utilized for oppressive political aims, to this day.[71] As Emilie Townes will remind us later in this chapter, though iron shackles have been loosed, the Black body remains bound by institutionalized and internalized racisms and white hegemonic systems of social, psychological, physical, and carceral control. If freedom is to be-come truer, more realized, more unbound, then these shackles also must be abolished, both from within and from without.[72]

In this context, in the US, long after traversing what was perceived to be the path trod to freedom, many find that their humanity is not yet affirmed, and that their dignity is still questioned. Shouts of "Black Lives Matter!" are *not* met with abundant affirmations, not even in most of our churches. Instead this cry is deemed controversial. These voices are si-lenced once again, or worse, explained away and deradicalized, sanitized for suburban ears. At other times, they are arrested and detained or disap-peared. Spaces such as churches, classrooms, and the like, potential spaces of becoming, insofar as they are spaces which are okay skewing or silencing

68. Douglas, *Stand Your Ground*, 52–54.

69. Douglas, *The Black Christ*, 10–19.

70. Douglas, *Stand Your Ground*, 53.

71. Perhaps one of the clearest and more accessible accounts of the perpetuation of white supremacist oppression, seen through slavery, Jim Crow, and into the carceral sys-tems of the present, is found in Alexander, *The New Jim Crow*.

72. Townes, *Womanist Ethics*.

liberative and life-affirming cries, are unhelpful, to say the least. Indeed, they are spaces of perpetuated harm. So those who desire life simply leave. Thank God. If, with Cone and Williams, we cling to the assertion that each life is a sacred and holy beloved life, a reflection and embodiment of the *Imago Dei*, and yet we doubt, with Williams, that the world (and perhaps even our churches) may ever reflect that assertion, then what does our project become? What spaces might we be called to create? How might we make space in a hostile and unbecoming world to reflect and to foster this unpromising, yet very real, life-sustaining hope?

The Work of Ornery Hope

"Ornery" is an American dialectic pronunciation of the English empire's word "ordinary." As a colloquialism, it has taken on connotations such as "of the people" while simultaneously, as a colloquialism, actually *being* "of the people." Over time, it has also come to take on connotations such as "cranky," "uppity," "failing to conform to societal niceties," and so on. As such, ornery and womanist (from the phrase "You are acting *woman-ish!*" mentioned above)[73] have a similar rootedness in a transgressive act of speaking out (and speaking out *of* prescribed character) in the midst of oppressive situations and contexts, disrupting unjust and unequal power structures. Emilie Townes wonderfully names her womanist task as "the work of ornery hope."[74]

The Fantastic Hegemonic Imagination

In her work, *Womanist Theology and the Cultural Production of Evil*, Townes speaks of the "fantastic hegemonic imagination."[75] *Hegemony*, "initially a term referring to the dominance of one state within a con-federation, is now generally understood to mean domination by consent. This broader meaning was coined and popularized in the 1930s by Antoni Gramsci, who investigated why the ruling class was so successful in promoting its own interests in society. Fundamentally, hegemony is the power of the ruling class to convince other classes that their [ruling

73. Walker, "Womanist," xi–xii.

74. Townes, *Womanist Ethics*, 145.

75. Townes, *Womanist Ethics*, 7.

class] interests are the interests of all."[76] Hegemony, hegemonic power, is reflected most clearly in domination that dominates seemingly *by the consent of those who are dominated.*

The fantastic hegemonic imagination, Townes argues, is a product of hegemony. As we conform to hegemony's structures, we not only think under hegemonic control, imbibing and believing its knowledges, but we therefore imagine under hegemony as well. We create and reproduce hegemony for future generations. The source of this *imagining*, the *fantasies* that lead to the production of images, particularly *stereotypes* for Townes, is called *the fantastic hegemonic imagination.* This imagination produces and reproduces cultural stereotypes, stereotypes that play similar roles, but take on new shapes and forms in each generation. These stereotypes serve to block Black women, as well as other oppressed and marginalized groups, from being seen, heard, or acknowledged as actual complex humans with complex and dynamic personalities. These stereotypes, so to speak, "put them in their place," as that place is dictated by hegemony. Related to the problem of "scientific sight" discussed in Chapter 1, at their strongest, these stereotypes then disallow Black women to *become* outside the frames of these images themselves. That is, they are a tool for hegemonic control, and they suppress becoming.

Such frames are especially reinforced by hegemonic history or *dominant narratives.* Such history erases character complexity. It generalizes, which is a form of erasure. It washes over accounts of divergence by Black people and Black women from these stereotypes. The many are painted as one.[77] As a result, a subjugated person, in the case of Townes' work, a Black woman, exists in the eyes of others (and especially white, ruling-class others), *and quite often even in the mirror,* only as this imposed hegemonic caricature, as this stereotype, and she cannot be noticed or *become* as otherwise.

In other words, these images, life constricting and reductive, are a perpetuation of slavery's shackles, built upon the foundation of the dehumanization that chattel slavery produced and necessitated. As long as the fantastic hegemonic imagination endures, a cycle yet unbroken, so does, in a real and embodied sense, enslavement.

---

76. Ashcroft et al., *Post-Colonial Studies*, 116.

77. "When memory and imagination impersonate history, they are fruits of the fantastic hegemonic imagination." Townes, *Womanist Ethics*, 18.

Localized Memory, Counter-Hegemonic History

Townes sets as her task to dig up these fantastic images, many of which have become the official history or concrete narrative of the hegemonic. Digging up historic manifestations of these images and stereotypes, Townes then attempts to disrupt that official history produced by hegemony, so as to shatter those images and to free subjugated minds and bodies from their control. Her tools for shattering the fantastic hegemonic images, are "localized memories" and "counter-memories."[78] These memories are to be mined from hyper-local histories and everyday stories from everyday people. In contrast to the univocal and official history produced by the hegemonic, these are to be multi-vocal and cacophonous. As such, when voiced, they truly become counter-hegemonic. Contradicting hegemonic images and narratives, they put a crack in the caricatures, hoping we might see something deeper, something truer underneath.

As a tool to shatter these fantastic hegemonic images and stereotypes, these localized- and counter-memories allow those of us who become exposed to them, perhaps, to become just a little bit freer from our own embedded, internalized, fantastic, hegemonic, and dehumanizing stereotypes. We might become freer to receive others as dynamic and becoming. We might become freer to *become* a bit more ourselves.

Creating Topsy, Defining Self and Self Becoming

It is near the end of her work that Townes summons the image of Topsy, a character first imagined (read: *imaged*) by the abolitionist Harriet Beecher Stowe in her now famous/infamous *Uncle Tom's Cabin*.[79] The character, given animal-like traits, says Townes, was intended to elicit empathy and compassion in white upper class audiences, so as to move them to want to abolish slavery. Despite her good intentions, and though she talked to white organizers and abolitionist activists, Beecher Stowe, it seems, never had any actual contact with real and living enslaved women. Said again, *Beecher Stowe did not talk to enslaved Black people*, even though these were the people she set out to portray (and even to liberate). This means Topsy was produced from Beecher Stowe's "fantastic" and hegemonic

---

78. Townes, *Womanist Ethics*, 21–27.

79. Townes, *Womanist Ethics*, 141.

imagination in the context of silenced Black women (specifically those to whom Stowe did *not* listen).

The character of Topsy subsequently became the grounding for a stereotype that would be picked up by the especially infamous Tom plays. These plays, in turn, re-distorted this already distorted imaginative character into something cute/funny meant to be paid for, consumed, and laughed at by white racist audiences. Rather than eliciting empathy, the image, by way of these plays, would perpetuate a stereotype about "savage" Africans, unable to care for themselves or to be "civilized." These "savage" bodies are safer, and it is safer for everyone, hegemonic logic reasoned, if they remain under the control of white handlers/owners/police. Besides, "they are happier this way!" "It really is better for *them!*" Again, we see a reincarnation of the image of "the happy slave."[80] The hegemonic imagination enforces hegemony: the way things are, are the way that they should be.

Of course, these stereotypes (derived from and fed by the image of Topsy, among many others), endure today, fueling white territorialism and mass incarceration, as well as white paternalism in the workplace, and so on. Hegemonic images reinforce hegemonic behaviors and relationships, marginalization, dehumanization, and continued and ongoing racist oppression.

The work of *Ornery Hope*, the work of counter-hegemony mentioned above, then, Townes says, is the work of a hope which engages the question: *What if a white woman had not been the author and creator of Topsy?* What if Topsy had not spoken a white woman's imagined words? Looking to Alice Walker's *The Color Purple*, for inspiration, Townes tasks herself and other womanist theologians with the work of "voicing Topsy, knowing Topsy, being Topsy, growing Topsy." That is, it is the work of "allowing Topsy and all of her friends to speak."[81]

This task is engaged, for Townes, through the work described already above: the work of *retrieval*, of digging up racist/white supremacist/hegemonic histories (for example the image of Topsy) and disrupting them by digging up also localized and complexified counter-memories. It is also done through engagement in the work of "voicing" today, empowering those to speak, in solidarity, who are still rendered silent. Topsy *becomes* as the histories that have skewed, defined, and imprisoned her, become shattered (a) by the coming to voice of counter-hegemonic memories, and

80. Townes, *Womanist Ethics*, 141.

81. Townes, *Womanist Ethics*, 145.

(b) by the speaking out and speaking up of voices that hegemony has long repressed and still seeks to silence. To remember and to speak *through* hegemony's frame is to puncture it and transgress it. And to puncture and transgress it is to begin a process of shattering and disintegration which leads to a new becoming, a new heliotropic ascent.

Spaces of Counter-Hegemony

For bell hooks, such hegemony-transgressing work is also the work of education.[82] The educator, true to her etymological roots (*edu-care* meaning "to draw out" or "to lead out" rather than "to pound in" or "to indoctrinate") may become a guide to help the silenced "come to voice," learning to tell one's own story, and even to tell it strategically.[83] For hooks, this happens best in the space of a classroom.[84] The classroom serves as counter-hegemonic space.

Counter-hegemonic space is also the space of hope: the space where we are able to encourage students to transgress the limits that would define and restrict them. That is, it is the space where students might *become*. Hope is fostered; indeed, it is created, even born anew, in such a space of transgressive becoming. Such a space, for hooks, as for Townes, is a space that names and challenges "fantastic images" and hegemonic histories, but also other delineating, defining, and therefore restricting structures: heteronormativity, patriarchy, racism, capitalism, and the like.[85]

Counter-hegemonic spaces are spaces that allow for the testimonies of the ancestors to crack the drywall of hegemony, where the voices of the centuries speak, and where the voiceless come to voice today. Counter-hegemonic work is long and hard, says Townes, but it is the work of *ornery hope*, and "ultimately," says Townes, this work, a slight trickle though it

---

82. "We learned early that our devotion to learning, to a life of the mind, was a counter-hegemonic act, a fundamental way to resist every strategy of white racist colonization." hooks, *Teaching to Transgress*, 2.

83. hooks, *Teaching to Transgress*, 148–51.

84. "The academy is not paradise. But learning is a place where paradise can be created. The classroom, with all its limitations, remains a location of possibility. In that field of possibility we have the opportunity to labor for freedom, to demand of ourselves and our comrades, an openness of mind and heart that allows us to face reality even as we collectively imagine ways to move beyond boundaries, to transgress. This is education as the practice of freedom." hooks, *Teaching to Transgress*, 207.

85. hooks, *Teaching to Transgress*, 28.

starts, eventually becomes a mighty stream, and "the water wears the rock away through an unwillingness to alter its course."[86]

Spaces of counter-hegemony produce hope, yet at the same time that hope is needed in order to keep up the work of hope itself. As we said of Bloch's Utopian Surplus, so we might say of Towne's *work of ornery hope:* hope is produced by the work, yet the hope in turn feeds the work. Hope is produced, and the hope that was produced feeds hope so that the production of counter-hegemonic spaces, fostering liberative memories and human becoming, will not cease. Hope is a commitment, in other words, a task, and also a reward. It is the work of the whole heart, soul, strength, and mind, for it "begins . . . with the rending of the marvelously complex interlocking character of our humanity."[87] The *work of ornery hope* is embodied and existential and it involves one's whole being, even as it involves one's whole *becoming.*

Local Churches, Localized Memories, Testifying Counter-Hegemony

Community-centered congregations (churches, synagogues, houses of worship) should take note of this method and its tools. Many congregations hold detailed stories and accounts of hyper-localized memories and communal becoming "under the radar" of hegemony. If one finds the right person in such a local congregation, and asks about their particular community's story, it won't be long before there emerge for the careful listener some cracks in the stereotypes about the people who gather there, their neighborhood, their racial or ethnic groups, and so on.

Such stories may serve as a source to counter anti-Black stereotypes. They may also serve to challenge the myth of one, homogenous, "white" history, challenging "uninterrogated whiteness," where it persists.[88] Such stories hold the possibility of revealing the diversity of ethnic struggles and stories at the micro-level before certain groups (for example, Irish, German, Italian, French, etc.) became assimilated into an evolving whiteness and what in the US has become white hegemony. Such stories (though weaponized against Black stories in bizarre instances of *othering*[89]), could

86. Townes, *Womanist Ethics*, 163.

87. Townes, *Womanist Ethics*, 163–64.

88. Townes, *Womanist Ethics*, 70.

89. For example, when I lived in Bridgeport, Chicago, when certain Irish residents

also be sites of intersectional solidarities, where, perhaps, there could be a new becoming, perhaps even beyond the Manichaeistic frame which remains largely intact today.[90] That is to say, the privileging of cacophonous localized stories may allow for an intersectional approach of understanding oppression which combats the oppressor/oppressed dualism, without giving up the very real struggle against oppression. These intersections of oppression may also serve to foster intersectional solidarities uncovered by the communal voicing of localized narratives.

Lastly, as is attested by various Black and Womanist theologians, the age old practice of *testimony* holds in itself the potential of being counter-hegemonic.[91] A testimony that testifies to one's pains and sorrows, and yet perhaps also God's faithfulness in the midst of that pain, serves both to condemn the world and the systems that produce suffering, while simultaneously

---

heard anything about *slavery* in conversation around continued African America oppression, they would often evade any sense of solidarity, instead remembering aloud that "My people were also enslaved," or oppressed, or so on, a phenomenon popularly known as "the oppression olympics." Rather than finding overlapping history as a space to stand in solidarity, this would become, instead, a debate about who deserves sympathy and who does not. What a world if these groups could use shared pain to unite! For more on intersectionality and oppression olympics, see Jha, *Pre-Post-Racial America*, 138.

90. Angela Davis has recently pushed the work (and language) of intersectionality toward what she is calling, with the movement, *intersectional solidarities* or *intersectional struggles*. Proceeding from the question of the intersectionality of privilege and oppression, the question of intersectional solidarities arises: How do we foster a space of acknowledged and shared pain not to measure, name, compare, and contrast, alone, but also, beyond description and into a space from which we might start to imagine and resist together? This is not a fully new idea. However, the union of intersectionality with solidarity into one is quite helpful and brings a new sense of awareness and community to the work of solidarity. Kimberlé Crenshaw is most often credited for developing and popularizing the concept of intersectionality, having received it from forbears such as the Third World Women's Movement in New York. The members of TWM named their own "triple jeopardy," existing as women, women of color, and as women of color from the global south. These "intersections" (the *intersectionality* embodied in their everyday) created a unique matrix of oppressions, each of which, intersecting, shaped and threatened their lives, their relationships, their families, and their bodies. To reiterate, Davis' important and perpetual contribution is her emphasis upon intersection not only as a measurement of oppression, privilege, and pain, but also as a space where solidaritous bonds might be formed across difference. When I use the term *intersectional solidarities* here, it is with Davis' meaning in mind. Davis, *Freedom is a Constant Struggle*, 17–18, 144; Aguilar, "From Triple Jeopardy," 415–28; Crenshaw, *On Intersectionality*; Crenshaw et al., *Critical Race Theory*, 58–74.

91. See Douglas, *Stand Your Ground*, 139–49; Williams, *Sisters in the Wilderness*, 1–14; Butler, "Testimony as Hope," 24–32.

articulating the possibility of solidarity: I'm suffering. God is with me. You all are with me. We are in this together. As a counter-hegemonic response to hegemony's slogan, "Pull yourself up by your bootstraps!" which is a very isolating imperative, Lee H. Butler Jr. affirms that Black faith offers the following. "Our hope lies [not in a narrative about bootstraps, but, rather] in the African concept of 'lift as we climb.' [This faith proclaims that I am not an island to myself, but that] I am related to everyone and everything that contains life."[92] Again, we are all in this together.[93]

One powerful testimony, spoken in the days of slavery, yet still received today, Kelly Brown Douglas notes, is as potent as it is brief: "God does not consider us as chattel."[94] *God does not consider us as chattel.* In these words, spoken as testimony, we hear a counter-hegemonic narrative affirmed. Declared to the community, the words may, in turn, become for others a source of humanization asserted against the dehumanizing forces all around. That is, received as God's truth, these words then hold the power to create in the listener an opening for renewed human becoming. In contrast to the false and oppressive worldview perpetuated by slaveholders, their systems, and their laws, the truth told in the realm of testimony affirms Black reality, Black hope, Black worth, and Black life.[95]

Without a Need to Believe?

The hope born of counter-hegemonic narratives in counter-hegemonic spaces may be, indeed, a hope that is born adjacent to belief and certainly hope that is born in the hearts of committed believers. Nonetheless, counter-hegemonic *ornery hope* is also hope that is born from the transgression of belief and the transgression (or disruption) of hegemonic dogmas themselves (theological or otherwise). Dominant narratives, official histories, stereotypes: as these are cracked open by the introduction of localized, particular, and existentially experienced contradictions to hegemonic normality, beginning to free subjugated people from conformity to hegemonic control, so localized theologies will, by extension, or by the same action, be seen as disruptive and transgressive (and so also heretical) as personal *testimonies* come to flow beyond a hegemonic framework from the lips of

92. Butler, "Testimony as Hope," 29–30.
93. Shaw, "Black Club Women," 10.
94. Douglas, *Stand Your Ground*, 149.
95. Douglas, *Stand Your Ground*, 139.

those declared by hegemonic theological productions to be abominations, criminals, (again, heretical) or *damned*. Yet, when hegemony cries "heresy!" or "unclean!" we may confidently reply "freedom!" and "becoming!" and "a New Creation!" for hegemony loves to cry "Crucify!" when hope begins to lift the lowly, when hope begins to exalt the humbled, when hope preaches a new Reign, born within and among the poor. Hegemony loves to cry, "Crucify!" when hope begins to transgress the hold of hegemony's empire on the heart and the mind, declaring "The new Reign of love is already within/among you," a transgression which is a mustard seed. This is because as the seed climbs toward the sun and becomes a great shrub, as the pinhole becomes a web, in is spreading, creaking, cracking, in the digging-in of its roots, slowly there becomes a shattering of hegemony's foundation and an ajarring of hegemony's frame.

Here, *faith* or *belief* may not find its opposite as *doubt* or as *unbelief*. Rather, we find that if hope finds its fruition in the freedom of *becoming*, a becoming beyond hegemony's frame, then a faith that is rooted in hope must constantly have something to do with *becoming* itself. It must transgress itself, shed old skins. As Tillich might say, it must be *dynamic*. It must be this way so that it does not become a prescribed dogmatic or orthopraxic "cookie cutter" to which the *believer* might conform in thought or action, but rather a resurrective-transgressive force. Truly, for the Christian, this faith encounters the messiah not as the catechetical instructor, or the giver of the New Testament or Law, but rather, at least in moments and at least in some spaces, as "the Resurrection and the Life" (John 11:25), the source of becoming power that transgresses hegemony and overcomes the death that is dealt by a world that would crucify.

And yet, neither belief in a *god* nor belief in a *promise*, for the one who finds hope in counter-hegemonic activity, is a requirement. The work of *ornery hope* is, for Townes, aided by faith. It is fed by the God of the ancestors, the Most High God. This is clear *for her*. However, the work of *transgression* transcends a need to believe. Unbelief itself, insofar as it challenges the static dogmatic believer may certainly be perceived, from this perspective, as even more "faithful" to the project of *ornery* and *counter-hegemonic hope* than the belief of one whose faithfulness offers no disruption to the principalities and powers and no transgression to the systems that perpetuate their oppressive hold.

Where might we look for hope outside of promise? Where might we find hope for an agnostic church and for those of us who find it hard to believe?

Ornery hope, counter-hegemonic hope is yet another possibility. Belief may aid such hope and may be formed and reformed by it. Yet this hope, beyond belief, is both born and nourished in acts of hegemonic disruption and transgression. Such hope makes no promises and demands no dogmatic conformity. It is *ordinary,* it acts *womanish,* it *testifies* against hegemony, and it carves out *spaces of becoming* in a hellish and damnable world.

IV. Hope in *the Holler*: Extracting Counter-Cultural Faith from the Historic Holler

Hope's Bridge

A. Elaine Brown Crawford, building on the works of Townes and Williams, engages *hope* in and from the emotional and physical spaces and matrices of *the Holler*.[96] Born from such contexts—hope emerges as a passion for the possible, and, for Crawford, specifically a "passion for [that which is] possible *in this life.*"[97] This means that, for Crawford, hope's object is neither infinite nor breaking-in from an imagined future, but, rather, is limited by the time, space, and circumstances into which the hoper is born—by the existential location of those who would hope, and by the intersection of privilege and oppression at which she finds herself.[98] Said differently, *hope in the Holler* is both instigated and limited by *the Holler* itself.

For Black women, under the weight of slavery and racist oppression, and in the context of sexual, emotional, and physical abuse, this passion for the possible takes on a unique shape.[99] From this perspective, and from this unique space, womanist hope and womanist theology speak. As distinct from white theologies of hope, Womanist theology, and Crawford's own theology of hope, begin with *the Holler* experienced by

96. Crawford very neatly merges what we have spoken of as Townes' project of counter-hegemonic retrieval and her own question regarding the hope that brought historically abused women through *the Holler*. Crawford doesn't ask "what must we create anew?" but "How did we get this far [perhaps by faith] without giving up completely?" In bringing these narratives to the fore, listening for hope, Crawford seeks (in her own language) a counter-hegemonic hope, a hope that is not controlled or imposed by the hopes of the white American faith that enslaved her forebears.

97. For this expression, Crawford credits Patricia Hunter and Søren Kierkegaard, noting that it is also used by Moltmann. Crawford, *Hope in the Holler,* 20.

98. Crawford, *Hope in the Holler,* 75.

99. Crawford, *Hope in the Holler,* 16.

Black women. Such suffering, Crawford describes as having three defining characteristics. It is maldistributed. It is enormous in severity. And it is transgenerational. That is, (a) Black women and Black people suffer more (and differently) than other groups; (b) the suffering is so great that it literally causes diseases and lowers the life expectancy of Black people; and, (c) it lingers on for generations.[100]

At the same time, Crawford claims, and as a result, hope, likewise, becomes disproportionate. It is larger among those who suffer the most. As pain is immense, spanning generations, so is the hope, the passion for the possible that gets Black women through. It must be so. How else could one endure *the Holler* of existence every day?

Our Hope Is In, Our Hope Is Of

In what is such hope grounded? Out of what is it made? From what does hope spring (eternal or not)? What is the source and power of this hope, that it endures even *the Holler*? These are a few of the questions that Crawford asks.

To arrive at responses, Crawford embarks on a womanist task of *retrieval*.[101] Mining historical texts, specifically narratives from women

---

100. In describing the three marks of black suffering, Crawford relies on William Jones' work on theodicy as a source. Crawford, *Hope in the Holler*, 17.

101. Retrieval, in womanist theologies, is a method by which "Womanist theologians can bring the experience and knowledge of the marginalized to the center by standing aside to let the community speak for itself." Thomas, "Womanist Theology." Crawford picks up this task in her utilization of Black women's narratives. It is their voices to which she turns in search of prolegomena of her own. As Crawford affirms, "part of what is lacking in the discussion of hope [and womanist hope] is attention to the actual voices of abused African American women. [Crawford's primary intent] is to capture the perspectival lens of the slave women whose voices have been virtually silenced in history." This work of *retrieval*, itself, to use Townes' frame, is counterhegemonic. It is the lifting of voices from a space of silencing. It is allowing for testimony which holds the possibility of shattering stereotypes that form in the imagination when a vacuum is created by hegemony's silencing of subjugated and multiplicitous images and voices. Of course, the narratives themselves, written under slavery, were an assertion of self in a world that abused these women and made them into sub-human property. As such, the very act of writing, says Crawford, is an act of asserting one's humanhood and stoking a passion for the possible right now. Again, by writing, and by using their gifts, these authors offered humanizing and counter-hegemonic narratives and images that were literally unheard and not listened to at the time, not even by the likes of white abolitionists. Crawford, *Hope in the Holler*, 16, 22–28, 90–107; Townes, *Womanist Ethics*, 139–41.

telling their own stories of enslavement, she then goes on also to explore narratives from women who have experienced emancipation, and, finally, narratives from women who have experienced abuse in contemporary times. At first glance, Crawford's answer to her own question is simple: this *hope*, born in *the Holler*, is always and ever grounded in "the Lord."[102] Hope and religious conviction go hand in hand. Hope springs from faith which is articulated with theological words.[103] Spiritual emphases and languages shift with time.[104] Yet, nevertheless, this groundedness-in-the-Lord remains—at least among the subjects Crawford chooses to engage as her sources and interlocutors. In these forebears, Crawford clearly uncovers a counter-cultural faith that stokes a counter-cultural passion for the possible even in seemingly impossible, hopeless circumstances and times, even in the depths of *the Holler*.

"Ole Satan's Church is Here Below":[105] Passion for the Possible in a Counter-Cultural Faith

Crawford's first set of narratives, those to which we turn now, are narratives written or dictated by Black women while they were enslaved in North America. This is a uniquely formative period, says Crawford, a time in which Black women's hope took on shapes and contours that remain to this day. As such, it is a reality any student of hope must attempt to grasp if that student is to better understand the present.[106] Here, Crawford uncovers what she calls a counter-cultural theology and a counter-cultural hope.[107] This "theology of hope, born in slavery," Crawford holds, "was

---

102. Crawford, *Hope in the Holler*, 109.

103. Crawford, *Hope in the Holler*, 109–10.

104. Crawford, *Hope in the Holler*, 64.

105. These lyrics are from a spiritual quoted by Harriet Jacobs in her book *Incidents in the Life of a Slave Girl*, and cited in Crawford, *Hope in the Holler*, 31.

106. Crawford, *Hope in the Holler*, 34.

107. As "counter-cultural," such theologies, as is the case with those mentioned above in our work with Douglas and Townes, will be counter the culture of white Christianity and white supremacy, as well as counter the images and stereotypes pushed upon Black women and the enslaved. Crawford highlights the "negro wench," "Jezebel," and the "Mammy." These are just three stereotypes that, perpetuated, portray black women as hyper-sexualized and "wanting to be raped" on the one hand, and asexual on the other (even as they are being raped or molested by slave masters). Again, this is the "culture" that these theologies served to counter for those who embraced them. Crawford, *Hope in the Holler*, 20–22.

a resisting and active hope."[108] It was a hope grounded in a religion that served not as "an opiate to soothe the brutalities of slavery, [but rather as a] fire that ignited [a] passion for justice and full humanity,"[109] even if justice was not immediately achievable. Crawford finds this faith articulated in Mary Prince, Sojourner Truth, Old Elizabeth, Harriet Jacobs, and others. Following are a few very brief examples.

Forced to work on the sabbath (something she was convinced was a sin), Mary Prince, in her time, comes to offer her critique and ultimately her judgement upon the masters for the "breaking" of the sabbath. "It is very wrong . . . to work on Sunday or to go to market," she affirms, "but will not God call the Buckra (white) men to answer for this on the great day of judgement—since they will give slaves no other day?"[110]

In her raising of this question, of course, Mary Prince subverts the judgement that white religion and white slaveholding Christianity would cast upon her for working on the sabbath. There is no doubt that, contrary to their judgement, it is in fact the economic system, and the institution of slavery itself, that mandate her work and create said infraction. If there is *sin* to be named, it is certainly to be found embedded in the people and in the systems that those people created and perpetuated in order to enslave—and not in the forced actions of the enslaved, themselves.

Likewise, Sojourner Truth made a clear distinction between the Religion of Jesus and the Religion of America, as did Old Elizabeth.[111] Harriet Jacobs, too, drew a hard line between what she dubbed as the Religion of the South and *actual* Christianity. "If a man goes to the communion table [in the South], and pays money in the treasury of the church," she observed, "no matter if it be the price of blood [or gained through the enslavement of Black bodies], he is called religious."[112] Faithfulness is an illusion, she illuminates. Christian identity, in this false expression of the faith, is sold and bought alongside bodies. The church's true Lord, yet again, is gold. In contrast to this superficial display, Jacob's faith is internal, deep, and strong.

On one occasion, Jacobs' master tried to convince her to have sexual relations with him. First, however, he needed to convince her that it was morally okay. She need not worry, he contended, as in so doing she would

---

108. Crawford, *Hope in the Holler*, 15.
109. Crawford, *Hope in the Holler*, 28.
110. Crawford, *Hope in the Holler*, 28.
111. Crawford, *Hope in the Holler*, 32.
112. Crawford, *Hope in the Holler*, 29–30.

remain "as virtuous as [his] wife." Jacobs disagrees. "The Bible doesn't say so," she responds, holding up the symbol of her faith against her master's abuse.[113] Such moments are telling about the Religion of the South that was prayed and practiced alongside the evils of human enslavement. They are also telling about Jacob's faith, testifying both that the world is not as it should be, and that Jacob's God has more authority over her heart than her so-called master ever could.

The same Harriet Jacobs scolds Christians who hold slaves and yet do not allow Black folks into their church pews. "Talk to the American slave holders as you talk to the savages in Africa," she advises Christian teachers. "Tell *them* it is wrong to traffic in men. Tell them it is sinful to sell their own children, and atrocious to violate their own daughters. Tell them that all men are brethren, and that man has no right to shut out the light of knowledge from his brothers. Tell them they are answerable to God for stealing the Fountain of Life from souls that are thirsting for it."[114] "Are doctors of divinity blind," she asks, pausing pensively, about those who fail to speak such truths, "or are they [simply] hypocrites?"[115]

Sadly, James Cone will echo this exact sentiment a century and a half later when he asks, again, of the doctors of the faith: Where were you when they were lynching us? Were you there when they crucified my ancestors?[116]

The countercultural, counter-abuse, anti-enslavement faith expressed by these women is the faith which grounds and stokes hope in *the Hollers* of Black women even today, says Crawford. Because of such faith, enslaved women were empowered to resist, to cry out, and to endure, undergirding their ongoing and passionate quest, "for voice, humanity, and the freedom to control their lives and bodies."[117]

Doubt in the Holler?

Crawford's major deficit, insofar as it pertains to our own questions, is somewhat obvious. The women she chose to study were, to one degree or

---

113. Crawford, *Hope in the Holler*, 31.

114. Crawford, *Hope in the Holler*, 30.

115. Crawford, *Hope in the Holler*, 30.

116. Particularly, Cone struggles with Niebuhr's vocality on oppression, yet silence in regard to the injustice and terror embodied in the practice of lynching in the US. Cone, *The Cross*, 56–64.

117. Crawford, *Hope in the Holler*, 33.

another, women of faith in a God. That is, Crawford's sample is skewed toward the theistic. Had she intentionally sought out women who were atheists, for example, in contemporary times, she certainly would have yielded different results. Nonetheless, what Crawford finds in the faith of these women is indispensable and illuminating.[118] And of course, Crawford's own search is explicitly theological—her work itself a prolegomenon for further theological explorations into womanist hope.

Faith of Our Mothers

It is common in various African spiritualities to pour out libations as a spiritual practice.[119] The pouring out may be seen as a conjuring of ancestors, or a simple honoring of those who have gone on before. It may also be seen as a reminder that we have come this far by faith, and that there is a great cloud of witnesses, saints, and survivors who testified to the faith long before the present generation was named, but who testified to the faith that it might be received for strength and for salvific healing today. Libations may also simply name the presence of a physical absence of a loved one, due to death. There is no single meaning. Gestures and rituals always say more than words.

As Bloch, escaping fascist violence as a refugee, sought to mine Utopian Surplus in the hopes and dreams of the revolting peasants, the musical composers, and the utopian dreamers who had lived before him, and as Alves sought to dream his messiah's dreams of a banquet and playground where all may be childlike, free and happy; in similar fashion, from her own context, her own space of *the Holler*, Crawford mines the hopes and the faith of her ancestors, the ones who followed the faith of Jesus, the rock in a weary land. Such faith, though it shared a proper name (Christian) was not the same faith, and not the same religion, of those who enslaved Crawford's forebears.

As mentioned above, Crawford asks in her work specific questions regarding abused Black women's hope and *passion*. In what has such hope been grounded? Out of what is it made? From what does hope spring (eternal or not)? What is the source and power of hope, that it endures even the Holler? Although the answer is "the Lord" for Crawford, and although this hope in the Lord she calls "the bridge" that sustained Black women in

118. Crawford, *Hope in the Holler*, 11–12.
119. Nehusi, "Libation."

the seeming hopeless time of crossing between slavery and the present, it seems to me that, in Crawford, the ancestors themselves also function as something of a bridge—or perhaps as the power to cross.

That is, it is the narratives of Mary Prince, Old Elizabeth, Sojourner Truth, Harriet Jacobs, Priscilla Albright, Margaret Nickerson, Phyllis Green, and more, which are Crawford's pathway and connection back to the faith of Jesus. The narratives testify to these women's faith, faith in the Lord. Their stories and lives contain it, standing in direct contrast to the religion of America and its empty promises. With these women, Crawford writes her prolegomenon, and as she writes, she amplifies their voice.

In this sense, Crawford's work is a libation, a pouring-out, a conjuring of the faith of Jesus, discovered in the narratives, the words, the stories, the lives, and the testimonies of these women who were abused, commodified, raped, and beaten by "good, upstanding Christian men and women," and "good American citizens." Here, in the presence of these forebears, Crawford finds a "passion for the possible in their lives . . . grounded in belief in a God who aids the oppressed of humanity."[120] As these women arrive again in Crawford's work, they testify against slaveholding Christianity, and, at the same time, against any faith that would look the other way in situations of abuse or justify the oppression of any people.

Yes, hope is a bridge embodied and incarnated in the faith of these women. Hope carried them through the crossing, from the time of slavery and into the present. And though today literal chains are often less visible, the weight of oppression and a passion for the yet possible still remain and still anticipate something better and something new: a fuller voice, a fuller humanity, and a fuller freedom in which women might control their own bodies, free from abuse. Crawford sees these women's passion for the possible, and it becomes passion for her own *possible*, fuel for her work of ministry and recovery in a still (and often increasingly) hostile world that would un-voice, dehumanize, abuse, isolate, and incarcerate Black bodies and Black women.

May Crawford's work summon the spirits of these women for all who would struggle to find the energy and the will to survive.

---

120. Crawford, *Hope in the Holler*, 34.

A Need to Believe?

What does Crawford's work say to our questions: *Where might we look for hope outside of promise? Where might we find hope for an agnostic church and for those of us who find it hard to believe?* Crawford turns to faith, and indeed to the beliefs and theologies of her forebears, reminding us that Black women throughout American history had their own distinctive interpretive key, and that their faith was countercultural, as was their undying passion for the possible.[121]

Does a church and a people who find it hard to believe want more alternate beliefs from which to choose? More to pick from? Perhaps. Yet what is important to us here, in regard to our questions, is the following. Not unlike Townes' counter-hegemonic hope, the womanist hope of which Crawford speaks is also a rejection of the "religion of America," "the religion of the South," and any church that blessed slavery, did not respond to lynching, and today says little as Black lives are dehumanized and detained, and while black women are beaten and abused.

With her interlocutors, Crawford does not look for promise or hope in an institution that saw nothing promising or even fully human in her ancestors. In mining the faith of several women, Crawford finds several theologies, but in each piety she uncovers something common: reliance upon a God who is incarnate within, struggling and surviving within and alongside women who are doing the same, giving them power to survive, endure, overcome, and sometimes even to become free.

One need not become a pastor or theologian, as did Crawford, in order to live this faith. Neither must one join a church. This faith was not, as a rule, received or transferred by way of the churches and preachers. It was born more robustly in the fields, in the hush harbors, in the kitchens, and

---

121. Although this recreation/use of the oppressor's God may still entail *promise* as well as *belief*, it is not belief imposed from on high, from a magisterium or a white man (representing a white, patriarchal religion) in a white robe. On the contrary, such hope/belief is born in the body, in *the Holler* itself, at all of its intersections, and transferred, yet morphing, dynamic, generation to generation. It uses the Christian language, words similar to those used by the slaveholders and the conquistadors. And yet it is saying something quite different. This faith of Jesus, a fuel and vessel for a hope that is a *passion for the possible*, is not enslaving, but rather power for surviving in the midst of slavery, oppression, and abuse. It is not the justification of enslavement and dehumanization, but rather the urge and authority to claim one's own humanity and belovedness, and to fight for one's freedom and the freedom of one's people, despite *the Holler* of abuse and pain. Crawford, *Hope in the Holler*, 18.

in the hearts of those who endured unspeakable pain (and sometimes pain they spoke of anyway). It was born in the deepest depths of *the Holler*. The prayers whispered by these women, desire for a better life, a passion for the possible right now, may be whispered still today in hopeless situations and in the continued and perpetual *Holler* of the everyday. Perhaps they still hold power, whatever the pray-er believes, whatever her theological articulations, and certainly whether or not she's ever stepped through a Christian church's door. There is no promise of utopia born from such a prayer, but perhaps there might be a fire, a small flame, a flicker, and a passion for that which just might, right now, be possible. Such hope is *unpromising* even as it holds promise for the one emboldened to challenge *the Holler* right here and right now.

CHAPTER FOUR

Hope in the Key of *Chōra*

So Close You Can Touch It

WHAT IF, WHEN JESUS said the Reign of God is at hand, he meant *nearby*—not simply in time, but also in space? What if *at-hand* means *so close that we can touch it*? What if, contrary to those who would wonder about a delayed parousia or an unreturned messiah, Christ is already returning, coming near quite often, again and again? These eschatological questions are among the many that Vítor Westhelle engages.

As he builds new constructs and platforms from which to leap theologically into space (and spatial questions) one prominent and recurring tool he utilizes to do so is the Greek word *chōra*. *Chōra* "etymologically means to lie open, listen, be attentive, be ready to receive. It defines a space between places or limits, an adjacent ground."[1]

"Only for the sake of the hopeless ones have we been given hope."[2] This quotation from Walter Benjamin, Westhelle loves. Yet how does this translate? Who are the *spatially* hopeless? They are those who may inhabit choratic spaces, those who dwell at the limits, the *eschata*.[3] These are not imaginary people. For Westhelle, these are especially those landless siblings with whom he worked in his time as Coordinator of the Ecumenical Commission on Land (CPT) in Paraná;[4] those who had no place, who had been dis-placed—not by choice, but rather by force, to a choratic realm, to the limits, squatting between a fence and a runway on the side of

1. Westhelle, *The Church Event*, 128.
2. Westhelle, *After Heresy*, 163.
3. We will unpack this terminology below.
4. Susan Barreto, "Celebrated Systematic Theologian."

a highway, their situation the result of a long history of colonial exploitation and corrupt rule.[5]

There are those also who pass through these realms. Those who are fleeing. Those such as Jesus' family, traversing the wilderness when Herod decreed that children such as he should be slaughtered (Matt 2:16–18). Perhaps those who are passing through in such a way are trusting an angel's pleading: "Flee! Run! Be gone!" Even if this is so, they must be terrified. Is this not the country where our ancestors were enslaved? Is this not the sea that parted to deliver and united to drown? Traversing the *chōra* (a desert, an ocean, a sea, mountains, an arbitrary border, a border wall, or even the space between the bodies which define and separate us) holds no certain promise. Nonetheless, one finds oneself there, crossing, perhaps desiring. Will there be a sanctuary or an oasis? Will we find something of a home? Will love be consummated or end in bitter estrangement? Perhaps in death, detention, prolonged abuse? In the end, is there really an other side at which to arrive?[6]

Hope in the key of *chōra* is sweet and sour. It is tense and uncertain. The muscles in the neck and the gut are tangled in a knot. It mourns that which it has left behind, anticipating God-knows-what.[7] Perhaps God knows. In the *chōra*, there is no hope that is not laced with sorrow and hunger and aspirations and fear.

The choratic key sings something of the songs of Advent: in our mangers and inns, in the embrace of strangers at the rejection of others, here will be a holy, terrific and terrifying arrival of that which we do not know. Do we await a birth? What will it look like? Do we await destruction? Will there be salvation? A respite? A revolt? Will there be weeping and gnashing of teeth? For whom? Will the heavens become torn? Will a garden bloom and the moon be turned to blood? What of the grand wedding feast? Are my garments prepared?

Is it true? Is the reign nearby? Or is it Doomsday?[8] Hope in the *chōra* is saturated with inquisitive expectant emotion. It is timid. It is joyful. It is terribly afraid.

5. Westhelle, *The Church Event*, 165.

6. Westhelle, *The Church Event*, 140.

7. Westhelle, *Eschatology and Space*, 132.

8. Whereas much of the liturgical church prefaces Advent with Christ the King or Reign of Christ Sunday, the Church of Sweden observes Doom Sunday. In a Westhellian frame, the two of these together seem quite fitting—and make sense of the Revised Common Lectionary texts for the day. Haslanger, "Day of Doom."

Approaching the *Chōra*

Where might we look for hope outside of promise? Where might we find hope for an agnostic church and for those of us who find it hard to believe? These are the questions we have been asking along our way. In response, Bloch and Muñoz offered us *Utopian Surplus*, hoping the revolutionary hopes of belonging and becoming left to us by our aspirational ancestors. Alves offered us that we might dream the messiah's dreams—and also that, sacramentally, these dreams might become infused with our own, that ours and the messiah's dreams might become together. Crawford, Townes, Williams, and Copeland offered us *hope in the Holler* for survival and quality of life, a passion for the possible right now, grounded in counter-hegemonic spaces and the counter-cultural, slavery-denouncing faith of their Black Christian forebears.

This chapter will turn our attention to the eschatological thinking of Vítor Westhelle. It may seem a strange turn to make with our agnostic questions, turning to a theologian who makes such frequent use of thoroughly Christian theological categories. But it is not so strange. As indicated above, though Westhelle's vantage point is one often spoken using Christian language, it is also constantly seeking to transfigure and transgress.

Hoping from the *chōra* holds an agnostic sensibility. Whatever it understands of God-talk, and whatever categories serve to contain it, it is nonetheless uncertain. Like Bloch's *heimweh*, Alves' *saudade*, and Crawford's *Holler*, Westhelle's hope is often homesick, anxious, and screaming. It is *weak*.[9] Nonetheless, it is hope for the sake of the hopeless, hoping against hope.[10]

In order to engage our questions as we search for an unpromising hope in Westhelle, (and unpack that which we've said above), we will take a cursory journey through Westhelle's use of eschatological and liminal language, a language he uses to speak of the apocalyptic emotions that liminal situations produce. In sections one and two we will begin by taking a look at Westhelle's spatial approach to the eschaton, as well as his conceptualization of those he calls the eschatoi. We will connect these to his conceptualization of the choratic realm. In section three, we will touch upon the transgressive connotation of crossing that the *chōra* elicits, including a brief

---

9. Westhelle often refers to Benjamin's conception of *weak* messianic power. Benjamin, "Theses on the Philosophy of History," 197.

10. Westhelle, *After Heresy*, 163.

detour into Foucault, in order to speak of transgression, discipline, and the norm. This conversation will lead us into section four, where we will look at Westhelle's use of *hybridity* as a concept for speaking of community, Christ and church-places. Finally, we will return to Westhelle's use of the term *apocalypse* as it pertains to our question of hope without promise. We will close the chapter with an embrace of the apocalyptic, choratic, unpromising hope which runs through the pages of Westhelle's works, as well as some brief remarks in the form of an after-word.

I. Ends and Crossing

Eschatology and Ends

For Westhelle, talk of liminality is eschatological-talk. This is because, for Westhelle, eschatology as a discipline ought to be held to its etymological roots. These have to do with limits and ends. Though the scope of eschatology has been often restricted in theologies to end-times, Westhelle insists upon the importance of space as a "lost dimension" in eschatological discourse, without which eschatological understanding is bound to suffer a terrible anemia.[11] If we displace God's reign, the kin[g]dom, even *God godself* (as that which we hope for) to a teleological end/consummation of time, or if we speak of God "breaking" or "slicing" into time from outside of time, in an eternal now, a moment of authentication, or the like, we have already begun to fall astray from faithfulness to a God who, in Christ, is revealed in flesh, and indeed in the stuff and the matter of the world. That is, a God who exists as the future, *alone*, is a God who is not fully present, sacramentally everywhere, in stuff and in flesh.[12] An end-time theology disembodies and un-matters God. "God is in matter, or else God does not matter," says Westhelle (with Keller).[13] Likewise if eschatological God-talk has not to do

11. Westhelle, *Eschatology and Space*, 1–20.

12. Westhelle is quite fond of recalling Luther's remarks from his *Confession Concerning Christ's Supper* that if Christ sits "at the right hand of the Father," as the Creeds maintain, then Christ sits everywhere. Christ, who is fully present in bread in wine, is fully present, albeit perhaps differently, in every speck of dust and every atom in the universe. That is, again, God is in matter and not simply disembodied in *time* or an abstract, non-physical *eternity*. Westhelle, *Transfiguring Luther*, 159; Luther, "Confession Concerning Christ's Supper," 262–79.

13. Westhelle paraphrases Catherine Keller. Westhelle, *Transfiguring Luther*, 160.

with spatial matters, and with *taking place*, then that God-talk does not hold much weight upon a Westhellian scale.

What, then, does matter? The following paragraphs will help us to understand. Here we will explore Westhelle's use of *eschaton*, eschata, and the eschatoi,[14] as well as what Westhelle refers to as spaces of *crossing, chōra,* or choratic realms.[15] We will do so using an illustration occasionally utilized by Westhelle himself.

Xenodoxeion

More than once, Westhelle recalls a story about Saint John Chrysostom. The story is a story about a preaching event. At the time John was to deliver this specific homily, we imagine, he climbed the stairs to the pulpit and peered out at his gathered flock below. It was a proud day. The assembly was celebrating the birth of the first Christian Charities.[16] The first xenodoxeion, as they were called, very lovely little houses that were commissioned and made "to deal with the homeless problem," had finally been constructed. In fact, as the people settled in for John's homily, in honor of the celebration of this concrete solution, several families had already been settled into the developments.

As John began to speak there, in the midst of the congregation's anticipated reception of praise, he made eye contact with each—perhaps especially with the richest among them—and he asked a holy question to the gathering. First: a pregnant pause . . . Then: "What have you done?" He *said* the question, rather than asking it. "What have you done?" Presenting the question, John confronts his churchgoers, giving his admonition in place of their anticipated laud and praise. "What have you done?" "In hiding away, these least of these, you have hidden away Christ himself, who calls you to encounter him in each one."[17] In hiding away the poor (and in calling "the

14. Westhelle, *The Scandalous God*, 156.

15. This is a borrowed Derridian term. Westhelle, *After Heresy*, 87, 131–32; Westhelle, *Eschatology and Space*, 78; Westhelle, *The Scandalous God*, 97–100; Westhelle, *The Church Event*, 127; Westhelle, "Liberation Theology," 320–23; Westhelle, *Transfiguring Luther*, 152–53.

16. I am speaking hyperbolically to illustrate a point. The church had been charitable for quite some time, including Paul's congregations who were urged to remember the poor at the church in Jerusalem and to contribute to them (Acts 11:29; Rom 15:25–32; Gal 2:10). See Johnson, *The Acts of the Apostles*, 202–8.

17. The sermon to which Westhelle refers is Chrysostom's *Homily 45* on the Acts

homeless," rather than the system that produces homelessness, a problem), the Christians are hiding away Christ who claims that where two or more gather he will be present, and who claims that he is present always in "the least of these" (Matt 25:40). In the name of the first charities, these well-intended Christians have created ghettos.[18]

In the Ends: *Eschata* and *Eschatoi*

As mentioned, an *eschaton* in Westhelle's work generally refers to an end or a limit, as the term *eschatology* etymologically suggests. Moving beyond time-bound eschatologies and into spatial/geographical realms, in Westhelle's conception, *eschaton* points to other *ends*: physical boundaries, geographic borders, societal margins, city limits, and the like. As these are plural, they are called (using the Greek language) *eschata*. These are spaces often represented (but simultaneously "crossed out") on paper by cartographical delineations.[19]

For example, from where I am sitting, these include the gray dotted line that separates Illinois from Indiana on Google maps, or the solid gray line that separates the US from Mexico. In biblical narratives, these spaces are often sites of crucifixion, places of skulls, the spaces where Jesus is lynched by Rome. They are often spaces where garbage and waste are heaped up, Gahennas and Golgothas, where we put the items and the people we choose to discard.[20]

---

of the Apostles. Westhelle, *The Church Event*, 134; Westhelle, *Transfiguring Luther*, 152.

18. In his reading of Chrysostom, as well as elsewhere, Westhelle relies heavily on Segundo's interpretation of Matt 25. Segundo argues that unlike much of the world who may not know that kindness to others is kindness to God (represented by the questions in verses 37–39, "Lord, when did we see you hungry and feed you, or thirsty and give you something to drink?"), Christians, the community called *church*, are those who actually do know. The church is "those who already know," and therefore should respond to Christ the o/Other accordingly. Segundo, *The Community Called Church*, 63.

19. Westhelle, *Eschatology and Space*, 55–56.

20. At the edge of Chicago, these include our own county dumps. They include the spaces where people live under bridges and viaducts, on Lower Wacker (beneath the city), and under the Stevenson Expressway, near Archer and Lock. They include coal-ash sites in South Chicago and unremediated coal-fired power plant sites on the river between Pilsen and Bridgeport, and at the riverbank in Little Village. Each exists at/as a border, a margin, an end. They include the Dan Ryan expressway, placed to separate Black and white communities. They include the displaced spaces of Palestine, barbed wire, "security" guards, and checkpoints. In Brazil, for Westhelle, these include the

The physical boundaries that are often constructed at, in, or around eschata serve as roadblocks to our senses. They keep us from perceiving those others who are relegated to such spaces. Westhelle calls these people, those who dwell at the eschata of the world, the *eschatoi*.[21]

In the story of John's congregation, the poor homeless (and subsequently housed) are the eschatoi, the particular eschaton in which they dwell is the literal margin of town. They are covered by walls constructed by Christian charity and Christian builders. The xenodoxeion are shelters. They protect and give cover from the elements. Yet they also serve to hide. They cover up the eschatoi. In building these covers, the Christians house people. However, simultaneously, and "by virtue of [their] wealth [they shield themselves, knowingly or not] from the unpleasant reality of the o/Other."[22] So there, at the eschata the eschatoi remain, unencountered, tucked away, hidden, and housed.

The eschaton has to do with ends, limits, and margins. There is not one *eschaton*. There are *eschata*. The *eschatoi* are those who inhabit the *eschata* of the world. They are often hidden, intentionally or unintentionally, from hegemonic or dominant-class/cultural senses.[23]

---

spaces into which displaced (and therefore landless) people are forced—neither the new plantation nor the highway, but that space in-between where displaced people squat. We tarry in these spaces a while, at least until the alderman or ICE or Streets and Sanitation kick us out. *Eschata* include our prisons and our concentration camps, spaces where people remain unheard by power—and unseen, either intentionally or unintentionally, trapped or silenced behind bars, iron, concrete, guards, walls. Westhelle, *Transfiguring Luther*, 114; Westhelle, *The Scandalous God*, x; Westhelle, *The Church Event*, 116–18.

21. The *eschatoi*, are those whom the epistle to the Romans, in chapter 4, notes are without *ousia* (aousia), without being, but that God calls into being, as God "calls into being those who have none." For a helpful discussion that links those who are a-ousia in Romans 4 to the marginalized and subaltern "nonbeings" of the world, see Caputo, *The Weakness of God*, 78–82.

22. Westhelle, *Transfiguring Luther*, 152.

23. It is my belief that the emotions of the in-between were important for Westhelle because the people he worked with found themselves in choratic spaces and sought to name something of the divine in them. His eschatological descriptions are less an invitation for those already compromised to go deeper into the desert sand, but rather a language for those in the crossing to name the sacredness and the terror of their crossing space.

Chōra, the Crossing, and Choratic Spaces[24]

The third Westhellian eschatological concept illustrated by Chrysostom's congregation is that of *the crossing*, that of *choratic spaces or realms*. This concept can be tricky, as it tied up with the others. Each liminal space, each eschaton, is a choratic space, yet in potentiality. Because of this potentiality, it can sometimes seem that Westhelle uses the terms interchangeably. Generally, however, this is not precisely the case. The following paragraphs will help us to clarify Westhelle's use as well as our own.

In some anthropological circles, both *chōra* and *choratic space* are terms that can be used to describe the spaces (and sometimes the movements) which take place, to use a phrase from Victor Turner, "betwixt and between" the beginning and the end of a ritual or rite of passage.[25] As the rite portrays a journey and a turning point, so one's own life journey and one's own identity are often also at something of a personal or communal turning point when the rite is enacted. For example, if the rite of passage is that of a child walking across a bed of hot coals, after which the community declares that child to be an adult, then the choratic space is the space in which the crossing takes place. It is the path of coals which is walked upon, *the crossing*. It is the space in which the person is neither a child nor an adult, but in transition, in transit, "betwixt and between," on the way, and becoming.[26]

In Christian traditions, baptism, though sometimes stationary, nonetheless signals a space of change in the pouring of water over a body, in some cases, or in an immersion of the body beneath water, in others, with plenty of variations and localized adaptations. In any of these baptismal gestures, the encounter of water with body becomes a space between symbolic death and symbolic rebirth (Rom 6:4; Gal 2:20) or perhaps symbolic "uncleanliness" and ritual cleansing (Acts 22:16). It is for many a soteriological space of justification: a deliverance from damnation into that which is considered salvific. For others it is a door into the process and journey of sanctification, and so it is a new beginning. In liturgical traditions, other water-related *crossings* or choratic spaces are recalled at baptism: the flood,

---

24. This is a borrowed Derridian term. Westhelle, *After Heresy*, 87, 131–32; Westhelle, *Eschatology and Space*, 78, 97–100; Westhelle, *The Church Event*, 127; Westhelle, "Liberation Theology," 320–23; Westhelle, *Transfiguring Luther*, 152–53.

25. Turner, "Betwixt and Between," 93–111.

26. Snepvangers et al., *Embodied and Walking*, 223.

the passing from enslavement to wilderness through the Red Sea, and even the crowning of birth itself.[27]

The graduation stage a high school senior walks across, becoming a graduate, is choratic space. Walking the aisle for a wedding or an altar call is, likewise, a choratic crossing. The seminary classroom, it has been argued, may be called choratic, as it is the space of becoming between the life of preparatory study and the life of fulfilled vocation.[28] The desert wilderness of the exodus and of Joseph's and Mary's flight to Egypt, and every desert or sea crossed by migrants and refugees: all of these crossing-spaces are choratic.

There is a popular etymology about a particular choratic space which is told of in Ireland. If one visits certain castles there (which are now small museums) the tour guide will often offer the following story. In the bedroom of a castle, it is said, the family used to keep straw, or thresh on the floor. This thresh helped to keep the room warm. It was also very messy. In order to keep the thresh mostly in the bedroom, so that it would not get tracked down the hall, it was found helpful to set up a barrier in the doorway. This way the thresh would be preserved. Appropriately, this barrier between one room and another, which is neither room, but the space of crossing from one into another, betwixt and between, is called the *threshhold*. The threshold, another space between spaces, is choratic. At Shinto shrines, the threshold between the outside world and a sacred space is marked by torii, sacred gates/entrances, so that one may acknowledge and be mindful in the crossing.[29] At dojos, martial artists bow as they enter the space of practice and growth. They also bow to one another as practice begins and ends.[30] Many Roman Catholics leave a *stoup* or small bowl filled with holy water near the entrance of their homes.[31] Other Christians also mark doorways with chalk, crosses, or other symbols in the blessing of a building or home.[32] These monuments, marks, prayers, and gestures are all intentionally mindful of the choratic.

---

27. Carson, "Liturgy Betwixt and Between," 85–88.

28. Billman, "Classrooms and Choratic Spaces," 150–59; Carson, "Higher Education as Liminal Domain," 75–80.

29. Kasulis, *Shinto*, 27.

30. Toguchi, *Okinawan Goju-Ryu*, 60.

31. Kosloski, "3 Powerful Sacramentals."

32. Ramshaw, "Bringing the Blessing Home," 19.

The crossing, the *chōra*, is often a space of transition. As such, it may be a space of transformation or growth (sometimes marked *by*, sometimes acted out *through*, ritual). One's identity may be less defined here, in the crossing, and exist more as *becoming* (as Bloch would have it) or *queer-becoming* as conceived by Muñoz.[33] Definitions and delineations are elusive and classifications are blurred in the *chōra*. Emotionally, for the subject, the crossing may be a space of anticipation: a space of loss, hope, fear, excitement, and so on. That is, it may be a space of the expectant emotions discussed in Chapter 1.[34]

Choratic Potentiality

In the case of the story of John and his assembly, we read of a missed crossing, a choratic space that could have, and yet did not take place. Said differently, there was a stage, but there was no play. There was an opening, but the crossing itself remained only in potentiality, suppressed. The potential crossing in this setting was a communal/social crossing. It was to be the crossing of one set of *others* into o/Other(s), forming a space called community, and the community called church, as Westhelle understands it.[35] In such a crossing (the one that, in this case, did not take place) Church takes place as/in/with the choratic realm. The reason this space did not emerge as a crossing in the story of John's gathering is that it was prevented by those new dwellings which claimed to be *for* the o/Other, the dwellings that the church people built. The walls of the xenodoxeion blocked one from an o/Other.[36]

33. Bloch, *The Spirit of Utopia*, 199; Muñoz, *Cruising Utopia*, 10.

34. Bloch, *The Principle of Hope*, 1:11.

35. Westhelle draws again on Segundo's understanding of the church as the community who "already knows" that Christ is present in the encounter with the o/Other. He simultaneously names this space created in encounter as Church Event itself. This space is akin to what Bhabha calls a "Third Space." In my use of *o/Other* I am replicating Westhelle's use, which is not entirely consistent, but which retains an incarnational affirmation that Westhelle holds dear: that God is in the o/Other. As we will touch on later, this does not mean that the o/Other brings along salvation. Indeed, our neighbors may in fact be plotting to murder us. Whatever the character/intent of our neighbors, this is the best short-hand reminder of an essential element in Westhellian understanding. I will use it throughout the chapter with intention. Segundo, *The Community Called Church*; Bhabha, *The Location of Culture*, 36–39; Westhelle, *The Church Event*, 39.

36. Westhelle, *The Church Event*, 128; Westhelle, *Eschatology and Space*, 99–101; Westhelle, *Transfiguring Luther*, 132.

When one misses an other, it is not always because of this kind of barrier. Such an encounter-via-crossing (even without the xenodoxeion) is often prevented by social walls, walls built by class constructs and wealth inequality, walls built by ideologies that distort one's perception of an o/Other, and even other literal walls, such as those of the church building where John was called to administer the Word. Whatever form they may take, the choratic, the crossing, is often prevented by barriers. Here, they are built at the intersection of class, sect, and/or an alienating conception of otherness. Here they are built as walls at the edge of town.

There is yet another element of the choratic which is important for any interaction with Westhelle. Specifically, for Westhelle, the choratic has to do with the Divine. For this reason, missing the *choratic* that is so nearby entails more than missing a certain kind of "becoming." As we have said, becoming is not all that John's community avoided with their walls. For Westhelle, the choratic, the crossing, is the space where God, the sacred, the fleshy Divine is encountered, touched, even loved (as well as, perhaps, fed or visited). These spaces, the crossings, the communities that create and emerge from them, are the matrices through which one might pass to encounter God the o/Other. In the crossing, on the Way, as the early Christians called it, there is Christ: on the Emmaus Road (Luke 25:13–35), on the way to Damascus (Acts 9:1–9), in the life of following on-the-Way (Acts 9:2, 19:9–23, 24:14–22), in the transgression of locked doors and cultural divisions into the prophetic space of Pentecost moments (Acts 2), in meeting the least of these (Matt 25:31–46), and in the giving up of the ghost (Mark 15:37–39). God *happens* here, in the crossing, in the *chōra*. God and Church take place.[37] The Reign of God is near-by, at hand. Will we look for it in the crossing? This is the eschatological and ecclesial question which Chrysostom asks.

To review, eschatology has to do with limits and margins. The eschaton may be a geographic, spatial, or material end/limit. There is no one eschaton. There are eschata. The eschatoi are those who inhabit the eschata. The choratic space is the space of the crossing and potential encounter/becoming. It is a threshold. In the crossing, the *chōra*, Church may "take place." It may show up as an event, a moment.

37. Westhelle, *The Church Event*, 128.

II. Choratic Encounters

The Choratic without the Encounter

Not every *chōra* will bring us into the kind of encounter that Westhelle and Chrysostom desire. In the film *Pervert's Guide to Ideology*, Slovenian scholar, Slavoj Žižek speaks precisely to a phenomenon of crossing in which, though a physical barrier is transgressed, and a choratic space opened, an ideological barrier, nonetheless, remains. As a result, in this physical crossing, exposure to the o/Other does not take place and a becoming is prevented. Žižek calls this phenomenon (just one example of an ideological barrier) Hollywood Marxism.[38]

To illustrate, Žižek recounts a journey through the *chōra* of class delineations, as represented in the movie *Titanic*. In *Titanic*, the main character, a rich young woman named Rose (perhaps the epitome of Western privilege and a benefactor of colonial/imperial wealth—perhaps a modern-day equivalent to the members of Chrysostom's congregation) has a crisis in meaning. Moved by her crisis, Rose descends from the deck, full of the yawning upper-class, and into the depths of the boat, *crossing* from one level to another, to another, to another. In the lower levels, among the lower economic strata, she dances and romances with "The Poor," (and with a young lover named Jack) apparently becoming freed from the anti-sensual meaninglessness and despondency produced in the presence of her wealthy peers. At the end of the movie, Rose, reflecting back, shares memories of meaning and joy from her experience. She can share these memories because after the ship was sunk, she survived, returning to the upper deck of a privileged life.

In this analysis, "The Poor," though they welcomed her, fed her, showed hospitality and so on, were still remembered as little more than Rose's helpers, her saviors, those she escaped into on something of a vacation, a tour, an immersion experience, and from which she emerged with meaningful memories. Here lies the problem. These people (these eschatoi) were to Rose objects, property, tools for meaning-making. They were meaningful *to her*.[39]

---

38. This term specifically refers to James Cameron's "ridiculous fake sympathy with lower classes." It is a term in circulation among movie critics. Žižek, *The Pervert's Guide to Ideology*.

39. Gaulke, "God's Work? Our Hands?"

In Rose's frame, these people existed *for her,* and they could only be seen as commodities created for her use and enjoyment. Rose was unable to listen rightly to them, even those she may have claimed to love.[40] Unable to perceive her o/Other, Rose is able to relate to her o/Other as one relates to a favorite skin moisturizer: I love this because of what it does for me. But Rose was not able to be transformed or changed by proximity or even by a love-feeling. Said simply, with Rose, there is no two-way relationship. There is no reciprocity. Rose's o/Other is never fully received or perceived. Her o/Other is simply used, an object.

As a result, the power and class differentiations that create Roses and Jacks in the first place remain intact. Whatever love or passion Rose might have felt as the result of her romantic fling (and even the choratic motion of sexual intercourse), it was not a love that moved her to live or to die for the object of her love. Neither was Rose ignited with any fire or outrage that such people were forced to the bottom of the ship and deemed dispensable at its sinking. She did not protest that fact that these eschatoi, Jack and Jack's peers, were the first to be sacrificed as the Titanic submerged.

Rose's ideological frame, not jarred by her encounter, prevented her from learning that the class/caste system which she observed on the ship, a quite visible and marked segregated hierarchy, through which she (a rich person) could travel downward, but through which the poor could not ascend, was simply a snapshot of the world to which she comfortably returned, and in reality had never fully left. She was personally changed, meaning she had new memories and new emotions. Yet her changedness didn't do anyone any good. It was not what we will refer to in our next section as *metanoietic.* Her experience felt meaningful, but in reality, it was meaningless to any cause bigger than her scrapbook. It did not provoke love or love's fruits. It did not produce community, let alone solidarity. Her "I" never became an "us" or a "we."[41]

Said differently, this encounter, and this crossing, as meaningful as it may have felt, was another example of the poor being exploited, used as tools for the benefit of the dominant class, something to talk about at the next cocktail party, an adventure to be recalled.

40. To return to our conversations in Chapters 1 and 3, Rose's perception was blocked by her skewed classist "scientific sight" and her stereotypes of the poor, produced by the fantastic hegemonic imagination.

41. Bloch, *The Spirit of Utopia,* 200.

It is said that when Dives was in Hades, he saw Lazarus in the distance, on the far side of a great chasm. From the distance, wealthy Dives called out to the patriarch Father Abraham to send Lazarus, as a slave, to dip his finger is some water so that Dives, now suffering and thirsty, might have something to drink (Luke 16:24–26). Like this rich man who called out from Hades for Lazarus to serve him water, those who suffer from an ideological lens of Hollywood Marxism fail to be transformed by the crossing.[42] They only ever see Lazarus, Jack, the poor, as a servant, a fling, a tool, an object, a slave. They look but do not see. They listen but do not hear God the o/Other in their midst (Isa 6:9; Luke 8:10).

The Choratic Encounter: Parousia, Krisis, and a Metanoietic Relocation

Westhelle recounts more than once the story of Copernicus and his worldview changing work, *On the Revolutions of the Heavenly Spheres*. Contrary to the teaching authorities of the Church, Copernicus' work argued that the sun, and not the earth, was the center of the universe. The planets, travelling via heavenly spheres, said Copernicus, revolve around the sun.[43] When Copernicus wrote of *revolution*, it was in order to describe the revolving. After Copernicus, however, *revolution* became a word that has also to do with the radical recentering of one's entire universe. This radical sense of *revolution*, a re-centering, a re-orientation, is perhaps the closest sense we have to understanding both Jesus' and the Baptist's cry for metanoia: *Repent! Be transformed! Be radically re-centered! God's reign of love in nearby and at hand!*[44]

What made such a cry palatable to the crowds who were attracted to Jesus and John? Why did people respond to the prophets' cry? Such transformation was perhaps made possible for the crowds who gathered around Jesus and John precisely because they were gathered, listening to a word, sharing loaves and fishes, proximity and company. There, many stood and many communed in the presence of their radically o/Others. This coming, or arrival, of one's o/Other, for Westhelle, is to be considered, in space, the *parousia* of Christ, Christself. The coming and arrival of the other is the

42. Žižek, *The Pervert's Guide to Ideology*.

43. Weinert, *Copernicus, Darwin, & Freud*, 20–36.

44. Westhelle, *The Church Event*, 120; Westhelle, *After Heresy*, 67.

parousia of Christ the o/Other.[45] People gathered, hungry for God's reign and for bread. And there, there were o/Others. When the parousia takes place, both *krisis* and *metanoia* also lay nearby.[46]

The Parousia of the o/Other as Metanoia-Sparking Krisis

Contrary to Rose's personal adventure through the class *chōra* of Žižek's *Titanic*, contrary to Dives upon Lazarus' approach at the choratic threshold of his property, and contrary to the community of Chrysostom's hiding of the echatoi in the distant, invisible eschaton, forcing the choratic into perpetual potentiality, "the church . . . happens [for Westhelle, in] allowing the other, the poor, and the stranger [the hidden and unacknowledged eschatoi of the world to actually] emerge, to have a voice, to have a face."[47] If pushed, I think Westhelle would agree that "allow" is not quite the correct word. That is, Church happens when the voices of the eschatoi bubble up, speak, sing, whether they are allowed to do so or not.[48] Said negatively, if the subaltern cannot speak, then church community has missed both communing and the Church event itself.[49] When Church takes place, and the path to the o/Other opens up a space of mutual becoming, "the time of silencing is over."[50] Church is marked by cacophonous glossolalia.[51] The subaltern preaches in her own voice.[52] Such voices are not one, but polyphonical. Yet voices which speak matter little if, as a result of their speaking, no matter is transformed.

---

45. Westhelle, *The Church Event*, 116, 127, 147; Westhelle, *Transfiguring Luther*, 160.

46. Westhelle, *The Church Event*, 116.

47. Westhelle, *Transfiguring Luther*, 153.

48. In an interview with Graham Hill, Westhelle lifts up postcolonial voices, as well as Black theologies as examples of voices that have been made *eschatoi* and othered by hegemony. These voices, introducing themselves, even in academia, which had traditionally silenced them, may be thought of as that which creates bubbles in the lacquer of hegemony. To those who placed the lacquer, the woodwork seems to be ruined, but to those bubbling up, there is something of salvation (and new becoming). Global Church Project, "Vítor Westhelle."

49. Westhelle, *The Church Event*, 11; Westhelle, *After Heresy*, 39; Spivak, "Can the Subaltern Speak?"

50. Westhelle, *Transfiguring Luther*, 153; Luther, "To the Christian Nobility," 7.

51. Caputo, *Cross and Cosmos*, 268; Westhelle, *After Heresy*, 22–24; Bloch, *The Spirit of Utopia*, 187.

52. Westhelle, *After Heresy*, 163.

Tension and Turning

The Rev. Cheryl Rivera is a pastor in East Chicago, Indiana, and director of the Northwest Indiana Federation of Interfaith Organizations. As is common practice, after events or direct actions, Pastor Rivera debriefs with leaders, listening for feeling words and points of tension, as well as leading leaders in evaluating their own performances and letting others give feedback. Rev. Rivera often prefaces the *tensions* portion of her evaluations positing that, "without tension there is no turning." Tension is that choratic space, to use her wheel simile, where "the rubber meets the road." The point of tension is the point of motion, and of *turning!* If the rubber does not meet the road, there is no turning (and even if there is spinning, there is certainly no directional movement!). The voice of the o/Other, where it takes place as church, is a voice that speaks not simply to be heard, but to instigate a "turning," a radical reorientation, *metanoia*. The metanoietic tension (the *krisis*) brought by the word of the eschatoi to the space of the *chōra* holds the potentiality of transforming and revolutionizing (in a Copernican sense) all parties involved. There is a mutual becoming.[53] The proximity of communities, gathered around Jesus and John, hear the cry to be metanoietically transformed. Their proximity, their adjacency to the o/Other, empowers and/or instigates them to respond when they receive it.

In the gospels, the presence of Christ, when Christ is encountered, may mean woe to the rich and blessed happiness for the hungry and thirsty poor (Luke 6:17–26); in other words, God's nearby Reign and God's fleshy presence (God's eschaton and incarnational parousia) is metanoietic for all. The tension born from an encounter with the o/Other, changes the powerful and the poor into something new (2 Cor 5:17).

The presence of Christ the o/Other is the presencing of a *krisis*, the confrontation of a word, a turning point, a revolutionary, metanoietic spark. As a result of such a spark, a community may become an uprising body of solidarity.[54] Such uprising becomes possible in choratic community, where an other meets and perceives an o/Other in a choratic, krisis-inducing metanoietic encounter-event, moving each from isolation and

---

53. For example, according to the baptizer, mutual becoming includes unique becoming for those who are transformed. Tax collectors are to quit ripping off their neighbors. Soldiers are to stop abusing their power. Anyone who has more than one shirt is to share the other with another (Luke 3:10–14). Mutual becoming includes unique transformation for individuals depending on their place in societal relations.

54. Westhelle, *The Church Event*, 116–20.

from a space of o/Other-distorting ideological sense-inhibition, into a deeper, relational solidarity.[55] All parties are renewed. All parties become together, uniquely and mutually.

Metanoietic Relocation

Said spatially, those who are encountered and transformed, those who experience a parousia (the coming of the o/Other) and the metanoietic in the *chōra* that is opened by converging community and radical commun-ing/communion, may no longer sit in isolation, alone, but rather become relocated to stand together, as one body at "the front," (the front being yet another *end*, or eschaton!). The front is a space where we might say, with Fanon, and indeed with Christ embodied that "our minimum demand is that the last become first."[56]

When metanoia is spatialized, it may be seen as a relocation from isolation, estrangement, and the hiding of the o/Other at the eschaton, into a standing-with in solidarity, together, the becoming of a new eschatological community, a new Body, *at* the eschatological front. Here, there is no safety, but the bursting out of salvation."[57] Spatially, metanoia is a radical relocation, even as it may be a radical reorientation of hearts and minds.

III. Choratic Transgressions of the Norm

The Realm of the Norm

Michel Foucault is famous for his work exploring "transgressors"—deviants, outliers, those who lie outside the territorial bounds of normalized behavior, those who lie outside the territorial bounds of what is called *normal* or *sane*. Among his famous works on these subjects are *Discipline and Punish* and *A History of Madness*.

55. Describing deep solidarity, Westhelle sometimes speaks of "the solidarity of the shaken." This is a term borrowed from Patočka. I would add that, as the shaken become the solid, stable, and sometimes fixed establishment, they too must be destabilized and transgressed. If the last become first and reproduce the mayhem that created last-ness and first-ness in the first place, there is locational and spatial change without metanoietic transformation. There is movement without becoming. Westhelle, *The Church Event*, 120; Patočka, *Heretical Essays*, 105.

56. Fanon, *The Wretched of the Earth*, 10.

57. Westhelle, *The Church Event*, 123.

Historically, thinking with Foucault, *insane* as a descriptor has described "anything other than middle class [thought, behavior, and so on]."[58] In order to enforce the norm, to keep it normal or normalized, punishment has arisen, and arises always as a practice, from among those who are invested in the norm. Punishment forces conformity to normal behavior using violence (by inflicting pain or by controlling the body through other threats of violence, marginalization or incarceration). It is norm-enforcement and norm-augmenting behavior.

In places designated for punishment: in the mad house[59] or in the sanitarium, and even in the prison, the patient/inmate is taught to be grateful for receiving punishment, a paddling, confinement, incarceration, electric shocks, and the like. Why? Gratitude is due, one is to believe, because the punishment has been given as medicine. It is a cure for the prisoner's abnormal deviancy. The punishments here will restore them to health, sanity, normalcy. So the reasoning runs. If alignment with the norm is not a result of the discipline, then one at least *deserves* such abuse as punishments for one's ongoing existence as an abnormal/insane/perverted/bad person.

The All-Seeing Eye of Power

In the famous case of Tuke and Pinel, discussed in *Discipline and Punish*, it was found that subjects were able to be controlled (to have their bodies and behaviors modified) via three techniques: (1) hierarchical observation (the Gaze), (2) the normalization of judgment, and (3) the examination.[60]

In short, after a time of discipline and punishments, the doctors could come to control people simply by looking at them. If the abnormal patient did not behave, they knew what they had coming. Being watched by the gazer, being observed, is enough to make one conform to normalizing powers.[61] Cured by such healthy fear, the patients were now assimilated,

58. Torre, *Embracing Hopelessness*, 22.

59. Here I am using Foucault's language of *mad house* to emphasize the labels placed upon those considered outside the norm—they are "mad." Though it may seem appropriate to be mindful of those designated as such to use other, softer, or kinder language, Foucault's use is evidence of his mindfulness. That is, Foucault does not wish to conceal the reality that people considered deviant from the norm are relegated to an incarcerated/marginalized reality. To soften language is to disguise the dynamic of oppression and marginalization enacted in institutional imprisonment of deviance/abnormality.

60. Torre, *Embracing Hopelessness*, 22.

61. Torre, *Embracing Hopelessness*, 22.

conforming, and therefore *sane* (a word that etymologically can mean both *healthy* and *correct*). Contrary to the apostolic charge, they became conformed to this world by the renewing of their minds (Rom 12).

In his famous elaboration in *Discipline and Punish*, Michel Foucault engages Tuke and Pinel's study using Bentham's theory of the panopticon. The panopticon (as the name suggests) is a conceptualized prison/jail in which every prisoner has the sensation (and real spatial possibility) of being watched at all times. If one were to actualize Bentham's panoptical proposal into a physical prison where inmates could be assured that they were constantly being observed, then they would come to police themselves—so the theory runs. Knowing they were being watched, they would act *normally* and *behave*. They would no longer be out of control, but would, rather, conform. The gaze of the unknown guard would be enough to maintain normal and under-control bodies and behaviors among patients/prisoners.[62]

The phenomenon of control by violence (and implicit threats of violence) by way of the Gaze, is not restricted to the sanitarium or the panopticon in our age of video and internet surveillance. To use an Orwellian term, control by threat of Big Brother or Big Someone watching is everywhere.[63] It permeates our every reality. We bow to the gazer. We conform. If we do not, certainly there may be consequences. Perhaps there will also be crosses.[64]

Our mission, Foucault contends, is to challenge what is called *right* by society, knowing that *right* is generally code for *norm*, which means, as we have been saying, that which is normalized by the control of power and the maintenance/reinforcement of hegemony. We should seek to uncover and expose "the fact of domination . . . [as well as] its latent nature and its brutality," and how *right* reinforces the structures of domination.[65] "The system of right, the domain of law, are permanent agents of [the] relations of domination, these polymorphous techniques of subjugation. Right

62. Foucault, *Discipline and Punish*, 202–3.

63. Orwell, *1984*, 2.

64. Again, once truth/behavior in constructed/controlled by power, as per Tuke and Pinel, to deviate it from it makes one to be regarded as "insane." If one is insane, one becomes institutionalized, or at least regarded as "perverted" or weird, and therefore discredited/marginalized. The maladjusted one is pushed outside the territory or sequestered inside of it—institutionalized in hospitals or prisons, unable to check out of one's own accord. Witches are burned. The elderly are caged in homes "for their own good." Christ is crucified. Paul and Silas are hidden away in jail.

65. Foucault, *Power/Knowledge*, 95–96.

should be viewed . . . not in terms of a legitimacy to be established, but in terms of the methods of subjugation that it instigates."[66]

In the case of Chrysostom's community, the eschatoi, certainly those afforded no power whatever (not even to name themselves as other than *the Poor* or *the eschatoi*), were considered a blight because of their poverty, their smells, their hygiene, their lacerations (Luke 16:20). They were perceived as infecting the normal and sane/sanitized spaces such as John's church. Their very presence was considered a transgression and an offense to such a civil, sane, and quite reasonable society. That they were homeless was not the sin. That *the homeless* were present among the wealthy: now this was an offence!

The response to the presence of the eschatoi was a normalizing response: these poor people are out of place when they are in our space. Therefore, let us build a space for them so that this transgression ("the homeless problem") no longer occurs. Let us put them away if they are not able to conform. For Foucault, this has always been the function of charitable institutions: the lepretorium, the sanitarium, and of course the prison.[67] In the name of *good* (read: normal) we hide away the *bad* (read: those outside the norm). It is always "for their own good," as it is for "ours."

John's community members become something of a panopticon themselves. Rather than metanoietically becoming with their o/Others in an eschatological space of becoming, they choose to suppress becoming, and instead they reinforce the delineations of the norm. They were normal, and so they benefited (derived comfort) from this behavior and unbecoming.

Yet John would not have it. He did not bless the xenodoxeion. He understood that these houses of charity were houses of alienation and of punishment/incarceration. Such normalizing oppression was not to be blessed in John's eyes. On the contrary: Woe to you who hide away your neighbor. "Blessed are these poor." The reign of God is already theirs (Luke 6:20). Blessed are those who move into choratic becoming and metanoietic relationships with the abnormal and non-conforming. Blessed are those who open up the choratic via a transgression of the norms and the profanation of the usual. There, in the presence of the radically o/Other, there is something eschatological and something divine taking place—in the crossing, in the *chōra*, in the transgression.

---

66. Foucault, *Power/Knowledge*, 96.
67. Foucault, *History of Madness*, 596.

IV. Choratic Creation: Hybridity and the Apocalypse

We cannot speak for too long of *crossing* in Westhelle without bringing to the fore Westhelle's utilization of the concept of *hybridity*, a term for which he relies heavily on Homi K. Bhabha.[68] Though the term itself is not without contention in post-colonial and de-colonial discourse, Westhelle clearly finds it an important and useful tool for his own transgressive, choratic, theological project.[69] Indeed, Westhelle's work itself is something of a monument to hybridization (as a phenomenon and as a disruptive/ transgressive tactic), the grafting of post-colonial sensitivities, connotations, gestures, and movements into hegemonic discourse, indeed into (and from within) Christianity.[70]

Hybridity

Though the term is derived from the horticultural practices of "cross-breeding . . . two species by grafting or cross-pollination [in order to] form a third, 'hybrid' species,"[71] generally speaking, in lands where colonization has taken place, the term *hybridity* has come to refer to "cultural mixing or mingling between East and West."[72] The term has been applied to describe hybridical phenomena across varied fields. Armadeep Singh has made distinctions between what he identifies as unique forms or types of hybridity, each possessing their own contours. These include racial, linguistic, literary, cultural, and religious.[73] It would be helpful, perhaps following Bhabha, if he also added *political* as a category outside of or complementary to the

68. Bhabha, "Signs Taken for Wonders," 144–65; Bhabha, *The Location of Culture*; Bhabha, "Of Mimicry and Man," 85–92.

69. Westhelle, *Transfiguring Luther*, 95–109, 213; Westhelle, *The Church Event*, 111–12, 143–47; Westhelle, *Eschatology and Space*, 77.

70. "Postcolonialism indicates a crossing over, transgression of the boundaries, the *eschata*, of the colonial world, simultaneously incorporating some of its values and accomplishments while abandoning others in a dynamic process. This process called as 'hybridization' thus has an eschatological twist to it. Just as hybridization brings together incongruent entities resulting in hybrids that are unique in character (the god-man, Jesus), the language of postcolonialism has the unique character of 'heteroglossia,' an intersection of different semantic fields producing unexpected communicative effects." Westhelle, *Eschatology and Space*, 76–77.

71. Ashcroft et al., *Post-Colonial Studies*, 118.

72. Singh, "Mimicry and Hybridity."

73. Singh, "Mimicry and Hybridity," 6; Ashcroft et al., *Post-Colonial Studies*, 118–21.

cultural.[74] Singh, as others, sees the term as useful for naming hybridical phenomena, yet lifts up some clear precautions, especially in terms of understanding racial distinctions, and subsequently identifying racial "admixtures." Following Singh, to the best of our abilities, we are to avoid using such categorization and the imposition of such frames in a disempowering or alienating manner, especially as, quite often, minoritarian communities of multiracial people have already named themselves (i.e. Eurasians in India, and Mestizo communities in Latin America).[75]

Extending Singh's remarks, we might infer that, contrary to Fanon, with whom we spent a bit of time in the previous chapter, *hybridity* itself may serve conceptually as a sort of disruption or transgression of a strictly Manichean (or dualistic) lens, whether that lens is utilized to oppress or to liberate. This is because *hybridity* itself is the born/grafted "third" mentioned above. It does not fit neatly in a dualistic frame. It is born of the mixing of once dualistically dichotomized realities, and so exists itself as a transgression of such distinctions.[76] However, Bhabha argues that the uprising in Algeria and anti-colonial revolution, though it fuels its base with dualistic frames, is itself actually the result and image of a type of hybridity. Those who are uprising and consequently rebuilding after revolt, necessarily are the *third* created from the interaction of the dualistic *two*.[77]

It is helpful to say what *hybridity* is not. *Hybridity*, in Westhelle, is distinct from *mimicry*, a term sometimes used to describe the phenomenon produced when a colonized people wishes to survive while being dominated. At times, *mimicry* is met with critique and insult. It especially comes under attack from those whose goal is *not* assimilation (or survival), but revolt at any price and by any means.[78] Nonetheless, *mimicry*

---

74. Bhabha uses the term, among other ways, to describe the installation of postcolonial governments. For example, when a colonized group wins independence, they often mimic the government of the colonizer, yet infuse local sensibilities/practices, creating a government that is a hybrid of the colonized people's culture and the governmental practices of the colonizing West. Bhabha, "Of Mimicry and Man," 86–87.

75. Singh, "Mimicry and Hybridity."

76. Fanon, *The Wretched of the Earth*, 6–15, 43; Westhelle, *After Heresy*, 141.

77. Bhabha, *The Location of Culture*, 38.

78. That is, those who live a dissimulated existence, are often deemed as weak or "sell-outs" by those who wish them to stand up and speak out. This tension is especially observable in the US between generations of immigrants. Children of immigrants who become activists seeking to change oppressive systems often express frustration toward parents whose main goal was to assimilate and to create a space for their children to survive/thrive. In *ad hominem* attacks, terms like "Twinkie," "Oreo," or "coconut," are

is one way colonized, oppressed, or marginalized communities may resist (or survive) in a *dissimulated* manner.[79]

Dissimulation (or mimicry as dissimulation) may be used as a survival tactic. Etymologically, *dissimulation* derives meaning from the act of concealing/covering-up *and* mimicking/copying. "The effect of mimicry is camouflage," says Lacan. "It is not a question of harmonizing with the background, but against a mottled background, of becoming mottled - exactly like the technique of camouflage practiced in human warfare."[80] Camouflage protects one against one's aggressor. In the context of oppression/colonization, *dissimulation* takes place when and where a people or person acts in a way that the oppressor wishes in order to blend in and even not to be seen so that the oppressor does not get irritated or enraged by their difference. One does not "act out" of one's place and one does not "get out of line" (in the sight of the oppressor) so that one is not "put back in one's place" or "knocked back into line" by an act of discipline or punishment.[81] Instead, one seeks to "blend in." Dissimulated mimicry, then, involves one's dress, one's behavior, one's speech, one's gestures, one's clothing, one's laugh, one's religious practice and symbols and so on. One covers one's difference, as one's un-covered existence itself may be perceived by the oppressor as a deviation or even perversion, and therefore another opportunity for punishment. Said again, dissimulation is a mask that the oppressed wear when the power dynamic would render them dead or disciplined without a mask. To dissimulate is to "show the master what he wants to see," to hide one's Blackness, one's queerness, one's ethnic expressions, one's desire to be free. What the master would love to see is well behaved subjects, happy and ready to serve the empire, the throne, the flag, the country, the queen.[82] Dissimulated existence pledges allegiance to the flag even when one secretly detests it and burns it in one's home. "Authentic expression" or "being oneself" is not an option if doing so would put one's life on the line. From a dissimulated point of view, activism may be seen as an act of privilege.

---

often used to accuse one of being "white on the inside." These insults and slurs dismiss the complexity of the need to survive in a world where one's existence itself is constantly threatened, and therefore existence itself becomes a form of resistance against the constant threat of annihilation. See Singh, "Mimicry and Hybridity."

79. Westhelle, *After Heresy*, 39–42.

80. Lacan, *Of the Gaze,* as cited in Bhabha, "Of Mimicry and Man," 85.

81. Westhelle, *After Heresy*, 39–42.

82. Westhelle, *After Heresy*, 39–42; Bhabha, *The Location of Culture*, 90; Fanon, *Black Skin, White Masks*, 159; Bhabha, "Of Mimicry and Man."

Dissimulation is expressed negatively in a common phrase heard in capitalist spaces. Generally, it is utilized to speak of the physical absence of *the boss*:[83] "When the cat's away, the mice will play." The implication is that when the representative of the center of power is present, one behaves as one is expected to behave by those who hold power. "Free space," if it exists, is relegated to the hidden spaces of the eschata, spaces which remain in the absence of the boss and beyond hegemony's panoptical gaze, spaces where the figurative mice might yet actually play as mice, free from the cat's tyrannical prowling.[84]

Yet free spaces are generally not fixed. They are always at risk of being taken over, gentrified, or colonized. For example, Kelly Brown Douglas demonstrates that, in the United States, white places and spaces move and expand *with* white bodies. That is, white space, since the displacement of indigenous peoples, seems to be anywhere the white body goes. Said differently, when the boss, when the colonizer, when the white body, when the one with power (and often violent reinforcements) arrives, the space is now "his."[85] A flag is planted. A claim is staked. The police are on his side.

Despite this reality, in private spaces, in the absence of dominators or hegemonic representatives/officials, freedom may remain intact in pockets.[86] Here one may disengage from a dissimulated presence and become or behave with greater freedom and ease. For example, James Cone has identified such spaces, historically, in juke joints, as well as some Black churches for some Black North Americans.[87] This is also how Toni Morrison describes the space of *the Clearing* in *Beloved*.[88] Orwell, likewise, finds such spaces in

83. The term *boss* is itself an American English use of the Dutch term for *master*. In the early years of the US, it was distasteful for free people to refer to their employer as *master*, as that was a term reserved for those in charge over enslaved people.

84. When one exists as an outsider/marginalized person, play itself (and the freedom it represents) is seen as a threat to hegemony. Playing is a sign that one is "out of control." It is profaning/transgressive. Agamben, *Profanations*, 77.

85. Douglas, *Stand Your Ground*, 23–44.

86. Some of these we discussed in Chapter 3 using Townes' understanding of counter-hegemonic narratives and spaces. Townes, *Womanist Ethics*, 8.

87. Cone, *The Cross*, 12, 28.

88. Bostic makes a point of connecting Morrison's *Clearing* with an eschatological (and even heavenly) landscape, ripe for salvific becoming. Bostic, "Flesh That Dances," 277–96; Morrison, *Beloved*, 99–121.

the country "in the shade of hazel bushes," and off the grid, theoretically out of the sight/surveillance of Big Brother.[89]

Using again the story of Chrysostom, let us imagine that the poor in the story, receiving graciously the gift of the xenodoxeion, smiled in the fashion of John's churchgoers, perhaps parting their hair at the side, perhaps donning a suit and tie. They took photos: thumbs up! They said cheese. They received the charity which condescended upon them by the hands of the powerful. They said, "God bless you!" the same way that John's community did in worship, or in the passing of the peace. It warmed the hearts of the philanthropists to see the eschatoi smile and behave in this manner, to smile and to behave "normally." They placed a picture of it on their website. They patted themselves on the back.

In behaving as expected by the powerful (many of whom are unaware of their own power), these people, the eschatoi, were able to take what they needed to survive, in a system that had allotted a disproportionate abundance of food and shelter to John's community. Perhaps, later, the eschatoi spoke their own prayers, in their own dialect in their own out-of-sight quarters. In this way, the eschatoi, behaving in public so as to make John's parishioners happy, were utilizing dissimulating mimicry as a tactic for survival.

Hybridity, for Westhelle, is more than dissimulating mimicry, though it may begin as such. Yet hybridity moves outside of the colonizer/colonized dichotomized frame.[90] By nature, the hybrid reality is a disruption of such frames. Likewise, hybridical aims (and tactics) move from survival toward liberative transgression/disruption. Perhaps a hybrid may do so precisely because it is *post*-colonial (as mentioned above), because hegemony is already weakened, more ajar, and perhaps more penetrable. She who was *other* is now also a part of the body, she has been incorporated to some degree, even if she behaves within hegemony as an irritant or an allergy.[91]

Let's return to Chrysostom's flock. Perhaps some who dwell in the xenodoxeion decide to pay a visit to John's church. They find it quite

89. Orwell, *1984*, 123.

90. Westhelle, *After Heresy*, 138.

91. "Post colonial theologies can be broadly defined as an indisposition or inquietude toward the hegemonic canons of Western theology, in short: a dis-ease, which means not being at ease with. Or still better one could call it an allergy in the hegemonic systems. The word 'allergy' means an adversarial—from the Greek alla (work) and ergon (within a system), a practice of rubbing against the grain of a hegemonic system." Westhelle, *After Heresy*, 147.

strange. What are these powerful people looking at from their rows? Do they not realize that they are praising a very poor man, executed by a very wealthy king? Their worship is strange. Their Jesus is fascinating. The eschatoi pick up the words and the ritual, the gestures and the song. They pick up Jesus. They receive the faith. It feeds them. They feel strong, as if they are resurrecting.

Or another scenario: perhaps the xenodoxeion were provided by John's community to the eschatoi under a condition. They were allowed to live there only if they were willing to "convert." This was not a horrible deal, it seemed. So, in a dissimulating move, they faked it. They worshipped in the style of John. They praised in the language of the king: Thees and Thous and Thys and Thines. "Glory to You, O Lord!" They did as they were told. And after a while, the gestures, the language, the stories, infused with their own. They were Christian, it's true. And they were more.[92]

Whatever the exact scenario, the eschatoi are eventually moved to build their own church, to practice and to proclaim their faith. They cut the ribbon just outside of their blessed xenodoxeion. Soon they start incorporating local stories and songs. They speak their own languages. They ordain their own pastors and produce their own educational curricula. They raise their children in the faith. They even launch initiatives: let us give our gifts to the world, even as we have once received! Of course, to give gifts and not to receive alone, is to increase in ability and power and influence. Perhaps one of the eschatoi runs for office against a member who belongs to John's church, after which there is a Johannine "backlash."

But perhaps before all of this happens, someone from John's church shows up to see the church of the eschatoi. He is greeted, welcomed, even given a seat of honor! There he sees for himself that there is singing and dancing and joy. There is prayer and scripture. There, at the head of the

---

92. It is important to note that Chrysostom is traditionally credited in Eastern Catholic and Eastern Orthodox traditions for editing and producing a normative liturgical shape for orthodox worship, *against heresies*. Whereas retaining a unifying (liturgical and dogmatical) shape has been important to many traditions, including my own Lutheran tradition, it is important to revisit questions of orthodoxy always with the question: who benefits? Who benefited from what became known as correct? Whose kingdoms expanded? Who was killed as a heretic? Were they a threat to someone in power? In this paper, the illustration about Chrysostom and the xenodoxeion serves a useful (and quite malleable) illustration, but it should be used as a canon within the canon itself. We cannot take Chrysostom wholesale. He must be checked against his own distortions and dismissals of the o/Other (especially, for example, his venomous attitude toward the Jewish people). See Leighton, *A Guide*; Chrysostom, "Eight Homilies."

church, is Jesus, just as he hangs, nails and thorns, in John's cathedral, a poor man, fastened to a cross commissioned by a king. Above Christ is scrawled in red, "As He has Arisen, Rise Up, O Church, O People of God!"

The wealthy visitor, a lifelong, baptized member of the big church downtown, writes a report: "Your Holiness," he greets John, "I am contacting you to inform you that these folks are not *behaving* like *true* Christians." This the man deeply believes. Why are they not *true*? Because in this man's frame, one is either Christian (someone who thinks or acts like the members in John's congregation), or they are poor, helpless heathens in need of Christian mission/charity. They are poor heathens who rely on the powerful, kind, and giving Christians of John's community. In this frame, there can be no hybrid, no in-between, no mutual becoming. There can be no rising up of the poor ones who are fastened to crosses, no Christian *empowerment*, no Eschatoi Power. There can be only Christian charity, condescending from the church-people onto the poor eschatoi below. Jack may never rise to the top of the ship. He may only be visited by Rose.

Yet, by the time this man realizes it, hybridity has emerged. These people are Christians. And they are poor. And they are rising. They are becoming. There is no longer exclusively the prior either/or. There is both/and. And there is more. The members of the xenodoxeion church become members of the synod council. They join task forces and commit-tees. Eventually a bishop arises from their ranks. Perhaps the bishop asks the question: why must we rule in this manner? Why this hierarchy? Why these rigid delineations?

In more nationalistic or fascist times, perhaps the backward-glancers seek to suppress these hybrid Christians, the Christian Poor, the Eschatoi Rising as *heretics*. The man who wrote the letter now rallies an angry mob. Perhaps they are invaded by heresy police and accused of transgressive thoughts or behaviors or other offensive "impurities." Perhaps they yell "Crucify him! Lock him up!" reenacting the lynching of Jesus by the mob in Rome. Yet for now, they enter into and transform the system as they cross the choratic threshold and continue to create new communities, new hybridities. They transgress, they disrupt, they transform, they re-center and re-orient a system, even as they become it.[93]

93. Westhelle, *After Heresy*, 140.

Of Christ and Nephilim: Westhelle's Hybridity as Choratic Matrix

For Westhelle, hybridity is also of great Christological import. Indeed, for Westhelle, Christ Christself is *hybridical*.[94] So Christ is also by nature a *transgression*. That is, Christ *transgresses* simply by Christ being Christ. In the messiah, there is a *crossing*, a blending, an impurity according to hegemonic purity codes that legislate for differences to be separated and kept apart. For Westhelle, this is what Chalcedon holds to be at the very core of the Christian faith and salvation (Christ). Christ, in whom Christians claim the salvific, is fully human and fully divine.[95] A hybrid! A transgression! How are we to speak of this?

Westhelle notes that according to some Talmudic traditions, rather than the stories of the first humans in Genesis, the story of the Nephilim in the same book would be better described by what the post-Augustinian West has come to refer to as the Fall. In the story, the sons of gods visit earth so as to *come into* (בוא) the daughters of men, creating "the giants/mighty ones (גבּור) of old" (Gen 6:4). Such transgression of worlds, argues Westhelle, according to this tradition, could result in no imagined good. And so, via the crossing (the *chōra* crossed between the sons of the gods and the daughters of men that lead to a hybrid or "third" kind of being), something of a curse would ensue—a flood, a reset button, after which the remaining animals and the people would re-conform to their *natural* and *normal* named and pure states.[96] The crossing led to a certain kind of damnation (drowning) and a certain kind of salvation (starting creation anew).

It is apparent that the condemnative tradition, even where it clings to or emphasizes the salvific which is allegedly delivered by God to Noah and his family, fails to emphasize that Adam was charged with the *naming* in the first place (Gen 2:20). Why is this detail important? Names help us to call one another. As such, they may serve as a nonviolent way to identify and communicate with one another. Yet one possible result of naming is that the body may become imprisoned by the name. The body (and the *being*) becomes that which it is called. The name becomes a prison.[97] *Como se llama?* "What are you called?" Tell me what you are called so that I can

---

94. Westhelle himself encourages reading in a "post-colonial, transgressive hybrid key." Westhelle, *After Heresy*, 159.

95. Leith, *Creeds of the Churches*, 34–36.

96. Certainly, the flood waters here are also a choratic space.

97. Alves, "The Name," 117–21.

know *who you are,* so that I know where to place you in my memory and in my charts and in society.

If a name in this way becomes a restricting label (or a label becomes one's name as in the case of scientific sight[98]), a category out of which one may not move, then the name/label acts as a holding cell, a barrier to becoming. A name is a barrier, a limit imposed on us, that may inhibit us from moving into choratic realms of metanoietic possibility. Understanding the story of the Nephilim (and subsequent flood) as a return of earth's creatures to their proper places/names/categories, misses the point. Adam imposed names (not God). In so doing, he bound himself and the other creatures to a delimited/defined/confined existence.[99] Here is another kind of alienating Fall.

As the condemnatory/soteriological lens misses the mark, For Westhelle, hybridity and the choratic themselves become clarifying lenses with which to better view this story. This lens, coupled with an insight from Matthew and Luke, offers us a new vision. For Westhelle, where the space of the crossing/mixing was seen as a sort of Fall to Talmudic interpreters, so it is in a similar mixing/transgression of the Holy Spirit and another daughter of humans that God is born human, and at the same time a human, called by the name Mary, becomes *theotokos*.[100]

Here is what we uncover with a choratic/hybridical/eschatological lens: that mixing which was imagined as leading only to the terror of a flood (condemnation and death) is seen by the gospel writers as precisely that which gives birth to human salvation by the action of God. That is,

98. We discussed "scientific sight," in a Westhellian frame in Chapter 1. Westhelle, "Scientific Sight and Embodied Knowledges."

99. As discussed in Chapter 1, in anti-choratic circles, the mixing of categories, species, races, and the like suddenly becomes labeled as a profanation, a sin, "unnatural" to one's named (and therefore true/normal) being. As in the flood, the wages of such a choratic excursion into or with the o/Other is death (Rom 6:23). This is especially the case when the choratic that is crossed is the crossing of and intermingling of body/skin in sexual intercourse. As a result, one must be wiped out, flooded, drowned, and so on. Such sentiments are repeated today, of course, by the Alt-Right and other white supremacist and white nationalist groups in the US who make similar charges against "myseginization" or the mixing (and love) between races. These sentiments are repeated also by what has popularly been called "purity culture," often anti-LGBTQIA+ love, often anti-intercourse in general. Such fear of the choratic (of the crossing) by self-proclaimed Christians is not dissimilar from the covering of the eschata and the prevention of the choratic performed by the community of Chrysostom. Lemire, *Miscegenation*; Bolz-Weber, *Shameless*, 25; Valenti, *The Purity Myth*.

100. Westhelle, *Eschatology and Space*, 25.

the mixing itself—the hybridical and choratic space of crossing (and its fruits)—is the matrix through which salvation and damnation both appear to lie nearby and at hand.[101] As such, the space is *apocalyptic.*

And this is the apocalypse: in the crossing, in our exposure, in rising through a barrier, we might find our life's final end and oblivion. In the crossing, we might find born something of life made new. In hybridity, in the transgression of delineations and dividing lines (including those that separate our bodies, our skin) there is a possibility that something of God is revealed. There, at the eschaton, among the eschatoi in Bethlehem, God passes through the *chōra*, from Mary's womb into the stable's midnight light. A transgression from the start, there God is targeted by the normalizing violence of the king (Matt 2:7–12).

There, in the crossing, in the eschata, in choratic space between places, we ourselves may come upon junkyards and graveyards, and perhaps even the one we once loved deeply, our rock and our redeemer, our cornerstone, now rejected, now in prison, now thirsty, now hung violently from wooden beam.[102]

Hybrid Church Spaces

For Westhelle, churches also have to do with hybridity. Churches themselves are hybrid spaces, or what Bhabha has called a Third Space (or Third Space of enunciation).[103] In using this term it is helpful to remember that, as in horticulture, a hybrid is understood as a unique and distinct "third" created from the cross-pollination of two others.[104] The *third* in this instance takes shape from the two places from which cultural identities are gleaned—namely, the house (oikos) and the street (polis). Unlike the home where one is given a name, and unlike the street, the political arena, where one makes a name for oneself (via political transactions and relations to others), the church, a *third space* which is a hybrid of each, a space between these places, which is neither home nor street, is a space of sabbath.[105]

101. Westhelle, *Eschatology and Space*, 24–26.

102. Westhelle, *The Scandalous God*, 113.

103. Bhabha and Westhelle maintain capitalization of the term, *Third Space*, so I will follow their lead. Westhelle, *The Church Event*, 143–46; Bhabha, *The Location of Culture*, 39.

104. Singh, "Mimicry and Hybridity."

105. Westhelle, *Transfiguring Luther*, 149.

Here, also, identity may be given or made, but also removed and remade. It may become undefined. Here we may receive new names. The identity may become fluid and recreational. One may create and play with it. Here we may belong. Yet in our belongingness, we may still transgress that which has come to define/confine us. Here, Bhabha says, "we may elude the politics of polarity and emerge as the others of our selves."[106] Here, says Westhelle, we may be metanoietically "at ease" in the presence of the radically o/Other.[107] Here is a space of mutual becoming, of becoming together.

As touched upon in Chapter 3, the church as an institution and as it takes expression in local congregations has long been a space that has affirmed more than scientific sight.[108] Here people have sometimes learned to see and to sing and to feel beyond simple visual representation. Spiritual experiences themselves, though they may be spoken of in theological language and frames, also point beyond the frame. In the language of Tillich, faith does not settle simply for "signs." It also engages symbols. Signs point to a thing. Symbols both point to and participate in that which is beyond the frame, at the eschata—that which is beyond *inscription*, meaning that which cannot be contained in the script.[109] This practice (or possibility) of perceiving beyond representational frames, opens up the community to the possibility of perceiving beyond one's own framing, meaning beyond one's own body, one's own ideological lenses, one's own identity as given/constructed in the home or in the street.

As a communal space that holds the possibility of openness to varied knowledges, the church has the ability (and the task/vocation) to incorporate nearby transgressive voices by way of juxtaposition, proximity, adjacency. Here, *with one voice*, as aspirational metaphor for harmonious (homogenous) community, should be exchanged for the practice of *lifting every voice* into cacophony/noise/communication/Pentecost-sounds. Especially we listen for those which have been suppressed by hegemonic and normalizing forces.[110]

This becomes for Westhelle the work of the church, and the vocation of the church institution: to give space for the voiceless to speak, and for the invisible who wish to be seen to present themselves, to be(come) this

---

106. Bhabha, *The Location of Culture*, 38–39.

107. Westhelle, *The Church Event*, 132.

108. Westhelle, "Scientific Sight," 343–49.

109. Tillich, *Dynamics of Faith*, 47–50.

110. Westhelle, *After Heresy*, 163–64; Westhelle, *The Church Event*, 149–53.

space for those who are no longer content with dissimulated existence. As a Third Space, the church is positioned to live into its vocation. As a Third Space, it can become the stage upon which suppressed words may become the Word, and take new form in a space that is aspiringly free from the trappings of oikos and polis. When this happens there, when church takes place in/adjacent to them as event, church buildings may become a space of becoming, for individuals and for communities. In the *chōra* created by hybridity, we may transgress our names. In the space between places, we may create new and fluid imaginings regarding what might yet be, for us and for the world—with all the terror, desire and longing that those imaginings may entail.

V. An Unpromising Hope

Where might we look for hope outside of promise? Where might we find hope for an agnostic church and for those of us who find it hard to believe? One option is found in Westhelle's apocalyptic hope, a hope that is born of the *chōra*, open, shaped by space and motion. We call it *unpromising* because whatever expectant joy may be born in the crossing, it is a "hopeless birth of hope."[111] The flood and the Christ traverse the same matrix. Anticipated destruction and anticipated salvation are each *at hand*. As we noted above, this is the meaning of *apocalyptic*. Hope that desires from the *chōra* has neither promise nor guarantee. It hopes *against* hope (Rom 4:18). It desires with and yet against the fears that threaten to consume and annihilate.[112]

Here in the crossing, we may meet God the o/Other. Here in the crossing, an encounter with an other might be the end of our lives. Here we may find our voice. Here we may have our words appropriated or taken away. Beauty and biodegradation, the banquet and the threat of non-being are all always nearby, so close you can touch them, so close they can touch you. The path toward them, the threshold over which to step, the border to transgress, the crossing, the choratic space itself is neither sure nor certain. It is a risk—a holy risk, and yet a risk. It is a risk taken with a heart full of fear and uncertainty and longing.[113] It is a hopeful risk with no promise attached.

Hope, expectant emotion, hunger that moves the body is a risk. Nonetheless, perhaps out of desperation, perhaps out of fear, perhaps for

---

111. Westhelle, *Eschatology and Space*, 132.

112. Westhelle, *Eschatology and Space*, 132.

113. "Hope without risk is not hope." Camara, *Hoping Against All Hope*, 4.

threat of death or desire for life, we make the crossing. Or, perhaps (more Westhellian yet) we do not choose by reason or by instinct, desperation or desire. Perhaps, rather, we simply find ourselves here, in the midst of the crossing, in the choratic regions, Golgotha, Gehenna, the valley of the shadow of death.[114] Perhaps it is not so much by choice as it is by accident, by grace, by chance, by blessing, by curse. Yet here we are: in the wilderness. In the church. Drowning in or floating upon the flood. We have built our boats.[115] Still, it is possible that here, eating stale manna, singing praises stuck upon the mountain top, we may never be saved. Sending doves from the deck, we may never see dry land.

Afternote

Near the latter end of his life, Westhelle wrote clearly of another encounter he was having, this time with an unwelcome other. It was an encounter that could only be described as apocalyptic. An end was at hand. Westhelle's body had become a home for cancer. He was asked to reflect on his experience (somewhat appropriately in the choratic season of Advent). In reflection, he invoked a film which had fixated his interest for decades, and which had, at this end, taken on new meaning. In *The Seventh Seal*, a knight returns home from a crusade, and becomes engaged in a battle with death. The battle is depicted as a game played upon a chessboard. Revisiting the film, Westhelle offers his remarks.

> Cancer patients do not identify with any of the players, but with the chessboard and the pieces that keep on falling in moves being made on either side. We are the neutral ground over which a battle for life or death is being fought. This allegory of the chess game with death, a classic medieval motif, is quite depressing when one identifies oneself with an inert component of it, a chess board with its pieces. But it is realistic. It is not about the drama and search for a meaningful life. And it is not even about death and its stratagems either. It is about us, patients. Patients that

---

114. Westhelle, *Eschatology and Space*, 123.

115. The quotation (having to do with praxis and desire) that Westhelle chose for the header of his website (http://www.vitorw.com/) was the following. "If you want to build a boat, you don't go herd people together to collect wood and then assign them tasks. Rather, you teach them to long for the endless immensity of the sea." Interestingly, many churches built by Scandinavians are shaped as boats, boats having been popular metaphors for church by seafaring immigrant populations in the US.

do not have a scheduled release date, let alone the very idea of a release. Elusive remission, perhaps.

Except for some moments in which we are presented with an option for treatment (which happen only at critical moments in which the physician will not take full responsibility, and one has to sign a pile of documents that exempt everyone of responsibility if things turn out bad), we as patients, are not subjects, just chess-boards over which the game of life and death is being played.[116]

This was the sense of the end Westhelle lifted up near to his own. No longer do we inhabit the choratic (not as we are patients), but we become the chessboard, the space of the crossing. We become the eschatological opening, the board upon which the apocalypse takes place. We become the *third* hybrid space between life and death, adjacent to each. Perhaps this is what we were all along. So in the process of preparing papers and reflections (and for me, this chapter), we his students have continued to move our eyes across his works, his loving words meant for the joy and healing and voicing of the eschatoi, the hopeless, those stuck between spaces, falling between cracks in societies and economies, meant for those who administer the es-chaton despite the risk.[117] His pages for us become a space of crossing, eyes glancing, pens that underline, making marks adjacent to sites on the pages where epiphanies took place. Though Westhelle is gone, his work remains a *chōra*, an opening, an invitation, a reminder that we are to approach the other, the abyss, the unknown; a reminder that here we hear a weak call: to hope against hope for the sake of the hopeless, to claim a desire for a better next place and a radical reorientation of what is, knowing neither what the next place, nor the next hour, nor the next other might bring, but risking, nonetheless, on the side of an anxious hope.

116. Westhelle, "On Advent, Cancer, and Christmas."

117. Westhelle, *Eschatology and Space*, 122.

Conclusion

Two primary questions have given shape to this time spent together. *Where might we look for hope outside of promise? Where might we find hope for an agnostic church and for those of us who find it hard to believe?*

These questions arose from my experiences growing up in pockets of Lutheranism in the US which were heavily influenced, both in preaching and in theology, by Jurgen Moltmann's *Theology of Hope*. With all of its insight and activating power (moving those who pray to protest, too), Moltmann's theology nonetheless clung to the Christian tradition of associating *doubt* with *sin*, speaking of the "sin of despair."[1] It also retained an air of Christian supremacy, claiming that Christian hope alone is realistic.[2]

This Moltmannian hope was to take root through a person's ability, capacity, or even willingness, to embrace and rely on God's promise. It claimed that the resurrection is something of a proof or a sign that the promise of God's reign will yet come.[3] Inspired by the promise, Christian mission became in Moltmann the task of living into the promised and anticipated reign, proclaiming about and protesting for God's justice and peace in all the earth, more so in the here and now than in an other-worldly hereafter.[4]

When I became a Lutheran pastor, it did not take long for me to realize that the act of casting shame on despair and doubt could potentially have wildly oppressive effects on a person, doing lasting damage to a person's

1. Moltmann, *Theology of Hope*, 7–10.
2. Moltmann, *Theology of Hope*, 14.
3. To whom we should turn for proof of this proof, it was unclear.
4. Later, Moltmann would come to affirm the importance of this-worldly hope and the promise of an afterlife.

spirit. The act of casting such shame seemed to me like physically injuring someone who was already in bed, immobilized with the flu.

Secondarily, to treat despair or doubt as *sin* is also to ignore that physical, emotional (and sometimes specifically geographical) state—of *heimweh* and *saudade*, of *the Holler* and of the *chōra*—that demands hope in the first place.

Thirdly, using Bloch's *Principle of Hope* as a springboard into his own theological work, it is both insulting, and indeed quite dangerous, for Moltmann to claim that Christian hope is somehow the best (or the only realistic hope). Such a claim overlooks the broadness of Bloch's project, a project that searched for and found hope, daydreams of a better life, sweet utopian surplus, in many wells, not excluding Christian ones.

Bloch did not demand that those thirsty for hope should drink from just one reservoir. To do so would be to replicate the fascism that sought to take his life. As water is sought after both in desert cacti and in mountain streams (and is good for the body when consumed), so the question of hope is a question bigger than the bounds of one faith. Hope is to be sipped from wherever it is found.[5]

Lastly, the promissory motif means little to nothing for those of us who cannot or will not believe in a promise, in a god-of-promises, or in a god who is well defined. Instead, we search (and I have searched, in this text) for an *unpromising* hope, a hope that does not regard despair as a *sin*, but recognizes it as an existential reality—and as a springboard from which we leap, hopeful, terrified, and perhaps unpromisingly, into the unknown other-than-this.

Each of my interlocutors has offered us possibilities for speaking of and summoning an unpromising hope, each from their own spaces of pain, their own oppressive intersections, and their own emotional and spatial matrices, spaces from which they anticipate uniquely and creatively.

In the first chapter, Ernst Bloch offered us the gift of Utopian Surplus. Finding hope all around us, Bloch urged us to consume this hope, this surplus, and to avoid fascist longings and the mythologies that feed them. Consuming Utopian Surplus feeds our own *heimweh*, making us homesick for the Not Yet. *Heimweh* is a spiritual homesickness that may dwell in the

---

5. To reiterate, I have tried to enter the conversation contained in this text as a pastor and as a theologian, as a believer in community, and as a doubter who is not a stranger to despair. As I have entered the conversation, I have done so without a desire to restrict it to the discursive realms of church or theology, but to engage it from my context in order to bring it to a wider audience.

spirit of atheists, theists, and agnostics alike. It is not bound by belief or intellectual ascent. *Heimweh* feeds our desire for the *omnia sunt communia*, a revolutionary, reorienting desire shared by countless communities, ancestors, prophets, artists, and visionaries since ancient days.

José Esteban Muñoz further enhanced our understanding of Utopian Surplus. He spoke of the stage as a space to perform or rehearse our becomings together, naming the future as queer (and therefore open and undefined, defying binaries and delineations). Such stages aid our becoming and feed our desire for the Not Yet. We, too, as we become together, are open and undefined. We are not yet who we are becoming.

In M. Shawn Copeland, we were able to see *sass* as an event which contains a Utopian Surplus of its own. For a moment, in the act of giving the master a taste of his own medicine, we are able to get a taste of liberation. Roles are reversed. The silenced take voice. This taste feeds a desire for a liberation and an emancipation that might yet become.

Insofar as each of these speaks of Utopian Surplus, each also encourages readers to hope the revolutionary, liberative, queer hopes left to humanity by humanity's aspirational ancestors. These hopes were not received through a promise, but dreamt from a place of pain and hunger for a better life.

In the second chapter, we entered into Rubem Alves' poetic and saudadic hope. We reflected on his early task of "making and keeping life human in this world," and his understanding of the And Yet. We also highlighted his understanding of *aperitif* communities and their prophetic function in the world. In our search for an unpromising hope, we found Alves' early work somewhat lacking. The And Yet required us to affirm a memory not our own.

Yet then we turned to his theopoetic task of presenting the abyss so that dry bones might be stirred with desire, blush, and dance yet again. We looked at Alves' suggestion that a messianic community is one which dreams the messiah's dreams. Sacramentally, when dreamers take in the messiah's dreams, these dreams become infused with their own. When this takes place, the dreams of an individual, the dreams of a community, and the dreams of a community's messiah, *become* together. These are not defined as a promise received, but undefined and *becoming* as a communally shaped and reshaped longing.

For Alves, hope is fed in *aperitif* or sacramental communities, communities that desire in a similar direction, communities that bring us pleasure, while making us hungry for a better world, a world often envisioned as a banquet or a garden where children can freely play.[6] Here, the object of longing may be best understood as longing for the return to the mother's breast, or any new place where we might experience both pleasure and sustenance together, at the same time. Sometimes hope's object will not be reached. Yet, if desire is again stirred in bodies, if blush returns to warm the cheeks, the resurrection of the one who hopes anew is perhaps enough for Alves, even if the object of hope never comes, even if the object of hope remains as vivifying fantasy.

In the third chapter, we dug into the work of Delores Williams, Emilie Townes, and A. Elaine Brown Crawford, returning also to M. Shawn Copeland. We briefly visited both James Cone and Franz Fanon in order to clearly name the Manichean framework (and dualistic conception of liberation) from which many womanist theologies departed, adopting intersectional analyses as well as survivalist ethics, thereby forming a distinct framework and logic for womanist ethics and theological reflection.

Here we received a *hope in the Holler* for survival and quality of life and a passion for the possible right now, grounded in (and fed by) counter-hegemonic spaces and a counter-cultural, slavery-denouncing faith received from the Black Christian forebears of these writers.

Although theologies like Crawford's were still grounded in faith and beliefs, it was clear that the affirmation of these beliefs performed a liberative function and empowered bodies both to survive and sometimes to move toward emancipation.

We found that, though we are searching for an unpromising hope for those of us who find it hard to believe, we cannot deny that the formation of such beliefs in an oppressive context, such as those formed by the women that Crawford researched, affirms a freedom and openness toward belief-fluidity and becoming which is the other side of the agnostic coin.

The fourth chapter turned the questions of an unpromising hope toward Vítor Westhelle's eschatological work. Unpacking some of his key concepts (the *chōra*, the crossing, the eschaton, transgression, and hybridity), we found a hope that, unlike Bloch's revolutionary dreams, Alves' messianic dreams, or Williams' and Crawford's desires for survival and quality of life, is a hope that is conceived thoroughly (or especially) as spatialized, and so hopes expectantly but without any image of certainty. It is hope in motion or hope about to move. It is a hope that fills the body

6. Alves, *I Believe*, 43–50.

with as much fear and trepidation as it does with anticipated joy. It is a hope which risks and which "hopes against hope," in choratic spaces, in the crossing, even though hope's end may be death or increased despair. This hope is called *apocalyptic.* Salvation and destruction are at hand, so close we can touch them.

In each of these approaches to hope, despair is not a sin. It is a springboard from which we leap toward hope, grasping. Despair is pain. Despair is oppression and powerlessness. Despair is the Holler and the *chōra.* Despair is the geographic or emotional location or matrices from which hope is conjured anew. Despair is the space from which we anticipate, transgressively, unknowingly, with fear and anticipation, fantasies and desires, ready to pounce, ready to stretch toward the sun.

In each of these approaches to hope, even where a Christian faith or sensibility is expressed, or Christian language employed, it is understood that the conversation about hope is not restricted to Christian theology, and certainly not to Christendom or to the spaces or institutions of the church. Yet, theology and the church add to the conversation. Pastors, theologians, and worshippers bring an important perspective. Faith that creates hymns and art is faith that contains deep longing and surplus. Yet hope, understood well, is to connect churches (as communities of hope) to other communities of hope, to synagogues, temples, community centers, and societies of atheists. Hope does not convince us that we alone are realistic or right. Rather, hope drives us to form solidaritous and communal bonds across divides.

Hope as a discipline, as a conversation, and as becoming-in-community is a task we share. This task is bigger than us. It transgresses any bounds we fabricate. It is continually becoming, evolving, and expanding, even as we ourselves become. Bloch's saying holds true. "Who we are is [still] not yet."[7]

Where might we look for hope outside of promise? Where might we find hope for an agnostic church and for those of us who find it hard to believe? Here it is. It is the *heimweh* attached to utopian surplus. It is the *saudades* born of shared messianic dreams. It is screams in the Holler from which we might fight for survival, for quality of life, for human becoming, and for a culture that counters that which caricatures and enslaves. Hope is born in the anxiety of the *chōra,* in the crossing, the spaces from which we leap, into the unknown o/Other-than, in the songs we sing together as

7. Bloch, *The Spirit of Utopia,* 202–3.

we fumble on the stage. It is born for the sake of the hopeless, desiring, shaking, crying, and afraid.

Hope may be imbibed in the communities of hope all around us, places of the breast, counter-hegemonic, aperitif communities that are so close to us that we can touch them, taste them, communities that are so nearby that we may embody them if we get any closer. They give us pleasure and sustenance at the same time. These may become us, even as we become, even as we perform our own becomings, even as we become community together.

We need not believe in a promise, and we need not believe in a god of promises, or in a well-defined god. We need not believe in a god at all. We may remain belief-fluid, uncertain and swirling, and even afraid. There is no shame in this.

I write this conclusion in the final week of Advent 2019. It is my conviction, in this season of expectant emotions, that if pastors, community organizers, and community leaders in general, wish to speak of hope, to resurrect spirits, and to move bodies toward resurrective practices, that it is best to abandon the promise, and to work with our communities to mutually breathe life into one another, so that together we may hunger and become homesick for the Not Yet; so that together we may holler, desire, cross over into the o/Other, and dream waking dreams.

When the magi and the shepherds arrived at a manger, they embodied and represented divergent beliefs, social locations, and desires. They had received different visions and visitations. They had dreamt different dreams. Nonetheless, the desire they placed upon the child there allowed them to coexist, to commune in the child's presence! It allowed them to dance and sing. As they went on their way, their memories of that scene, the nativity, fed them and also made them hungry. They now hungered for a world at peace that reflected the proximity and ease in the presence of their radically others that took place in that holy night. They dreamt that in this child, that world for which they dreamt, that moment which they had experienced, might become more fully. As they went on their way, they felt enlivened. A spring had come to their step. They blushed a bit. They could do things that they could never do before. This vision, this memory, this dream even allowed them to defy a tyrant king who wished to sabotage such unlikely unity, who wished to murder the child who instigated dreams in mangers, in the Holler, in the crossings of the night (Matt 2:12).

Afterword

IN ALVESIAN TERMS, I entered the work of creating this text curious about how these authors approached the task of wishing dry bones into a crowd of laughing children. As I have said, I am very concerned for this task, for the resurrection of the spirit of our people. It may be said that this is the task of the seelsorger, especially when our people come tired and despairing into community. And especially when they have lost hope.[1]

After all of this writing, to speak of hope still remains difficult. Yet, hope is nonetheless clearly seen as embodied in various people I have been in community with, especially in the time I served as pastor at First Lutheran Church of the Trinity in Chicago.

One of these people is Ben. Ben volunteered in food pantries and community closets, and he was an active community member at our church. He had a fixed income and often had trouble getting around. When Ben learned that we had a chance at reinstating the 31st Street bus, a bus that would connect two food pantries to our church and our free-to-the-community clothing closet, as well as Mercy Hospital, it was clear to him that we should fight for it. We agreed at his impassioned urging.

This desire to win a bus breathed something of a resurrection into all of us. At one board meeting, we flooded the room with community members. Ben said to the CTA board members, looking them in the eye, "When you are denying one of us a bus, you are denying Jesus a bus!"[2] Ben understood that he was counted among the eschatoi. He spoke a variation on the words

1. Puleo, "Rubem Alves," 189.

2. This was said by Ben, August 12, 2015, to the Chicago Transit Authority board. https://www.facebook.com/bridgeportalliance/posts/860798507302971.

of Matthew 25. He spoke in the faith-language of those who ignored and neglected him. In the speaking, for a moment, Ben was a prophet.

On another occasion, Yami, who worked as a domestic worker, confronted the commissioner, on television for the first time, demanding to raise the minimum wage.[3] She herself would benefit from such a raise. As she spoke, she was surrounded by other community members, empowered in community to stand up. This act breathed life into her. Again, there was something of a resurrection in all of us. We who made up the community stood, proud of our leader.

Andrew, Diane and Erika were middle-class. They continue today to foster home and community in solidarity with community members who are regularly hungry and poor, transgressing delineations of class, race, and creed that often separate us, creating sanctuary and home even though they need not do so. They make it a practice of not only perceiving, but also being in relationship with those hegemony would suggest that they should not.

Each of these, in action, in proximity, in transgression of norms and divisions, expresses hope. Each person embodies it. It moves them. As this takes place, they induce hope in others, in those who encounter them, and sometimes even in those who observe from afar. They are, to return to Tillich, symbols of hope—they participate in hope, simultaneously pointing toward it. They are aperitif. They are carriers of Utopian Surplus. Hope, *heimweh*, *saudade* spills over to those who sit nearby, in their own Hollers, in their own choratic situations, in their own physical and emotional places of pain.

When communities take place in this way (and even when we intentionally try to create them), they might also be, as Westhelle says, spaces where one becomes "at ease" in the presence of the radically o/ Other, where one can speak in new languages and elicit new meanings and understandings. As Bloch said, these spaces can be spaces where the same Spirit gives both glossolalia and prophetic vision. Such transgressive spaces provide a space to become, to claim and to invent and reinvent one's own identity (and to shape and reshape one's community), transgressing identities that have been imposed or invented by the imposition and the

---

3. February 1, 2016, Yami lead a protest at a Walmart in Commissioner John Daley's district. This protest won us a meeting with John Daley, which was an early step in winning the battle for upping the minimum wage in Cook County, Illinois. www.facebook. com/bridgeportalliance/photos/a.932651463451008/932652530117568.

in-coming of hegemony's fantastic imagination, as well as its conquering and categorizing forebears.

These may be spaces of counter-hegemonic memory and ornery hope (Townes), sites of recovery (Alves), stages where we rehearse our becoming (Muñoz), spaces of solidarity on the Front (Cone, Davis, Fanon, Westhelle, Patočka), and collectives full of optimism of the will even if there remains a pessimism of the intellect (Davis, Gramsci).

What I remain uncertain about how to name (though I have tried with my interlocutors' help), is the life-giving nature and resurrective nature of one recognizing another, of community itself. This phenomenon is something of a bridge, connecting my primary interlocutors and experiences (including those cited above). Many of our church communities and organizing communities are made up of varied classes, of varied ethnicities, races, genders, and so on. Where these communities exist, and where these community members are committed to coexisting and becoming together, there is a certain new visibility that is fostered. Sometimes, in these communities, those who have been taught not to perceive one another, to avoid eye contact with one another, or to perceive the other as a caricature/fantastic hegemonic image, perceive someone anew, or perceive them for the first time.[4] When I know my neighbor's name, and cannot restrict her to a category or a reputation that precedes her, here there is something sacred that takes place, something sacred that is difficult to name.

I spent some time with a ministry in the South Loop of Chicago. Here we held community meals both with neighbors who were experiencing homelessness and college students. Those who were homeless, and the students alike, would prepare and then share a meal with others. It was a feast—something Westhelle or Alves might refer to as a sabbath banquet. We would always remind ourselves that "We don't do charity. We do community." This was the point: not hiding away in Chrysostom's xenodoxeion, but rather community together, a xeno-koinonia, if not a xenophilia. The results were often beautiful and often messy. After the meal we would invite folks out to deliver meals—to go outside of that safe

---

4. I think of one of the early "story-shares" we had at First Trinity. One member told her story of being a mom and struggling economically. She told her story in front of the whole congregation. She had been leading songs for a year or two by this point. Folks who never would've found the courage to ask were suddenly freed from projecting fantasies and caricatures onto her. That is, her story was humanizing. People saw the person that she offered for them to see. In the telling, her story also became a point of connection for those who suffered similar struggles. It was resurrective as well as unifying.

third space and into the literal streets—the spaces to which other home-less neighbors were exiled without a home.

As we debriefed one week, one participant, René, described her "learning" in this way: "I go to school downtown. And I work here. I have been taught not to look, not to see. But tonight, instead of looking through people, I found myself looking for them." It was in this looking, she said, that she experienced something holy. Church happened. Here, in the crossing and in the perceiving, in community, in the transgres-sion of bounds between hungry and fed, for a moment, there was present something of the divine.

Such moments, such people, such practices resurrect us. They are important to the work/play called community, the communities we call hopeful, and the community called church. They hold Utopian Surplus that is sweet. Most days, I am uncertain as to what I believe. Yet, I am aware when hope abides in proximity. I am uncertain about the use of a language of promise. But where hope is made flesh, I pray that we all will always be becoming nearby.

Bibliography

Agamben, Giorgio. *Profanations*. Translated by Jeff Fort. New York: Zone, 2015.

———. *The Time That Remains: A Commentary on the Letter to the Romans*. Stanford: Stanford University Press, 2005.

Aguilar, D. D. "From Triple Jeopardy to Intersectionality: The Feminist Perplex." *Comparative Studies of South Asia, Africa and the Middle East* 32.2 (2012) 415–28. https://doi.org/10.1215/1089201X-1629016.

Alexander, Michelle. *The New Jim Crow: Mass Incarceration in the Age of Colorblindness*. Rev. ed. New York: New, 2012.

Alves, Rubem. "Confessions: On Theology and Life." *Union Seminary Quarterly Review* 24.3–4 (1974) 181–93.

———. "From Paradise to the Desert: Autobiographical Musings." In *Frontiers of Theology in Latin America*, edited by Rosino Gibellini, translated by John Drury, 284–303. Maryknoll, NY: Orbis, 1983.

———. *I Believe in the Resurrection of the Body*. Eugene, OR: Wipf & Stock, 1986.

———. "The Name." In *The Best Chronicles of Rubem Alves*, translated by Glenn Alan Cheney, 117–21. Campinas, BR: New London Librarium, 2017.

———. *Ostra feliz não faz pérola*. Edited by Vanderlei Lopes. São Paulo: Planeto do Brasil, 2008.

———. *The Poet, The Warrior, The Prophet*. London: SCM, 2002.

———. *Protestantism and Repression: A Brazilian Case Study*. Translated by John Drury. Eugene, OR: Wipf & Stock, 1985.

———. "Ser Mais Religiosos Que Deus." In *Ostra feliz não faz pérola*, 189–90. São Paulo: Planeto do Brasil, 2008.

———. "A Theological Interpretation of the Meaning of the Revolution in Brazil." ThM thesis, Union Theological Seminary Press, 1964.

———. *A Theology of Human Hope*. St. Meinard, IN: Abbey, 1975.

———. "Theopoetics: Longing and Liberation." In *Struggles for Solidarity: Liberation Theologies in Tension*, edited by Lorine M. Getz and Ruy O. Costa. Minneapolis: Fortress, 1992.

———. *Tomorrow's Child: Imagination, Creativity, and the Rebirth of Culture*. Eugene, OR: Wipf & Stock, 2009.

———. *Transparencies of Eternity*. Translated by Jovelino Ramos and Joan Ramos. Series Sapientia. Miami: Convivium, 2010.

———. *What Is Religion?* Translated by Don Vinzant. Maryknoll, NY: Orbis, 1984.

Anderson, Justice C. "Alves, Rubem A., 'A Theology of Human Hope.'" *A Journal of Church and State* 18.2 (1976) 358–59.

Ashcroft, Bill et al. *Post-Colonial Studies: The Key Concepts.* New York: Routledge, 2002.

Baker-Fletcher, Karen. *Dancing with God: The Trinity from a Womanist Perspective.* St. Louis: Chalice, 2006.

Bakunin, Michail. "Federalism, Socialism, Anti-Theologism." https://www.marxists.org/reference/archive/bakunin/works/various/reasons-of-state.htm

———. "The Reaction in Germany: A Fragment of a Frenchman (1842)." The Anarchist Library. https://theanarchistlibrary.org/library/mikhail-bakunin-the-reaction-in-germany.

———. *Statism and Anarchy.* Rev. ed. Cambridge: Cambridge University Press, 2002.

Baldwin, James. "From Nationalism, Colonialism, and the United States: One Minute to Twelve-A Forum." In *The Cross of Redemption: Uncollected Writings*, edited by Randall Kenan, 9–15. New York: Vintage International, 2010.

Barreto, Raimundo César, Jr. "Rubem Alves and the Kaki Tree: The Trajectory of an Exile Thinker." *Perspectivas* 13 (2016) 47–64. http://perspectivasonline.com/downloads/rubem-alves-and-the-kaki-tree-the-trajectory-of-an-exile-thinker/.

Barreto, Susan. "Celebrated Systematic Theologian Westhelle Remembered for Faith/Science Contributions." Lutheran Alliance for Faith, Science and Technology, June 4, 2018. https://luthscitech.org/celebrated-systematic-theologian-westhelle-remembered-for-faith-science-contributions/.

Barros, Ernesto. *Sobre deuses e caquis: teologia, política e poesia em Rubem Alves.* Rio de Janeiro: Instituto de Estudos da Religião, 1988.

Beale, Frances. "Double Jeopardy: To Be Black and Female." In *The Black Woman: An Anthology*, edited by Toni Bambara, 90–100. New York: Washington Square, 1970.

Benjamin, Walter. "Theses on the Philosophy of History." In *Illuminations: Essays and Reflections*, 196–209. Boston: Mariner, 2019.

Bergen, Doris L. *Twisted Cross: The German Christian Movement in the Third Reich.* Chapel Hill: University of North Carolina Press, 1996.

Bergman, Ingmar, dir. *The Seventh Seal.* Stockholm: Svensk Filmindustri, 1957.

Berry, Wendell. "Manifesto: The Mad Farmer Liberation Front." In *A Country of Marriage: Poems*, 14–15. Berkeley: Counterpoint, 2013.

Bevans, Stephen, and Roger Schroeder. *Constants in Context: A Theology of Mission for Today.* Maryknoll, NY. Orbis, 2004.

Bhabha, Homi K. *The Location of Culture.* New York: Routledge, 1994.

———. "Of Mimicry and Man: The Ambivalence of Colonial Discourse." In *The Location of Culture*, 85–92. New York: Routledge, 1994.

———. "Signs Taken for Wonders: Questions of Ambivalence and Authority under a Tree Outside Delhi, May 1817." *Critical Inquiry* 12.1 (1985) 144–65. https://doi.org/10.1086/448325.

Billman, Kathleen D. "Classrooms and Choratic Spaces: A Meditation on Seminary Teaching." In *Churrasco: A Theological Feast in Honor of Vítor Westhelle*, edited by Mary Philip et al., 150–59. Eugene, OR: Pickwick, 2013.

Bloch, Ernst. *The Heritage of Our Times.* Translated by Neville Plaice and Stephen Plaice. Cambridge: Polity, 1991.

———. "Man as Possibility." In *The Future of Hope: Essays by Bloch, Fackenheim, Moltmann, Metz, Capps*, edited by Walter H. Capps, 50–67. Minneapolis: Fortress, 1970.

————. *Man on His Own: Essays in the Philosophy of Religion*. New York: Seabury, 1970.

————. *The Principle of Hope*. 3 vols. Translated by Neville Plaice et al. Cambridge: MIT Press, 1995.

————. *The Spirit of Utopia*. Translated by Anthony A. Nassar. Stanford: Stanford University Press, 2000.

————. *Thomas Münzer Als Theologe Der Revolution*. Berlin: Aufbau-Verlag, 1960.

Bolz-Weber, Nadia. *Shameless: A Sexual Reformation*. New York: Convergent, 2019.

Bosch, David. *Transforming Mission: Paradigm Shifts in Theology of Mission*. 20th Anniversary ed. Maryknoll, NY: Orbis, 2011.

Bostic, Joy. "Flesh That Dances: A Theology of Sexuality and the Spirit in Toni Morrison's Beloved." In *The Embrace of Eros: Bodies, Desires, and Sexuality in Christianity*, edited by Margaret Kamitsuka, 277–96. Minneapolis: Fortress, 2010.

Browne, Ray B. "Some Notes on the Southern 'Holler.'" *Journal of American Folklore* 67.263 (1954) 73–77. https://doi.org/10.2307/536810.

Butler, Lee H. "Testimony as Hope and Care: African American Pastoral Care as Black Theology at Work." In *Living Stones into the Household of God: The Legacy and Future of Black Theology*, edited by Linda E. Thomas, 24–32. Minneapolis: Fortress, 2004.

Camara, Dom Helder. *Hoping Against All Hope*. Translated by Matthew J. O'Connell. Maryknoll, NY: Orbis, 1984.

Caputo, John D. *Cross and Cosmos: A Theology of Difficult Glory*. Bloomington, IN: Indiana University Press, 2019.

————. *The Weakness of God: A Theology of the Event*. Bloomington, IN: Indiana University Press, 2006.

Carson, Timothy L. "Higher Education as Liminal Domain." In *Liminal Reality and Transformational Power*, 75–80. Lanham, MD: University Press of America, 1997.

————. "Liturgy Betwixt and Between." In *Liminal Reality and Transformational Power*, 85–88. Lanham, MD: University Press of America, 1997.

Carvalhaes, Claudio. "About A-Mazing Rubem Alves." *Estudos de Religião* 32.2 (2017) 305–16. https://www.academia.edu/34907311/About_A_Mazing_Rubem_Alves.docx.

Cervantes-Ortiz, Leopoldo. "A Theology of Human Joy: The Liberating-Poetic-Ludic Theology of Rubem Alves." *Perspectivas* 13 (2016) 6–26. http://perspectivasonline.com/downloads/a-theology-of-human-joy-the-liberating-poetic-ludic-theology-of-rubem-alves-3/.

Chrysostom, John. "Eight Homilies Against the Jews (347–407 C.E.)." *Patrologia Greaca* 98. https://sourcebooks.fordham.edu/source/chrysostom-jews6.asp.

Clauss, Ludwig Ferdinand. *Race and Soul*. Berlin: Büchergilde Gutenberg, 1933.

Coates, Ta-Nehisi. *Between the World and Me*. New York: Spiegel & Grau, 2015.

Cone, James H. *Black Theology and Black Power*. New York: Seabury, 1969.

————. *A Black Theology of Liberation*. 40th Anniversary ed. Maryknoll, NY: Orbis, 2010.

————. *The Cross and the Lynching Tree*. Maryknoll, NY: Orbis, 2011.

Copeland, M. Shawn. "Wading Through Many Sorrows: Toward a Theology of Suffering in Womanist Perspective." In *A Troubling in My Soul: Womanist Perspectives on Evil and Suffering*, edited by Emilie M. Townes, 109–29. Maryknoll, NY: Orbis, 1993.

Crawford, A. Elaine Brown. *Hope in the Holler: A Womanist Theology*. Louisville, KY: Westminster John Knox, 2002.

Crenshaw, Kimberlé. *On Intersectionality: Essential Writings*. New York: New, 2020.

Crenshaw, Kimberlé, et al., eds. *Critical Race Theory: The Key Writings That Formed the Movement*. New York: New, 1996.

Davis, Angela. *Freedom Is a Constant Struggle: Ferguson, Palestine, and the Foundations of a Movement*. Chicago: Haymarket, 2016.

Deloria, Vine, Jr. *God Is Red: A Native View of Religion*. 30th Anniversary ed. Golden, CO: Fulcrum, 2003.

Douglas, Kelly Brown. *The Black Christ*. Maryknoll, NY: Orbis, 1994.

———. *Stand Your Ground: Black Bodies and the Justice of God*. Maryknoll, NY: Orbis, 2015.

———. *What's Faith Got to Do With It? Black Bodies / Christian Souls*. Maryknoll, NY: Orbis, 2005.

———. "Womanist Theology: What Is Its Relationship to Black Theology." In *Black Theology: A Documentary History [Volume Two: 1980–1992]*, 290–99. Maryknoll, NY: Orbis, 1993.

Duncan, Mike. "True Liberty, True Equality, and True Fraternity." Revolutions Podcast, June 23, 2019. https://www.revolutionspodcast.com/2019/06/106-true-liberty-true-equality-and-true-fraternity.html.

Ellacuría, Ignacio. *El Pueblo Crucificado: Ensayo de Soterología*. Mexico: CRT, 1978.

Engels, Frederick. *Socialism Utopian and Scientific*. New York: International, 1935.

Fanon, Frantz. *Black Skin, White Masks*. Translated by Constance Farrington. New York: Grove, 1994.

———. *The Wretched of the Earth*. New York: Grove, 1965.

Fletcher, Jeannine Hill. *The Sin of White Supremacy: Christianity, Racism, & Religious Diversity in America*. Maryknoll, NY: Orbis, 2017.

Foucault, Michel. *Discipline and Punish*. New York: Vintage, 1995.

———. *History of Madness*. Edited by Jean Khalfa. Translated by Jonathan Murphy. New York: Routledge, 2006.

———. *Power/Knowledge: Selected Interviews and Other Writings 1972–1977*. Edited by Colin Gordon. New York: Pantheon, 1977.

Gaulke, Thomas. "God's Work? Our Hands?" *We Talk, We Listen* (blog), April 17, 2017. https://wetalkwelisten.wordpress.com/2017/04/17/gods-work-our-hands-rev-tom-gaulke/.

Gibson, Lee. *A Punk Rock Flashback*. CreateSpace, 2015.

Gill, Theodore. "The Ecumenical Movement Remembers Rubem Alves, 1933–2014." *World Council of Churches* (blog), July 24, 2014. https://www.oikoumene.org/en/press-centre/news/the-ecumenical-movement-remembers-rubem-alves-1933-2014.

The Global Church Project. "Vítor Westhelle | Listening Attentively to Prophetic Postcolonial Voices and to Our Scandalous God." February 22, 2017. Vimeo video, 22:33. https://vimeo.com/205199956.

Grant, Jacquelyn. "Black Women and the Church." In *But Some of Us Are Brave: Black Women's Studies*, edited by Akasha Hull et al., 141–52. 2nd ed. New York: Feminist, 2015.

———. *White Women's Christ and Black Women's Jesus: Feminist Christology and Womanist Response*. Edited by Susan Thistlethwaite. American Academy of Religion Academy Series 64. Atlanta: Scholars, 1989.

———. "Womanist Theology: Black Women's Experience." In *Black Theology: A Documentary History: 1966–1979*, edited by James H. Cone and Gayraud S. Wilmore, 273–89. Rev. ed. Maryknoll, NY: Orbis, 1993.

Günther, Hans F. K. *Rassenkunde des deutschen Volkes*. Munich: Lehmann, 1930.

Gutiérrez, Gustavo. *Teología de la liberación: perspectivas*. 3rd ed. Lima: CEP, 1981.

Harris, Jessica C. "Revolutionary Black Nationalism: The Black Panther Party." *Journal of Negro History* 86.3 (2001) 409–21. https://doi.org/10.2307/1562458.

Haslanger, Phil. "Day of Doom, Day of Hope." *Memorial United Church of Christ* (blog), November 21, 2015. http://www.memorialucc.org/day-of-doom-day-of-hope/.

Heschel, Susannah. "Nazifying Christian Theology: Walter Grundmann and the Institute for the Study and Eradication of Jewish Influence on German Church Life." *Church History* 63.4 (1994) 587–605. https://doi.org/10.2307/3167632.

Hill, Rene. "Who Are We For Each Other?: Sexism, Sexuality and Womanist Theology." In *Black Theology: A Documentary History [Volume Two: 1980–1992]*. Maryknoll, NY: Orbis, 1993.

hooks, bell. *Teaching to Transgress: Education as the Practice of Freedom*. New York: Routledge, 1994.

Inwood, Joshua. "White Supremacy, White Counter-Revolutionary Politics, and the Rise of Donald Trump." *Environment and Planning C: Politics and Space* 37.4 (2019) 579–96. https://doi.org/10.1177/2399654418789949.

Jackson, Ronald L., II. *Scripting the Black Masculine Body: Identity, Discourse, and Racial Politics in Popular Media*. Albany: State University of New York Press, 2006.

Jha, Sandhya Rani. *Pre-Post-Racial America: Spiritual Stories from the Front Lines*. St. Louis: Chalice, 2015.

Johnson, Luke Timothy. *The Acts of the Apostles*. Sacra Pagina 5. Collegeville, MN: Liturgical, 2006.

Jung, C. G. *Memories, Dreams, Reflections*. Edited by Aniela Jaffe. Translated by Clara Winston and Richard Winston. New York: Vintage, 1989.

Kamitsuka, Margaret. "Sex in Heaven? Eschatological Eros and the Resurrection of the Body." In *The Embrace of Eros: Bodies, Desires, and Sexuality in Christianity*, edited by Margaret Kamitsuka, 261–76. Minneapolis: Fortress, 2010.

Kasulis, Thomas P. *Shinto*. Honolulu: University of Hawaii Press, 2004.

Keefe-Perry, L. Callid. "A Song for Rubem Alves." *Tripp Fuller: Hombrewed Christianity* (blog), July 20, 2014. https://trippfuller.com/2014/07/20/a-song-for-rubem-alves/.

———. *Way to Water: A Theopoetics Primer*. Eugene, OR: Cascade, 2014.

King, Martin Luther, Jr. "1963 Address at the Freedom Rally in Cobo Hall." https://kinginstitute.stanford.edu/king-papers/documents/address-freedom-rally-cobo-hall.

———. "The Other America." http://www.gphistorical.org/mlk/mlkspeech/.

———. "'Where Do We Go From Here?,' Address Delivered at the Eleventh Annual SCLC Convention." https://kinginstitute.stanford.edu/king-papers/documents/where-do-we-go-here-address-delivered-eleventh-annual-sclc-convention.

Kosloski, Philip. "3 Powerful Sacramentals to Have in Your Home." *Aleteia — Catholic Spirituality, Lifestyle, World News, and Culture* (blog), July 5, 2017. https://aleteia.org/2017/07/05/3-powerful-sacramentals-to-have-in-your-home/.

Krabbe, Silas C. *A Beautiful Bricolage: Theopoetics as God-Talk for Our Time*. Eugene, OR: Wipf & Stock, 2016.

Kristeva, Julia. *This Incredible Need to Believe*. New York: Columbia University Press, 2009.

Lehmann, Paul Louis. *Ideology and Incarnation: A Contemporary Ecumenical Risk*. Geneva: John Knox Association, 1962.

Leighton, Pullan. *A Guide to the Holy Liturgy of St. John Chrysostom.* Scholar's Choice, 2015.

Leith, John H., ed. *Creeds of the Churches: A Reader in Christian Doctrine from the Bible to the Present.* 3rd ed. Atlanta: Westminster John Knox, 1982.

Lemire, Elise. *"Miscegenation": Making Race in America.* Philadelphia: University of Pennsylvania Press, 2002.

Linhares Junior, Bruno Mattos. "Nevertheless I Am Continually With You: A Cosmopolitan and Theopoetic Reframing of Pastoral Theology." PhD diss., Princeton Theological Seminary, 2008.

Lorde, Audre. *The Master's Tools Will Never Dismantle the Master's House.* London: Penguin, 2017.

Luther, Martin. "Confession Concerning Christ's Supper (1528)." In *Martin Luther's Basic Theological Writings,* edited by Timothy F. Lull and William R. Russell, 262–79. 3rd ed. Minneapolis: Fortress, 2012.

———. *Martin Luther's Basic Theological Writings.* Edited by William Russell. 2nd ed. Minneapolis: Fortress, 2005.

———. "To the Christian Nobility of the German Nation." In *Three Treatises,* 1–112. 2nd ed. Philadelphia: Fortress, 1990.

Marx, Karl. "Contribution to the Critique of Hegel's Philosophy of Right." In *The Marx and Engels Reader,* edited by Robert C. Tucker, 53–65. New York: Norton, 1978.

Miller, Gary. *Anarcho Punk Albums: The Band's Story behind Anarchist Punk Music.* Hedgehog, 2018.

Mitchem, Stephanie Y. *Introducing Womanist Theology.* Maryknoll, NY: Orbis, 2006.

Modood, Tariq. "Catching Up with Jesse Jackson: Being Oppressed and Being Somebody." *Journal of Ethnic and Migration Studies* 17.1 (1990) 85–96. https://doi.org/10.1080/1369183X.1990.9976223.

Moltmann, Jürgen. *A Broad Place: An Autobiography.* Minneapolis: Fortress, 2008.

———. *The Crucified God.* 40th Anniversary ed. Minneapolis: Fortress, 2015.

———. *Theology of Hope.* New York: Harper & Row, 1965.

———. *A Theology of Hope (Love: The Foundation of Hope, Part 1).* July 18, 2015. YouTube video, 12:31. https://www.youtube.com/watch?v=oGBb8--Ic3I.

Morrison, Toni. *Beloved.* New York: Knopf, 1987.

Muñoz, José Esteban. *Cruising Utopia: The Then and There of Queer Futurity.* New York: New York University Press, 2009.

Myers, Walter Dean. *Malcolm X: By Any Means Necessary.* New York: Scholastic, 1994.

Nancy, Jean-Luc. *Intoxication.* New York: Fordham University Press, 2016.

Nehusi, Kimani. "Libation: A Ritual in African Life." *African Holocaust Society* (blog), May 8, 2013. https://africanholocaust.net/african-libation/.

Nelson, Paul Raymond. "Lutheran Ordination in North America: The 1982 Rite." PhD diss., University of Notre Dame, 1987.

Nietzsche, Friedrich. "On Those Who Are Sublime." In *Thus Spoke Zarathustra: A Book for All and None,* translated by Walter Kaufmann, 116–18. New York: Modern Library, 1995.

Orwell, George. *1984.* Signet Classics. New York: New American Library, 2003.

Patočka, Jan. *Heretical Essays in the Philosophy of History.* Chicago: Open Court, 1996.

Plaice, Neville, et al. "Translators' Preface." In vol. 1 of *The Principle of Hope.* Cambridge: MIT Press, 1995.

Paul VI, Pope. *Lumen Gentium.* http://www.vatican.va/archive/hist_councils/ii_vatican_council/documents/vat-ii_const_19641121_lumen-gentium_en.html.

Puleo, Mev. "Rubem Alves." In *The Struggle Is One: Voices and Visions of Liberation*, 185–204. Albany: State University of New York Press, 1994.

Ramshaw, Elaine. "Bringing the Blessing Home: The Many Occasions for House Blessings." *Liturgy* 21.4 (2006) 19–27. https://doi.org/10.1080/04580630600872570.

Regis, Marco André. *A Magia Erótico-Herética de Rubem Alves*. e-galáxia, 2015.

Remak, Joachim. *Nazi Years: A Documentary History*. Prospect Heights, IL: Waveland, 1990.

Segundo, Juan Luis. *The Community Called Church*. Maryknoll, NY: Orbis, 1973.

Shaw, Stephanie J. "Black Club Women and the Creation of the National Association of Coloured Women." *Journal of Women's History* 3.2 (1991) 10.

Singh, Amardeep. "Mimicry and Hybridity in Plain English." *Armadeep Singh* (blog), May 8, 2009. https://www.lehigh.edu/~amsp/2009/05/mimicry-and-hybridity-in-plain-english.html.

Snepvangers, Kim, et al., eds. *Embodied and Walking Pedagogies Engaging the Visual Domain: Research Creation and Practice*. Champaign, IL: Common Ground Research Networks, 2018.

Sobrino, Jon. *No Salvation Outside the Poor: Prophetic-Utopian Essays*. Maryknoll, NY: Orbis, 2008.

Spivak, Gayatri Chakravorty. "Can the Subaltern Speak?" In *Can the Subaltern Speak?: Reflections on the History of an Idea*, edited by Rosalind C. Morris, 21–79. New York: Columbia University Press, 2010.

Thomas, Linda E. "Womanist Theology, Epistemology, and a New Anthropological Paradigm." *Cross Currents* 48.4 (1998). http://www.crosscurrents.org/thomas.htm.

Tillich, Paul. *Dynamics of Faith*. World Perspectives 10. New York: Harper, 1957.

———. "You Are Accepted." In *The Shaking of the Foundations*, 153–63. New York: Scribner's Sons, 1953.

Toguchi, Seikichi. *Okinawan Goju-Ryu: Fundamentals of Shorei-Kan Karate*. 22nd ed. Burbank, CA: Ohara Communications, 2005.

Tolstoy, Leo. *The Gospel in Brief*. Translated by Louise Maude and Aylmer Maude. CreateSpace, 2016.

———. *The Kingdom of God Is within You*. Translated by Constance Garnett. Mineola, NY: Dover, 2006.

———. *Walk in the Light and Twenty-Three Tales*. Maryknoll, NY: Orbis, 2003.

Torre, Miguel de la. *Embracing Hopelessness*. Minneapolis: Fortress, 2017.

Townes, Emilie M. *Womanist Ethics and the Cultural Production of Evil*. New York: Palgrave Macmillan, 2006.

Ture, Kwame, and Charles V. Hamilton. *Black Power : The Politics of Liberation*. New York: Vintage, 1992.

Turner, Victor. "Betwixt and Between." In *The Forest of Symbols: Aspects of Ndembu Ritual*, 93–111. Ithaca, NY: Cornell University Press, 1970.

Valenti, Jessica. *The Purity Myth: How America's Obsession with Virginity Is Hurting Young Women*. Berkeley: Seal, 2009.

Vandiver, Josh. "The Radical Roots of the Alt-Right." In *Political Extremism and Radicalism in the Twentieth Century*. Cengage Learning, 2018. https://www.gale.com/binaries/content/assets/gale-us-en/primary-sources/intl-gps/intl-gps-essays/full-ghn-contextual-essays/gps_essay_plex_vandiver1_website.pdf.

W., Bill, ed. *Alcoholics Anonymous : The Story of How Many Thousands of Men and Women Have Recovered from Alcoholism*. 4th ed. New York: Alcoholics Anonymous World Services, 2001.

———. *Twelve Steps and Twelve Traditions*. New York: Alcoholics Anonymous World Services, 1965.

Wald, Elijah. *The Blues: A Very Short Introduction*. Oxford: Oxford University Press, 2010.

Walker, Alice. "Womanist." In *In Search of Our Mothers' Gardens: Womanist Prose*. San Diego: Harcourt, 1983.

Warrior, Robert Allen. "Caananites, Cowboys, and Indians." *Christianity and Crisis*, September 11, 1989. https://www.rmselca.org/sites/rmselca.org/files/media/canaanites _cowboys_and_indians.pdf?fbclid=IwAR3iARjZQER-NR6v8hQ9oWsCiRmQJm1v BCoAzRLT8qRW1bqMMqrWGcWo-2w.

Weinert, Friedel. *Copernicus, Darwin, & Freud: Revolutions in the History and Philosophy of Science*. West Sussex, UK: Wiley-Blackwell, 2009.

Westhelle, Vítor. *After Heresy: Colonial Practices and Post-Colonial Theologies*. Eugene, OR: Cascade, 2010.

———. *The Church Event: Call and Challenge of a Church Protestant*. Minneapolis: Fortress, 2010.

———. *Eschatology and Space: The Lost Dimension in Theology Past and Present*. New York: Palgrave Macmillan, 2012.

———. "Liberation Theology: A Latitudinal Perspective." In *The Oxford Handbook of Eschatology*, edited by Jerry L. Walls, 311–27. New York: Oxford University Press, 2008.

———. "On Advent, Cancer, and Christmas – A Re-Posting in Honor of the Rev. Dr. Vitor Westhelle." *We Talk. We Listen.* (blog), May 14, 2018. https://wetalkwelisten. wordpress.com/2018/05/14/on-advent-cancer-and-christmas-prof-vitor-westhelle-2/.

———. *The Scandalous God: The Use and Abuse of the Cross*. Minneapolis: Fortress, 2006.

———. "Scientific Sight and Embodied Knowledges: Social Circumstances in Science and Theology." *Modern Theology* 11.3 (1995) 341–61. https://doi. org/10.1111/j.1468-0025.1995.tb00070.x.

———. *Transfiguring Luther: The Planetary Promise of Luther's Theology*. Eugene, OR: Cascade, 2016.

White, Rozella Haydée. "When I Found Out, Dylann Roof Was Raised in My Church." *The Salt Collective* (blog), June 28, 2015. http://thesaltcollective.org/when-i-found-out-dylann-roof-was-raised-in-my-church/.

Williams, Delores S. *Sisters in the Wilderness: The Challenge of Womanist God-Talk*. Maryknoll, NY: Orbis, 2006.

———. "Womanist Theology: Black Women's Voices." *Christianity and Crisis*, March 2, 1987. https://www.religion-online.org/article/womanist-theology-black-womens-voices/.

Wipf and Stock Publishers. "Theopoetics - An Interview with Callid Keefe-Perry." January 5, 2016. YouTube video, 26:44. https://www.youtube.com/watch?v=nHuHn3vxePg.

X, Malcolm, and Simon Starr. *By Any Means Necessary (Speech)*. CreateSpace, 2018.

Zeilig, Leo. "The Influence of Revolutionary Frantz Fanon Endures with Africa's Intellectuals." *Quartz Africa*, May 29, 2016. https://qz.com/africa/694858/the-influence-of-revolutionary-frantz-fanon-endures-with-africas-intellectuals/.

Žižek, Slavoj, dir. *The Pervert's Guide to Ideology*. New York: Zeitgeist Films, 2012.